THE GODLY REBELLION

THE GODLY REBELLION

PARISIAN CURÉS AND THE RELIGIOUS FRONDE, 1652–1662

RICHARD M. GOLDEN

THE UNIVERSITY OF NORTH CAROLINA PRESS

CHAPEL HILL

© 1981 The University of North Carolina Press

Manufactured in the United States of America

Library of Congress Cataloging in Publication Data

Golden, Richard M   1947–
The godly rebellion.

Bibliography: p.
Includes index.
1. Catholic Church—Clergy. 2. Clergy—France—
Paris. 3. Church and state in France—History—17th
century. 4. Paris—Church history. 5. Retz, Jean
François Paul de Gondi, Cardinal de, 1613–1679.
6. Jansenists—France—Paris—History—17th century.
7. Richer, Edmond, 1560–1631. I. Title.
BX1533.P3G6   282'.44   80-25282
ISBN 0-8078-1466-0

TO HILDA

CONTENTS

CONTENTS

LIST OF ILLUSTRATIONS

ACKNOWLEDGMENTS

Many people, perhaps too many, have helped me in the research and writing of this book. I thank them all for their concern and their criticism: Harvey Chisick, Robert Forster, Marie-Noële Grand-Mesnil, Albert Hamscher, André Katz, Joseph Klaits, Robert Kreiser, Susan Kupper, Charles Lippy, J. H. M. Salmon, Alexander Sedgwick, and Gary Stark. My colleagues in the History Department at Clemson University have provided me with an atmosphere conducive to professional work. I especially want to thank three other historians. Robert Isherwood, who over a decade ago introduced me to the study of French history when I was an undergraduate at Vanderbilt University, has constantly provided me with professional and personal encouragement. Were it not for him, I might now be reaping financial rather than intellectual rewards. Orest Ranum directed at The Johns Hopkins University the dissertation on which this book is based. I thank him for relieving my anxieties by always allowing me—no doubt against his better instincts—to follow my own inclinations, and for making me nervous by raising questions that would never have occurred to me. Alan Schaffer, with his friendship, humor, and cynicism, has made my life at Clemson very enjoyable. His comments on my manuscript have helped me to make it more comprehensible to nonspecialists.

The publication of this work was made possible, in part, by the assistance of the Faculty Research Committee of Clemson University.

I am also grateful to Betty Barrett and Flora Walker, who typed this book carefully and quickly.

My parents, Sylvia and Herbert Golden, kindled my interest in religion and politics by demonstrating that both are subjects worthy of critical discussion. Throughout the years of my extended education, they gave me encouragement and love.

I thank most of all my wife, Hilda, to whom this book is dedicated. She has spent many hours reading, typing, and criticizing it. I appreciate her understanding and forbearance. She deserves my heartfelt appreciation and gratitude.

THE GODLY REBELLION

INTRODUCTION

The period of rebellion and civil war known as the Fronde remains the "least completely understood" aspect of the reign of Louis XIV.[1] Historians of the Fronde have insisted on placing the period from 1648 to 1652 or 1653 into two phases, the Parlementary and Princely Frondes. Such studies of the revolts by the magistrates of the Parlement of Paris (the most important of the "sovereign" courts in the French judicial system, with jurisdiction over half the realm) and by the nobility have not taken into account either the severe problems or the ecclesiastical opposition facing the crown after 1652–53.[2] However, there was a third Fronde, the Religious Fronde, which lasted from 1652 to 1662 and whose major participants were the Parisian curés, the parish priests charged with the care of souls and with penitential discipline.

The Religious Fronde consisted of the curés' effort to achieve supreme authority over their parishes and thus independence from other ecclesiastical groups that sought to interfere in parochial affairs. This Fronde also entailed the curés' support of their archbishop, the cardinal de Retz, one of the major participants of the previous Frondes who continued to menace the government until 1662. As partisans of Retz, the curés opposed the crown. Furthermore, the third Fronde saw the curés adopt doctrines of Richerism, a radical view of ecclesiastical government formulated in the early seventeenth century by Edmond Richer, and Jansenism, a theological and political movement originating in the Counter Reformation. The curés were able to use Richerism and Jansenism in their battles against the Society of Jesus. The curés' bitter struggle with the Jesuits for control over the religious lives of the faithful formed the basis of the Religious Fronde. The years after 1652–53 were marked by violence.

The most common years given as the end of the Fronde are 1652 and 1653. On 21 October 1652, the young Louis XIV reentered Paris, signifying the reassertion of royal control in the capital, which had been dominated since the spring by his cousin, *le grand* Condé. Despite

3

his victory over government troops in April at Bléneau and in July at the Porte Saint-Antoine, Condé proved unable to control Paris. The masses reveled in his person and in his resistance to Mazarin, the hated Italian-born first minister, but the magistrates and the bourgeois increasingly found him to be a threat to good order. The 4 July massacre at the Hôtel de Ville, where Condé's soldiers killed approximately two dozen notables, destroyed his credibility and position. In October he left France to continue his rebellion at the head of Spanish armies. While the Parlementary Fronde had ended in victory—if only temporarily—with the Treaty of Rueil,[3] the Fronde of the nobles ended in ignominy.

The royal declaration of 22 October 1652, seemed to seal the crown's triumph by invalidating the Treaty of Rueil and by enabling the war against Spain to continue without interference by judges or nobles. The government could now reimpose taxes and restore the intendants.[4] Mazarin, around whom political and economic resentment as well as French xenophobia had crystallized, returned from exile on 3 February 1653. His presence appeared as a sign of government confidence and security.

Finally, the Ormée rebellion at Bordeaux, begun in 1651 and sustained with the help of Condé and the Spanish, ended in August 1653.[5] Provincial opposition had collapsed, the civil war had ended, reconstruction could begin.

But historical interpretations ending the Fronde in 1652–53 have ignored or minimized the conditions prevailing in the later 1650s that rivaled those plaguing the monarchy from 1648 to 1653. The war against Spain necessitated a level of government expenditure that once more resulted in higher taxes. The 1650s were characterized by tax rebellions throughout France. These rebellions continued into the personal reign of Louis XIV and posed a greater problem to the crown than the famous popular uprisings that preceded the Fronde.[6] One could view the years 1648–53 as the hinge of two great cycles of popular uprisings (from 1623–48 and from 1653–76).[7] But this chronology can be revamped because the Fronde lasted until Louis XIV assumed power following Mazarin's death.

The financial machinery of the government, owing to its structure and the fiscal demands placed upon it, was mired in a perpetual crisis in the 1650s. The trial of Nicolas Fouquet, *surintendant des finances*, and the transformation of the state's financial apparatus by Jean-

Baptiste Colbert in the early 1660s testified to the financial anarchy after the first two Frondes.[8] The nobility, losers of the Fronde of the Princes, still opposed Mazarin and royal policy. From 1657 to 1659, the aristocracy was rebellious in nine provinces, holding secret assemblies and terrifying the government.[9] The provincial Fronde had not ended with Condé's flight in 1652. On the contrary, Condé's traitorous activities offered to discontented French nobles the prospect of Spanish money and armies. It was by no means certain that France would defeat Spain. The seventeenth-century slide of Spain to the rank of a second-class military power is more obvious to us than it was to contemporaries. The hopes of aristocratic frondeurs ceased only with the defeat of the Spanish at the Battle of the Dunes (14 June 1658) and the Peace of the Pyrenees (7 November 1659), which ended the war.

The danger from Spain had been in the northern provinces of France, where the nobility could more easily establish contact with Condé's army. But even in the south the monarchy faced active opposition. Revolt flared in Provence in 1659 that was reminiscent of the Parlementary Fronde at Aix in 1649. Only severe repression restored royal control of Provence.[10] The king's voyage through the south in 1659 seemed more like a military expedition than a triumphal procession. The return to calm during the years that Louis prepared for his personal rule was only partial.[11]

Although on 22 October 1652 Louis had prohibited the Parlement of Paris from interfering in matters of state and finance, the judges continued to resist the government. The 1650s repeated the scenario of judicial conflicts with the monarchy, particularly over financial questions and over the crown's right to evoke cases from parlementary jurisdiction. Mazarin prevented overt revolt from the magistrates by altering or scrapping various policies. Only with Louis' assumption of power did the Parlement lose its political influence.[12]

Postscript to the Fronde, sequels to the Fronde, miniature Fronde—these and similar expressions have been employed by historians in their efforts to understand the tumultuous decade of the 1650s. Against the backdrop of the troubles—the war with Spain, financial crisis, aristocratic rebellion, and parlementary discontent—was the Religious Fronde. This Fronde has passed virtually unnoticed for several reasons. First, the religious frondeurs were the curés of Paris, who were important in their own day but who since have joined the faceless masses. Surely priests have lacked the glamour and the personal and

political notoriety of the much-studied upper clergy.[13] Recently, when
the lower clergy of the Old Regime have been researched, they have
usually been dissected economically and socially, but politically only
in the period prior to the French Revolution.

Second, the curés have remained unexamined because so little information about them has survived. Those sources that exist are
widely scattered throughout Paris; there is no continuous series. For
example, although the seventeenth century was an age par excellence
of letter writing, and while nearly all of the famous ecclesiastics have
left collections of letters, extant personal correspondence of the curés
is rare. Who would keep the mail of so many curés, even if they were
curés of the capital?[14] In addition, religious historians of the 1650s
have concentrated on the theological controversies between the Jesuits
and Port-Royal or on the last reverberations of the Catholic Renaissance.

Some nineteenth-century historians employed the term Religious
Fronde, but their understanding of it was different from mine. For
them the Religious or ecclesiastical Fronde encompassed Retz's resistance to the crown from his arrest in 1652 to his resignation as archbishop of Paris in 1662. These historians were concerned only with the
actions of great men. They concentrated on the high politics of Retz's
struggle and mentioned ecclesiastical involvement only in passing.
They failed to perceive the collective behavior of Retz's major adherents, the Parisian curés, except tangentially when they came into
contact with him.[15]

If biographers of Retz concentrated on him and so ignored the
rebellion within the Church of which he was only a part, historians of
the Fronde, by narrowing their scope to 1648–52, neglected the period of ecclesiastical defiance of the government (and of those groups
allied with it). Focusing on the rebellious behavior of parlementaires
and nobles, such historians failed to include in their studies that body
of clerics—the Parisian curés—who appeared on the stage of ecclesiastical politics after 1652. Also, historians working on social structure
have unfortunately ignored the curés, who constituted a professional,
not a social, group. That no work has placed the earlier Frondes in an
ecclesiastical setting is understandable, because relatively few clerics
participated to a significant extent.

During the first two Frondes the Parisian clergy did not repeat the seditious role they had played in the Catholic League during the sixteenth-century religious wars. Except for the case of Retz, the sermons of the Fronde did not mix politics and religion; the clergy for the most part remained faithful to the monarchy, desiring only peace.[16] Jean François de Gondi, archbishop of Paris from 1622 to 1654, sought to prevent clerical participation in the struggle, while directing the distribution of charity that was so needed during this period of troubles.[17] Internal disputes over grace and free will helped to divert the Church's attention from political factions.[18] The center of these theological debates, the University of Paris, therefore avoided taking sides in the civil wars.[19] While Port-Royal, the center of Jansenism, likewise was not involved in the early Frondes, the Society of Jesus remained tied to the government and solicited the expulsion of those Jesuits not devoted to Mazarin.[20]

Only the General Assembly of the Clergy, whose meeting from 1655 to 1657 was to assume significance during the Religious Fronde, entered into Fronde politics. The institution of the General Assembly developed out of the relationship between the monarchy and the Church in the Middle Ages and especially out of the crown's need for funds. When the Estates-General of 1560 and 1561 conducted a menacing campaign against the wealth of the clergy, the First Estate was scared into negotiating with the government. The result was the Contract of Poissy (21 October 1561), which established on a permanent basis the General Assemblies of the Clergy and which stipulated a sum to be given the king.[21] The monarch in return granted the clergy the right to collect its own taxes, the privilege of submitting complaints to the crown, and the right to appoint permanent deputies (the *syndics-généraux*, replaced in 1579 by the *agents-généraux*) to maintain the privileges of the clergy while the assemblies were not in session. Subsequent assemblies modified and regularized the institution whose major function in the eyes of the state was to grant subsidies, principally the *don gratuit* (literally, "free gift," the contribution granted by the clergy in return for general exemption from taxes).[22]

The quinquennial General Assemblies believed themselves competent to protect the clergy's interests regarding the wealth of the Church, matters of religion, and ecclesiastical jurisdiction.[23] Thus the Assembly of 1650–51 protested the government's imprisonment of the Prince of Conti, arrested in January 1650 along with Condé and his brother-in-law the Duke of Longueville. Conti was *abbé général* of the Order of Cluny and so shared clerical immunities. The Parlement's *arrêt* of 7 February 1651, which called for the exclusion from the king's Council of all foreigners and all those who took an oath to a foreign prince, also aroused the Assembly. Because the episcopacy dominated the General Assemblies, they were highly sensitive to encroachments on the "liberties" of the upper clergy. The Parlement's declaration was avowedly anticlerical because cardinals and bishops swore an oath of fidelity to a foreign prince, the pope. The clergy's opposition to the judges led the General Assembly to join with the assembly of the nobles, meeting in Paris during February and March 1651, in demanding the convocation of the Estates-General. Finally, taking advantage of the government's inability to impose its wishes amid the current disorders, the General Assembly diminished its subsidy. But, while securing its position against what it considered to be the abuses of absolutism, this Assembly was royalist. For example, by convincing the nobles to dissolve their assembly and to permit the General Assembly, which had greater legitimacy, to direct their affairs, the clergy helped save the crown from a dangerous situation. The regent, Anne of Austria, was able to promise that the Estates-General would be convened only *after* the majority of the king had been declared (7 September 1651). This amounted to a dead letter, as Louis could then legitimately repudiate his mother's pledge. The General Assembly affirmed once again that the clergy considered the just rule of an absolute king to be the strongest guarantee of the liberties of the Church.[24]

If most of the clergy devoted themselves to charitable rather than to political activities, there were some individual clerics deeply committed to either Mazarin or to his opponents. Those clerics who remained loyal to the first minister throughout his travails included Cordeliers such as François Berthod and François Faure; the Carmelite monk Léon; the king's confessor Charles Paulin; the abbé de Guron; Cardinal Antoine Barberini; Henri de Béthune, archbishop of Bordeaux; and Georges d'Aubusson de la Feuillade, archbishop of Embrun. Frequently, Mazarin's loyal clerics were endangered: Pierre Marca, archbishop of Toulouse, feared for his safety in Paris, while the Parlement arrested the bishops of Aire and Dol for relaying information to the first minister. Upon Mazarin's final return to Paris in 1653, he rewarded those clerics who had been faithful to him.[25]

Among the frondeurs, Retz had the greatest number of clerics in his entourage, including the abbés Guillaume Charrier and Gilles Ménage, the canon Claude Joly, and Félix Vialart, bishop of Châlons-sur-Marne. Jacques Carpentier de Marigny, another ecclesiastic tied to Retz, wrote numerous pamphlets against Mazarin as did abbé Jean Duval, who, however, was not attached to any faction. The princes too had their clerical retainers: the archbishop of Sens, Henri de Gondrin, favored Condé, while the abbé de La Rivière was associated with Gaston d'Orléans. The Parlement had its ecclesiastics, notably the councilor cleric abbé Pierre Longueil.[26]

While the Parisian curés did not take any collective action during this period, several were sympathetic toward Retz. In his memoirs he acknowledged the aid that curés rendered him, and in December of 1649 he wrote: "My strongest supporters in Paris were the curés. During the past week they worked with incredible zeal for me among the people."[27] Among those curés allied with Retz during the Fronde, and noted in his memoirs, were Henri Duhamel, curé of Saint-Merry, Pierre Loisel, curé of Saint-Jean-en-Grève, Pierre Marlin, curé of Saint-Eustache, and Jean Rousse, curé of Saint-Roch. Not surprisingly, these four were prominent in leading the corps of Parisian curés during the Religious Fronde, although the first two were soon exiled.

Duhamel and Loisel attained a certain notoriety at the time of the massacre at the Hôtel de Ville on 4 July 1652. The curé of Saint-Jean-en-Grève was wounded in the head and Duhamel, attempting to calm the crowd, was nearly killed.[28] This was the exception. Until the third Fronde, the curés were relatively docile. Instead of political or religious agitation, they preferred to aid in the mobilization of charity.[29]

This was not the case after the incarceration of Retz in 1652 and his accession to the archbishopric of Paris in 1654. The curés then emerged as vociferous defenders of the embattled cardinal-archbishop, and so of ecclesiastical immunities and the independence of the French Church from secular interference. Banding together as a corps, the curés met in regular assemblies to discuss common problems and implement collective strategy designed to increase their own authority. Confident of the support of their recalcitrant archbishop, they took advantage of the decade-long period of confusion and instability in the archdiocese to promote their own prerogatives. That is, the curés, though they sincerely believed Retz to be the legitimate archbishop and ardently opposed the government on his behalf, capitalized on the crisis in Church-state relations to further their own ambitions. The Religious

Fronde for the curés was the attempted elevation of their stature within the First Estate. They demanded recognition as a corporation having sole right to regulate parochial affairs.

Although the see of Paris was no longer the "second capital of Christianity" as it had been in the High Middle Ages,[30] it remained a focal point of Roman Catholic orthodoxy. The Counter Reformation saw an outpouring of religious fervor in Paris, most notably in charity, devotion, and in the establishment and reform of religious orders. The Sorbonne, though not the theological center of thought that it had been in the thirteenth century or during the conciliar movement, had great prestige. The "Most Christian King," unlike his sixteenth-century predecessors and unlike the mature Louis XIV, chose to live in his capital and so made the diocese all the more important. Because the diocesan revenues were so great,[31] the crown had more than a casual interest in having a friendly or a politically uninvolved prelate in control of such wealth.

This concern was well placed, for each diocese had its own personality[32] and that of Paris during the Old Regime seemed to be hypersensitive. The mix of religion and politics boiled with the League, the Religious Fronde, and the French Revolution. The presence of the Sorbonne, the meetings of the General Assemblies, and the residency of many prelates absent from their own dioceses made Paris the focal point of French religious controversy. By the 1650s there was a public fascinated by theological and political debate. This public's attitude was whetted but not satiated by the flood of pamphlets and works that burst forth during the Parlementary and Princely Frondes. These Mazarinades continued to be printed—though in diminishing numbers, to be sure—throughout the 1650s, but with a difference. Though only approximately 5 percent of the Mazarinades from 1648 to 1653 had religious overtones,[33] nearly every one from the end of the second Fronde until the death of Mazarin in March 1661 treated religious subjects or interpreted politics from a religious perspective. The content of these Mazarinades indicates clearly that the center of protest against the ministeriat (the government controlled by a chief minister) had shifted from judges and nobles to ecclesiastics.

In 1622, Paris had been removed from the jurisdiction of the archbishop of Sens and elevated into an archbishopric. The archdiocese was divided into three archdeaconries, which included the rural parishes, and two *archiprêtrés* (La Madeleine and Saint-Séverin), which were responsible for Paris and its suburbs.[34] The archbishop governed with the aid of his archdeacons and archpriests, who administered within the extent of their jurisdictions, and with his *vicaires généraux* (or *grands vicaires*), who were his principal collaborators. In the absence of the archbishop, the vicars-general governed the see. This was the case during the entire episcopate (1654–62) of the cardinal de Retz, when the vicars-general were absorbed with Retz's conflict with the government and with the Jansenist quarrels. As a result, the rural parishes had no direct contact with the archbishopric.[35] Ecclesiastical jurisdiction was handled in the court of the *official*, whose competence extended over all religious affairs. The tribunal pronounced only canonical penalties; for corporal punishment, the accused had to be handed over to a secular judge.

As head of an ecclesiastical province, the archbishop of Paris had the right to convoke the provincial as well as the diocesan synod. The Council of Trent had advised prelates to attend a provincial synod every three years and to hold a diocesan synod each year.[36] The diocesan synod was most significant, because it was the assembly of priests who were to render an account of their work to their bishop and to receive his instructions. Retz did not convene a single synod.[37] During the Religious Fronde, the curés filled this vacuum with their own assemblies. These became an instrument of their corporate self-interest and were not accountable to their archbishop.

Claiming the spiritual power that Jesus had given his apostles, the bishop was obligated to reside in his diocese, watch over his clergy and the faithful, take care of the poor and those worthy of pity, and supervise the spiritual life of the diocese. He judged matters of faith (and thus held synods and administered disciplinary power through the *official*) and exercised his sacerdotal power. Unlike other priests, the bishop alone could administer the sacraments of confirmation and ordination.

Nonetheless, the curé was the most important ecclesiastic in the diocese, for he brought religion to the populace. People in the seventeenth century identified themselves as parishioners; addresses were given by parish. A parish was a circumscribed area having a church in which the people were obliged to assemble on Sundays and holy days to hear Mass, participate in the celebration of the Divine Office, and receive instructions regarding their duties as Christians. The principal marks of a parish church which distinguish it from other churches are baptismal fonts and a curé having care of souls.[38]

The curé was responsible for the spiritual life of the parish, including the administration of the sacraments.[39] He was expected to preach on Sundays and holy days, instruct in the faith the children of the parish, visit and comfort the sick, provide charity for the poor, widows, and orphans, correct his parishioners' vices, and maintain a register of baptisms, marriages, and deaths.[40] To help him do these tasks, the curé could call on several types of ecclesiastics. His most precious auxiliary was his *vicaire*, whom the curé chose to help him propagate the faith and administer the sacraments. The *vicaire*, in the curé's absence, could discharge his functions. There might also be a *sous-vicaire* (also known as the *porte-Dieu* because he offered sacraments to the sick), who would, in turn, assist the *vicaire*. Chaplains, established in a parish as a result of a foundation, performed the religious services of their chapel and could maintain a degree of independence from the curé. At the lowest level of the parish clergy were the *prêtres habitués*, who lived off the revenues of an endowment and were obligated to be present in the choir during all church services. Sometimes assigned ministerial functions by the curé, the *prêtres habitués* tended to form communities of priests, living together and sharing their food.[41]

The temporal administration of the parish belonged to the parishioners. Their representatives, the churchwardens, were from well-placed social groups and regulated the *fabrique*, the wealth and revenues of the church. The churchwardens saw to the upkeep of the church, made payments for charity and priests, and often selected visiting preachers (a source of conflict with the curé, particularly if a Jesuit were invited).

The contending groups in the Religious Fronde included the curés, royal government, episcopacy, papacy, and Jesuits. All were involved in the drama of Retz's continued opposition to the ministeriat in the 1650s and in the controversies surrounding the elaboration of Richerism and Jansenism. Although it has not been interpreted as such, Retz's conflict was in a sense a Gallican one.

Gallicanism, a compromise between French national consciousness and Catholic universalism, designates French opposition to the authority of the pope without disputing the contention that the pope is the successor of Saint Peter with an authority extending over all local churches, all priests, and the body of the faithful. Though the seventeenth century was marked by conflict with the Holy See, schism was not possible.[42] The root of antipapal feeling was an episcopal and nationalistic reaction against the Curia's centralizing policies and against the idea of papal infallibility.[43] Originating in the early fourteenth-century struggle between Philip IV and Boniface VIII, Gallicanism culminated in the famous four Gallican Articles of 1682. These stipulated the king's independence of the pope in temporal affairs, the supremacy of General Councils over the papacy, and the validity of the customs of the Gallican Church. The last article proclaimed that the pope's judgment was not irrevocable.

Historians usually speak of three Gallicanisms: parlementary, episcopal, and royal.[44] Parlementary Gallicanism hailed the Parlement as the protector of the liberties of the French Church. The magistrates affirmed their right to exclude the pope from the Gallican Church and their right to interfere in episcopal jurisdiction. This interference was made possible by the procedure known as the *appel comme d'abus*, whereby a litigant could appeal to a sovereign court against an ecclesiastical judge suspected of exceeding his powers, encroaching on secular jurisdiction, or violating in any way the liberties of the Gallican Church.[45] Episcopal Gallicanism rested on the bishop's right to govern his diocese without hindrance from either the pope or the Parlement. The prelates therefore denied papal infallibility, saying that they held their office from God and from apostolic succession, and resisted the Parlement's evocation of cases from ecclesiastical courts. "Eldest son of the Church," the French monarch shared with bishops and judges their concern that papal authority be excluded when necessary from France. Royal Gallicanism, in addition, reiterated that the pope could not depose the king or remove his subjects from the obedience that they owed to him. The right, granted by the Concordat of Bologna (1516), to nominate to benefices gave the king direct and continuous influence over the French Church.

The three forms of Gallicanism were prevalent in the 1650s. The crown's attempt to remove Retz from the episcopal see of Paris amounted to secular interference within the First Estate. Retz had been declared the legitimate archbishop by two popes. The General Assembly of the Clergy at times sided with Retz and the papacy against the government, certain bishops, and French Jesuits. The last, usually viewed as ultramontanists, sided with Mazarin against Retz and the

papacy.[46] Jansenism clouded the Religious Fronde and demonstrated
how fluid Gallicanism could be. The Jansenists aided Retz, while the
monarchy, papacy, a majority of prelates, and the Jesuits labored to end
what they believed to be a sect and a heresy. The Parlement, although it
confronted Mazarin throughout the 1650s on financial matters and the
question of conciliar evocations, welcomed the crown's request to in-
dict Retz for treason, a request that offered the Parlement an opportunity to extend its jurisdiction into episcopal matters. On the other
hand, the Parlement, not Jansenist itself, consistently aided the Jansenists by resisting papal constitutions that attacked Jansenism and that
had been sought by the government. The curés, too, showed how flexi-
ble Gallicanism was. While doing their best to ensure that their archbishop would retain his see, they espoused Richerism, the Gallicanism
of the lower clergy, which forbade episcopal and papal interference in
parochial affairs.

Chapter one will examine the struggle Retz waged against the government and the curés' role in supporting him. The French Church in
the 1650s saw competing groups brought into the arena of ecclesiastical politics by Retz's fight. Because Retz was already the leader of
a faction, because the government faced other serious problems
throughout the decade (primarily the war against Spain and the recurrent financial crisis), because of his support by the curés, and because
of the increasing ecclesiastical importance of Paris,[47] his opposition
threatened the ministeriat. One aspect of the Religious Fronde was
therefore political, consisting of the struggle to control Paris.

Chapter two will treat the curés' own efforts to establish their sovereignty over the parishes of Paris. To accomplish this, the curés endeavored to create a corporate identity so that they could better challenge
those who denied their claims to parochial supremacy—the episcopate, the Society of Jesus, and the crown. The curés' institutional
means of promoting their identity was their assemblies, which they
held regularly to discuss collective grievances and to devise plans to
further their corporate interests. The intellectual basis for the curés'
ambitions was their Richerism. Richerism provided the curés with a
fund of arguments to undermine the obedience they owed to the pope,
to diminish the authority of the prelacy, and to exclude regulars from
interfering in the spiritual life of the parish. Adopting from Edmond
Richer a theory of their divine right as the descendants of the seventy-

two disciples that Jesus had sent out into the world, the curés were prepared to implement their extremist views. Their desire for a realignment of power through the realization of jurisdictional independence was an attempted revolution within the system of ecclesiastical politics: it aimed to place below the prelacy a stratum of curés having sole jurisdictional powers within the confines of the parish. This objective opposed the very foundations of Episcopal Gallicanism and the claims of ultramontanists.

Concurrent with this design, but not coincidental, were the curés' efforts to resolve the seemingly inexhaustible problem of regular-secular conflict in their favor. Basic to their ambitions during the 1650s was the desire to rid themselves of their competitors, the Jesuits. Chapter three will explore the curés' preoccupation, and virulent struggle, with the Society of Jesus, and the issues involved.

Until the mid-sixteenth century, all religious orders in France were bound by the rules of Saint Benedict, Saint Augustine, or Saint Francis. The Society of Jesus, founded by Ignatius Loyola and approved by Pope Paul III in 1540, offered a fourth alternative as well as a fourth vow, a special one of obedience to the pope. Unlike most of the old monastic congregations, the Jesuits did not have a particular purpose, such as preaching or charity, but instead embraced all forms of the apostolate—teaching, good works, missions. Monastic reforms, with the exception of the Dominicans and Franciscans, had strengthened the rules of enclosure; the Jesuits saw the entire world as their sphere of action. Their success was phenomenal.

But the Society soon made enemies. Some saw its churches as too luxurious; others objected to the very name of the new order. Nowhere was criticism greater than in France. Because the Jesuits were under the special protection of the papacy, they contradicted the very idea of an independent national church. The Jesuits were not French enough. Jurists and administrators opposed the increase in the numbers of the religious and the introduction of new rules. They were also jealous of the favor that the Jesuits received from French kings. A Jesuit education was soon very desirable; other *collèges* were irate at their loss of students and revenues. The Jesuit *collège* of Clermont in Paris, which taught theology, became a rival to the Sorbonne. Prelates detested the Jesuits because they had been declared exempt from episcopal jurisdiction. Resentment intensified with the attempted assassination of Henry IV in 1594 by Jean Chastel, a student of the Jesuits, and the Parlement of Paris banished the Society from France. Only in 1603 were the Jesuits allowed to return.

Nonetheless, opposition to the Jesuits continued. They did not appear any less ambitious or combative. Their cozy relationship with the aristocracy and their service as confessors to the three seventeenth-century kings exposed the Jesuits to the criticism that they were above all concerned with power. Such also was the curés' feeling. As early as 1580, the curés had been in conflict with the Jesuits in Paris.[48] The Jesuits had invaded parish life, encroaching on the prerogatives of secular priests. The curés ardently maintained that they alone had the right to supervise the spiritual lives of their parishioners. Jesuits and curés clashed over their respective places in the hierarchy of the Church and over the question of whether the parishioner had the right to go to the Jesuits for confession, Mass, and burial. One could not overestimate the Jesuits' importance in the formation of the curés' collective behavior. The hatred expressed toward the Jesuits not only induced the curés to adopt Richerism in order to proclaim their supremacy at the parish level, but also propelled the curés into opposition against the government. The crown was closely allied to the Jesuits and to a certain number of bishops willing to subscribe to Mazarin's directives. Thus, while the curés were political frondeurs through their support of the rebellious Retz, their struggle against the Jesuits likewise led the curés to confront the ministeriat and to direct their extremist thought against other ecclesiastical associates of the court.

Chapter four will discuss the curés' Jansenism. Jansenism offered a convenient vehicle with which to express dissent, both against the government and against the Society of Jesus. Politically, Jansenism had a tradition of confrontation with the government dating back to the 1630s. Theologically, the Jansenists accepted the Augustinian view that grace was given only to a select few and, when given, could not be resisted. This interpretation clashed with the Jesuit view, known as Molinism, which argued that sufficient grace was available to all men who had the free will to accept or reject it. In moral theology, Jansenists and Jesuits also disagreed, the former projecting a severe self-denying life for the Christian against the Jesuits' tendency to accommodate their teachings on moral issues to the foibles of human nature and to circumstances of time, place, and social status. Intellectually, the curés abhorred this so-called laxism, the theory that even a slightly probable opinion may guide conduct or belief. Practically, they were attracted to Jansenism because its doctrines served to elevate the power of the confessor over the parishioner.

As supporters of Retz, opponents of Mazarin, enemies of the regular clergy, as Richerists and Jansenists, the curés played a great role in the world of ecclesiastical politics of the 1650s. Along with other dissident movements, the curés threatened the ministeriat. The government's ecclesiastical allies, both bishops and Jesuits, certainly had much to fear from the curés. A study of the curés' corporate behavior and mentality will reveal a revolt against the government and an attempted doctrinal and jurisdictional revolution within the structure of the Church. The upheavals of this period enabled the curés to achieve a significance that reflected the importance of religious issues in seventeenth-century France. Although a failure, the Religious Fronde disclosed tensions within the Church and aspirations of parish priests that would culminate in the great Revolution of the eighteenth century.

CHAPTER ONE

THE PROBLEM OF RETZ
AND THE CURÉS

"The name [of Retz] alone was more capable
than entire armies of making Mazarin tremble."
Godefroi Hermant, *Mémoires*, 2:673

Retz's arrest, his disputed succession as archbishop of Paris, and his subsequent escape from prison incited the curés and other clerics, who had largely remained passive during the early Frondes, to activities in the realm of high politics that nearly toppled the government in the 1650s. We know now that this third, ecclesiastical or Religious Fronde was rooted in the corps of Parisian curés, for whom the struggle was more than a defense of the rights of the legitimate archbishop, and it entailed the propagation of their theological and moral doctrines and the enactment of their interpretation of curial jurisdiction and authority. Nonetheless, because they required the consent or at least the benevolent neutrality of Retz in order to realize these objectives, the curés were drawn into the nexus of the cardinal-archbishop's struggle with Mazarin.

As the background of the curés' behavior during the 1650s, this struggle determined the government's perception of the curés and afforded them the opportunity to challenge both Jesuits and bishops through the elaboration of Richerist and Jansenist doctrines. Indeed, Retz's battle was a precondition for curial rebelliousness, while his person was a unifying element in the curés' corporate activities. The conflict between Retz and the court that lasted from his incarceration on 19 December 1652 to his resignation as archbishop on 26 February 1662 centered on several problems. First, the imprisonment of Retz and the government's efforts to have him tried through other than the prescribed ecclesiastical formulas raised the question of the cleric's inviolability. Second, Retz's inability to function as archbishop because of the court's intractability brought charges of secular interference with the governance of the Church; this was aggravated by the problem of the spiritual administration of the diocese during Retz's absence. At issue was whose vicars-general, those of the frondeur archbishop or those appointed by the chapter of Notre-Dame under government pressure, would preside over the souls of Paris. Prominent among the vicars-general who defied Mazarin's designs were several curés. Next, the government placed the diocese in *régale*, invoking the king's right to the income of a see that had no bishop. Because the crown sequestered Retz's revenues, it once again appeared to encroach on ecclesiastical rights.

Concurrent with these matters was the government's incessant fear of a new uprising in Paris, another day of barricades, and a return to exile for Mazarin. What prompted this fear was that besides the persistence of conditions prevalent during the early Frondes—including economic depression and international war—the court now had to contend with those new threats peculiar to the ecclesiastical Fronde: interdict and excommunication. These spiritual weapons had awesome potential in a society just emerging from its Counter Reformation. An interdict on Paris would have closed the churches, suspended the sacraments, and would probably have driven a deeply religious population once again into open revolt against the detested first minister.[1] Since Retz possessed the authority requisite to place Paris under an interdict, the government constantly faced this potential crisis during the 1650s.[2]

The curés were seen as particularly significant in this regard. Their influence over their parishioners was great,[3] and it was assumed that the vast majority of them would obey and support an interdict issued in response to the government's actions against the Religious Fronde. Therefore, the possibility that curés would effect an uprising on such an occasion was taken very seriously by the court, which had suffered in the past through its miscalculation of the volatile situation in Paris.

Also important here was the matter of ecclesiastical *fidélités*, the mechanics of which remain unexplored by historians.[4] It would be profitable to speculate on the nature of these personal ties as they influenced the Religious Fronde. One reason the curés were not rebellious as a corps during the Parlementary and Noble Frondes was that their archbishop, Jean-François de Gondi, Retz's uncle, was loyal to the crown; the line of fidelity binding curés to archbishop was too strong for the company of curés to break for political reasons. On the other hand, when Retz assumed the archiepiscopal see, the substance of clientage commanded obedience to his rebellious person, and, with it, recalcitrance toward the crown.

Just as the system of *fidélités* worked from curé to archbishop, it also operated from parish priest to curé. The curé was at the center of a community of priests who assisted him in governing the parish. A community of priests could be fanatically devoted to its curé, as illustrated in the case of Duhamel, a curé exiled in 1654 for frondeur behavior. His priests (all Jansenists) were hounded out of the parish because of their devotion to the curé and to his sentiments.[5] On the other hand, a curé who endeavored to institute reforms among his parish priests might encounter opposition.[6] The relationship between curé and priests was not necessarily amicable upon the succession of a new curé; the system of *fidélités* only operated as each curé brought into the parish his own, personal choices as priests.

The number of priests in the parishes of Paris and the percentage of those who were firmly tied to their curé remain unknown,[7] but it is certain that Paris harbored thousands of clerics and that the court realized an uprising abetted by even a portion of this group could be very serious. When an assembly of bishops loyal to the crown met on 22 June 1659, it noted the potential for rebellion which the ecclesiastical system of clientage afforded the curés. It was contended that the Parisian curés "had caused all the other curés in the kingdom to revolt; that they were formidable men capable of troubling everything; and that, having under them four thousand priests who governed all souls, they were masters of everyone through this means. Because of these considerations, he [the archbishop of Rouen] concluded that it was of the greatest importance to abolish their assemblies."[8] An explosive situation persisted in Paris throughout the 1650s.

1. First Murmurings: Retz's Arrest

The arrest of Retz (19 December 1652), according to Hermant "one of the most celebrated events in the history of our century,"[9] was a calculated gamble by the court. Retz was an overmighty subject. Born in 1614, he became a canon of Notre-Dame, coadjutor and designated successor of the archbishop of Paris, his uncle, in 1643, and archbishop of Corinth in 1644. Since 1646, he had been vicar-general of the archdiocese of Paris. And, on 19 February 1652 he assumed the cardinalate. The strength of Retz in Paris, based on his offices, his reputation for seditious intrigue, and on his numerous and powerful allies, would have to be lessened in some way. After negotiations on the possibility of Retz becoming ambassador in Rome failed, the first minister agreed with the queen mother, Anne of Austria, to seize the coadjutor.[10] Mazarin detested Retz for his role during the previous few years. Since the Day of Barricades on 26 August 1648 and the siege of Paris in 1649, Retz assiduously and often mysteriously opposed the first minister and hoped to replace him. During the Noble Fronde, Retz had been the leader of one faction of the *grands* which, while at odds with the Condéan party, still aimed to overthrow Mazarin's administration.[11] Perhaps Retz's greatest and, from the government's view, most feared accomplishment was to bring the Parisian people into politics. Mazarin was always aware of the coadjutor's ability to foment disorder. Even by the end of the second Fronde, Retz still maintained supplies of munitions in the towers of the cathedral of Notre-Dame, which could serve him as a fortress.[12] The prospect of union between Retz and Condé frightened the cardinal-minister, and he constantly sought information on these men, their agents, and their negotiations.[13] Guy Joly, Retz's personal secretary, though writing after his estrangement from Retz, recognized his former employer's relationship to the government: "The cardinal de Retz rushed forward with the same presumptuousness that was the undoing of the duke of Guise at Blois. Without considering that the most dangerous position for a subject was to make himself feared by his sovereign, they both believed that no one would dare to attack them."[14]

To mitigate the repercussions that the arrest of Retz would have on Paris, Mazarin commanded that the public be informed of the coadjutor's unwillingness to accept the post in Rome, a refusal that necessitated his incarceration. A letter was also to be drafted to the Parlement and to provincial governors informing them of Retz's crimes and misbehavior. Such a document, stated Mazarin, should mention Retz's role in 1648 in detaching several members of the Parlement and others from obedience to the king, his seditious sermons, his scandalous life, his correspondence with enemies of the state, and his propagation of subversive libels that were capable of inspiring "a republican mentality."[15] Nonetheless, Mazarin was aware that he was on shaky grounds, for the arrest was a clear violation of the royal declaration of amnesty issued on 22 October 1652.[16] Mazarin recognized the enormous step he was taking in permitting a secular government to imprison a prince of the Church and the designated archbishop of Paris; he therefore attempted to justify the arrest before the public and to dissimulate his own role in ordering it.

On 19 December, Retz was arrested in the Louvre and conducted to Vincennes. There was no armed uprising, though Retz's partisans made several ineffectual attempts to arouse the people. Nothing shook the city, observed Retz: "Sorrow and consternation were visible enough, but they did not lead to an uprising. Either the people were too disheartened, or those who supported me lacked courage because there was no one to lead them."[17] The plans devised by Retz's noble friends, his relatives, and his creatures incurred the wrath of the court. The government ordered out of Paris the marquis de Sévigny, the former commander of the regiment of Corinth, which Retz had created in 1649. Charrier was sent to the Auvergne, but traveled to Rome to secure the pope's support. Guy Joly and the duc de Brissac went to Brittany to convince the duc de Retz to rebel on his brother's behalf. Others among Retz's partisans hurried to Mesières and Charleville to seek assistance from the governors of those fortresses. All who were solicited refused to revolt.[18]

Although armed aristocratic revolt was abortive, the arrest of Retz produced a violent reaction within the First Estate. This event drew nearly all clerical forces together: the chapter, curés, Faculty of Theology, those bishops resident in Paris, and the pope and his nuncio. Nearly the entire chapter, and every curé save one (Pierre Roullé, of Saint-Barthélemy) opposed the court's behavior.[19] On the day of Retz's arrest, the chapter, joined by several curés, assembled to debate alternative courses of action. Forty hours of prayer for the liberty of Retz were immediately ordered, along with the exposition of the Eucharist for three days in the hopes of exciting the population. In fact, the chapter and curés desired an interdict on Paris, and only the consent of the archbishop of Paris was needed; this, however, was not forthcoming.

The archbishop was far from outraged at the arrest. Contemporaries were in full agreement as to his feebleness and docility, and the hatred and envy he bore his nephew because of Retz's success during the previous crisis and his elevation to the cardinalate.[20] In spite of his family's entreaties, Retz's uncle refused to take this step, which at the very least would have severely disrupted the capital and would consequently have forced the court to release Retz.[21] The archbishop would consent only to public prayers on behalf of Retz and agreed to lead a deputation to the court the next day. At the Louvre, the archbishop halfheartedly pleaded for the release of his coadjutor.[22] The opportunity for an uprising was missed; Retz's uncle had effectively tied the hands of his clergy.

That same day, 20 December, an extraordinary assembly at the University of Paris decided to follow the example of the Parisian clergy by begging the king to accord Retz clemency, but its deputation, like the clergy's, turned out to be only a vain formality. No longer a powerful or respected institution, the university had gradually lost its ability to intercede in affairs of state. While the Parisian curés came to know their strength during the Religious Fronde, the university, conversely, became painfully aware of its lack of political influence.[23]

Although the great majority were doctors of theology, the curés now saw themselves as priests first, as theologians second. The corps of curés assumed, to a degree, its political-ecclesiastical role and particularly its doctrinal initiative and authority displayed in the quarrel over the Jesuits' laxism at the expense of the university. The strengthening of the company of curés occurred because the traditional structures (such as the university and the episcopate) could not adequately perform or satisfy clerical ambitions.

Most violent among the curés were Loisel and Duhamel, who excited their parishioners against the government and delivered heated sermons to this effect on Sunday, 21 December.[24] Nor was the pulpit quiescent after this date. Duhamel constantly reminded his parishioners that their sympathies should be with Retz: "since God says that he is with those who are suffering from oppression, we must not hesitate to be with him." And, while reading the customary prayers for the king, Duhamel added: "We thank God for the victories that he gives to the king. We pray that he pours royal and Christian virtues into the king's holy breast, and that he affords him victory over his passions more than over his enemies, grace in order not to be puffed up by the praise of the worldly, and a gentleness of heart toward his subjects. We pray that the king protect and defend his Church, which is so troubled, and that he send our dear pastor [Retz] back to his flock."[25]

René Rapin, a Jesuit biased against Retz, the curés, and Jansenism, worried—as did the court—that frequent repetition of such homilies favorable to Retz would stir the people and create sympathy for the coadjutor.[26] In fact, in the days following the seizure of Retz the only ecclesiastics vocally supporting the government were either clerical creatures of Mazarin—those who had clung to him even during his recent eclipse and persecution—or Jesuits, who steadfastly repugned the curés' views in politics, just as in doctrine, dogma, and moral theology.[27]

Later, in their assembly of 9 June 1653 the curés decided to renew prayers for Retz's freedom and to exhort their parishioners to ask God to console the archbishop and Retz. The curés resolved also to pressure the agents of the clergy and the nuncio to intercede with the king, queen, and Mazarin for Retz's release. These actions infuriated the government, which ordered the curés to the Louvre. There Rousse defended their assemblies, protested the curés' obedience, affirmed that their support for Retz was only spiritual, and begged the king to free the coadjutor. Chancellor Séguier replied that the curés were wrong to concern themselves with what was a matter of state; the king forbade them to continue their involvement with the Retz affair.[28]

Prelates in Paris also reacted to Retz's arrest. While those bishops resident in Paris during the 1650s normally were utilized by the court, particularly with respect to Jansenism and as an intermediary between France and the papacy, they could not at this time ignore the threat posed to their immunities by the highhanded treatment of the coadjutor. They assembled on 5 January, resolved to remonstrate in Retz's favor, and asked Marca to act as spokesman.[29] Marca, archbishop of Toulouse and advisor to Mazarin in the Retz affair, was to be an important force throughout the 1650s. He disliked Retz, abhorred Jansenism, and had become known for his book on Gallican liberties. His speech at the Louvre skillfully defended the episcopacy from secular jurisdiction by alleging that the threat to clerical immunities came from the Parlement. By shifting the subject of complaint from the imprisonment to the awaited trial of Retz, Marca satisfied both the clergy and the court. He approved the arrest as necessary for the conservation of internal order but requested that Retz be tried by his fellow ecclesiastics.[30]

Marca immediately wrote to Mazarin to explain that he had made the speech in order to weaken the protest of the episcopacy. He suggested that Retz be tried quickly and that his imprisonment be soon ended for that purpose.[31] Mazarin did not heed this advice which, if pursued, might have mollified the forces of ecclesiastical disorder. Retz was never brought to justice, a fact that worked in his favor, as he was then able throughout the Religious Fronde to cloak himself in his cassock and defend the Church against the tyranny of the first minister.

Retz's defense was presented to the public eloquently and often. On one level, the ecclesiastical Fronde was a pamphlet war. The spate of Mazarinades during the 1650s treated the conflict between Retz and the first minister. Mazarin saw to it that anti-Retz pamphlets were published. He aimed to separate Retz from public empathy, as well as from the coadjutor's creatures and adherents, and from Condé. Although Retz and Condé had opposed each other in the Fronde of the Princes, it was obvious now that their hope to overthrow the ministeriat could more easily be realized by a coalition of their forces. After all, with Mazarin back in control of Paris, Retz in prison, and Condé out of France, the situation was such that the two great malcontents needed one another. (But they never proved able to agree on a joint, effective course of action.) Condé appeared in 1653 to have posed the gravest danger to Mazarin. As even Guy Joly realized, "It is true that the court scarcely had anything to fear from either the partisans or the relatives of the cardinal de Retz, but it still had to fear their union with Condé's supporters."[32] Mazarin also feared an alliance between England and Spain and an English invasion to aid Condé and the Huguenots.[33]

Mazarin confronted another serious problem: the poor health of Retz's uncle raised the possibility that the coadjutor would soon succeed to the archiepiscopal see. Such an occurrence would threaten the ministeriat. A defiant archbishop, well-versed in intrigue and subversion, upheld by the myriad powers within the Church, might conceivably possess the capacity to topple the government. To prevent this, the court sought to have Retz renounce his right of succession. But a major obstacle loomed in the path of this plan—the pope.

Innocent X reacted strongly to the news of Retz's arrest. Although the pontiff personally detested the first minister of France,[34] he was sincerely outraged at the treatment accorded Retz. The pope had reportedly shouted at Charrier (Retz's agent at the Curia): "Give me an army, and I will give you a legate."[35] Certain frondeurs demanded

that the pope react by issuing excommunications which, he was assured, would be greeted favorably by the Parisian clergy, the *gens de
condition*, governors of provinces, and by the populace. In the turbu-
lent atmosphere of 1652–53, it was not at all certain that Mazarin's
days of exile were over. Only with hindsight could one discount the
possibility—even probability—of a new Fronde. In staunchly backing
Retz, the pope might be casting his lot with the next first minister.
Although he did not gamble on issuing drastic measures, Innocent
officially asked Valençay, the French ambassador to Rome, for the
liberty of Retz[36] and sent a letter to the king formally requesting
Retz's release. The court refused to receive the brief. Furious, Innocent
dispatched an extraordinary nuncio, Domenico Marini, archbishop of
Avignon, to aid the nuncio Nicolas Bagni, already in Paris, and to
demand an explanation for the coadjutor's incarceration. However,
Marini was stopped at Valence by a *lettre de cachet* and refused permission to proceed further. Even more outraged—and bolstered by
frequent letters from Bagni that had been solicited by the curés of
Paris—the pope was restrained from excommunicating Mazarin only
by the entreaties of the College of Cardinals. Innocent thus settled for
threatening Mazarin with censures, with the recall of the nuncio, and
with a rupture with France.[37]

On 3 March, Bagni at last had an audience with the king and asked
that Retz be transferred to the pope's care in Rome. It was the court's
position, however, that although the Concordat of Bologna reserved
jurisdiction over *causes majeures* to the papacy, this clause was so
contrary to the privileges of the kingdom that the king could not
possibly consent to its implementation.[38]

The Retz affair was at the same time clouded by the Jansenist question and the war with Spain. Mazarin desired the support of the pope
because he feared the latter's ability to thwart French policies both as
temporal head of an Italian state and as the leader of Catholic Europe.
Most important, Innocent could impede Mazarin's efforts against
Spain by appealing to the French episcopate to intercede with the king
for peace, or by offering to arbitrate the peace himself. At the very
least, therefore, Mazarin required the neutrality of the pope. To achieve
this (and to divert the pope's anger away from the injustice done to
Retz), Mazarin spurred the pontiff to exercise his spiritual authority in
the Jansenist affair.[39] Innocent sincerely wanted to dam the Jansenist
tide and therefore had to lessen his anger somewhat over the treatment

of Retz and the extraordinary nuncio, Marini. In this respect, Mazarin's policies complemented one another: his placation of Innocent reduced the possible repercussions of Retz's arrest and allowed the war against Spain to continue unabated; simultaneously, in allowing the pope to proceed freely against French Jansenists, Mazarin struck a blow at the staunchest allies of Retz. Indeed, it is apparent that Retz would not have posed such a threat in Paris had he not had the unwavering loyalty of Jansenists—most notably the curés.[40]

The result of these politics was the bull *Cum occasione*, promulgated on 31 May and welcomed in France by the court. Initiating a period of anti-Jansenists successes,[41] *Cum occasione* was for Innocent an *action d'éclat* which, through destruction of the Jansenists, would bring luster to his pontificate. For Mazarin it was an instrument for political purposes, conducive to the conduct of the war against Spain, to defusing the Retz affair, and to conciliating the government's principal supporters among the Parisian clergy, the Jesuits, who played a very real role in the attack on Jansenism.[42] But the pope did not cease to support Retz and fought the repeated attempts of the French court to negotiate Retz's resignation of his rights to the archbishopric. Innocent soon refused to name new prelates—twenty episcopal sees would remain vacant in France.[43]

In August 1653, in a discourse smuggled out of Vincennes and published in Paris, Retz categorically refused to yield his succession. This forced a decisive shift in government strategy. Unsuccessful in its attempts to persuade Retz to renounce his rights to the see and aware of the deteriorating health of the archbishop, the court now sought to prepare for the imminent archiepiscopal vacancy by denying Retz the seat. Marca prepared a memorandum, invoking canon law and reason of state, to the effect that the king could prevent a bishop-elect from taking possession of his see on the merest suspicion of treason.[44] In brief, Marca recommended that Retz be forced to resign. After the death of the archbishop, an *arrêt* of the *Conseil d'en haut* could deprive Retz of the bishopric and place the diocese in *régale*.

This memorandum formed the basis of government strategy, as the court waited anxiously for Retz's uncle to die. It was apparent that the chapter would ardently back the coadjutor's claims, while the curés posed no less of a threat to Mazarin's plans.[45]

2. *The Death of the Archbishop*

At 4:30 a.m. on 21 March 1654 the archbishop of Paris expired. One half hour later the chapter convened and, after deliberating, officially recognized Retz as archbishop.[46] In retaliation, the court that afternoon issued an *arrêt* which declared the diocese to be in *régale*. The chapter was to nominate officers to administrate spiritual affairs, while the government would appoint an *économe* to manage the revenues of the archdiocese.[47] The court was able to sequester the temporal fruits of the see,[48] but the administration of the spiritual proved another matter.

The ecclesiastical situation had become even more complex. Until now, it had been simply a question of Retz's person, of determining who would judge the coadjutor. While the Parlement had asserted its claim as judge because of the exceptional nature of the charge of lese majesty, the pope had been just as intransigent in upholding his prerogative to try cases involving cardinals. But, as of 21 March, there emerged the question of the spiritual government of the diocese. Nearly every element of the clergy—the chapter, the curés, the nuncio, and the papacy—recognized Retz as the legitimate archbishop. They all affirmed that during Retz's absence jurisdiction must be exercised by those vicars-general chosen by the archbishop. The court, however, stubbornly refused to allow Retz to take the oath of fidelity and declared the seat vacant for the very reason that he had not taken the oath.[49] On this issue, the opponents of the ecclesiastical Fronde converged.

The position of the frondeurs was that legally, owing to the rights of future succession contained in his charge of coadjutor and to the recognition granted him by the chapter, the archiepiscopal seat unquestionably belonged to Retz.[50] As outlined by Marca, the government's strategy revolved around two problems: how to insure the nullification of Retz's accession to the archbishopric, and how to oblige the chapter to perform its duty (i.e., reject Retz's vicars-general). With regard to the oath, Marca assured Mazarin that it was obligatory for bishops to swear their fidelity to the king because of the authority which the prelate exercised over the monarch's subjects. As for the chapter, Marca suggested that an appeal to the primate of Lyon might result in the overturning of Retz's accession and so induce the chapter to establish new vicars-general. On the other hand, these problems would be solved if the court could force Retz to resign.[51] But the pope again frustrated the government's renewed steps in this direction.

Meanwhile, after the *arrêt* of 21 March, the court ordered the chapter to send deputies to the Louvre. The canons requested that the king grant Retz his liberty. Rejecting this plea, chancellor Séguier showed them the *arrêt*, which enjoined the chapter to assume the spiritual administration, and insisted that the king did not recognize Retz as archbishop. Forbidden to speak again, the canons were dismissed. After their representatives returned to Notre-Dame, the chapter replied to the government by naming as vicars-general the two clerics—Nicolas Ladvocat and Paul Chevalier—designated by Retz. Immediately, following the precedent set after the arrest of Retz, the two vicars-general ordered public prayers of forty hours for Retz's release and the exposition of the holy sacrament in every parish church.

Once more, the threat of an interdict hung over Mazarin and Paris. The curés, chapter, and pope waited for Retz to act. Quiescent since June of 1653, the curés now reaffirmed their ardor for Retz's cause. In an extraordinary assembly held on 22 March, the company claimed that Retz was the duly constituted archbishop by virtue of his having been coadjutor. They therefore rejected out of hand the government's position with respect to the oath of fidelity. And, because they believed that the bishop's presence in a diocese was necessary, the curés resolved to do everything in their power to secure Retz's deliverance. Specifically, they determined to write to the king, to send a deputy to plead with Louis, and to offer continual public prayers for the freedom of Retz. Finally, they recognized the defiant vicars-general, Ladvocat and Chevalier, and thus enthusiastically obeyed their instructions.[52]

Retz paid tribute to this support: "The curés grew more inflamed than usual, and my friends fanned the fire."[53] The curés made no attempt to hide their feelings toward Retz, although public display of such loyalty was considered seditious. Mazure, appointed by the 22 March assembly to deliver the funeral oration of the late archbishop, did not fail to laud Retz, referring to him as "the archbishop's learned nephew, Doctor of the Sorbonne, Cardinal of the Roman Church, powerful in deeds and in words, the light of truth, the Gospel's support, and, finally, the protector of the hierarchy."[54] It is significant that Mazure depicted Retz as the protector of the hierarchy, implying the curés' conception of the hierarchy, one that excluded Jesuits from a meaningful position. The sides in the Religious Fronde were already

drawn. There was no question at the time that if there were an interdict, the curés would close their churches but the regulars would decline to do so.

Backed by the curés, chapter, nuncio, and the pope, and in position
to issue an interdict, Retz appeared to pose a grave danger to the
government. Other groups were also causing the government concern:
"The people, who were not at first moved by Retz's imprisonment,
began to grumble and catch fire over religion. Condé's friends did
what they could to excite them."[55] Indeed, the adherents of Retz
certainly took heart when he acceded to the archiepiscopal see, an
important power base, as Mazarin's mania to keep Retz from utilizing
it amply demonstrates. It was thought that an interdict might be forthcoming during Easter week.[56] No doubt an interdict would have
forced Mazarin to grant Retz his freedom, but the archbishop did not
display his customary audacity. Retz's failure to employ an interdict
against the government remains one of the great puzzles of the Religious Fronde. Certainly there were many opportunities for him to do
so. After the death of his uncle, Retz was entering a state of depression
and may have feared for his life. He failed to recognize the power of
his supporters and perhaps believed that the potential utilization of an
interdict was of more benefit to him in his negotiations with the
crown.[57] Whatever the reason, Retz dismayed his staunchest supporters, which included every major group within the First Estate,
except the regulars and the University of Paris, which prudently bowed
out of the Religious Fronde.[58]

Unaware of Retz's hesitancy to take drastic action, Mazarin moved
to nullify the effects of clerical unrest. On 27 March, an *arrêt* of the
Conseil d'état commanded Chevalier and Ladvocat to relinquish their
charge, prohibited anyone from recognizing them as vicars-general,
and threatened printers who might work for the two canons. The
next day the vicars-general met with the chancellor, who tried unsuc-
cessfully to browbeat them into resigning.[59]

Mazarin also continued to press Retz for his resignation. Although
the latter was aware of the cardinal-minister's anxiety about the ecclesiastical uprising,[60] sixteen months in prison, during which he had
vainly anticipated an armed rebellion, sufficiently discouraged Retz.
Now despairing that his ecclesiastical supporters would ignite a revolt,
Retz on 28 March exchanged his office of archbishop for seven ab-
beys. However, he fully intended to renounce this resignation at the

first opportunity. According to the terms of the agreement, Retz would not be freed until the pope had accepted his resignation. In the meantime, Retz was transferred to the château of Nantes under the benevolent guard of his old friend, marshal de La Meilleraye. Ironically, Innocent refused to accept Retz's resignation; the pope contended that it had been signed under duress and was therefore null. That act, in the eyes of the Holy See, was an affront to the Church and to the College of Cardinals. Retz's freedom was now blocked by his staunchest ally. To compound Retz's predicament, the court became convinced that he had stiffened the resistance of the pope through his intermediary, Charrier. Incensed, his patience exhausted, Mazarin ordered Meilleraye to resume harsh treatment of his prisoner. Faced with the prospect of the rigor he had undergone during the early period of his incarceration at Vincennes, aware that accommodation with Mazarin was at best remote, and with his resolve fortified by a warning that he was about to be led to much less congenial conditions at Brest, Retz decided to escape. Such an act could, it was hoped, rouse the forces of ecclesiastical disorder and carry Retz to his rightful place as archbishop in the capital.[61]

3. Retz's Escape

On the evening of 8 August 1654, Retz made good his escape. Escorted by twelve hundred cavalry, most of them Breton noblemen, he eluded his pursuers.[62] Retz had originally intended to go to Paris, take possession of his archbishopric, and see what effect his daring would have on the populace. He had hoped that Condé's siege of Arras, which had already excited the populace, would combine with the cardinal-archbishop's presence in the capital to rally the forces of discontent, including the Parlement, the Hôtel de Ville, and both Condé's and Retz's adherents.[63]

The possibility of Retz's inciting a rebellion in Paris was very strong. Added to the ever-present "ill intentions of the Parisians toward cardinal Mazarin"[64] were several factors that fomented discontent bordering on open revolt. First, Retz's escape coincided with agitation by the Parlement on behalf of those, including many magistrates, who held rentes (government bonds) on the Hôtel de Ville of Paris. The Parlementary Fronde had been occasioned in part by the crown's refusal to pay interest on the *rentes* and now, spurred on by Nicolas Fouquet (appointed *surintendant des finances* in 1653), the government resumed traditional financial policies that again brought *rentiers* into opposition. Mazarin informed the Parlement that its involvement in the dissidence encouraged the Spanish. Abel Servien, who shared the office of *surintendant* with Fouquet, feared another rebellion by the judges. One spy warned Mazarin that the assemblies held by the Parlement to discuss the question of *rentes* could lead to another Chambre Saint-Louis. In charge of the government while Le Tellier and Mazarin were in Péronne, close to the fighting, a frightened Séguier wrote to the cardinal-minister of the increased threat the Parlement posed after Retz had regained his liberty.[65]

Furthermore, the war with Spain was at that moment in delicate balance. The French siege of Stenay had stalled, while Condé pressed vigorously at Arras. A victory by Condé would open the road to Paris for the Spanish army.[66] International war threatened to become civil war, and Retz prepared to take advantage of this prospect. War with England in the summer of 1654 was also possible and caused Mazarin great concern.[67] However, Retz's plan to go to Paris was thwarted by a dislocated shoulder he suffered during his escape. Instead, he was forced to allow his shoulder to heal before he set out again, this time to Spain, and then to Rome, where he arrived at the end of November.

The month of August was therefore critical with respect to a reawakening of armed rebellion. Until the Spanish lines at Arras were broken during the night of 24–25 August, the French government faced collapse at the hands of domestic malcontents and foreign powers. The fall of Arras would have signaled an overwhelming conjuncture of antigovernment forces: the Spanish army victorious in the North, an uprising in Bordeaux, English entry into the war, and Retz in Paris.[68] Mazarin kept a wary eye on the provinces, on the "new disturbances" in Bordeaux, and on the union of Retz and Condé.[69]

But it was from Paris that Mazarin had most to fear. A certain level of provincial revolt could be withstood—indeed tolerated as but one drawback pursuant to the excesses in governing that seventeenth-century warfare seemed to require—yet only Paris could topple the ministeriat. Ranum's explanation of the traditional Fronde, which could serve as a model for the events of the Religious Fronde, emphasized the strong possibility of a new day of barricades in August 1654. In his analysis, the "*Fronde* consisted of a series of extensive rural rebellions which eventually gained the towns and finally the capital."[70] It was Paris, then, drawing on previous outbreaks of provincial unrest, which rebelled and so in effect formulated a Fronde. August 1654 possessed the same preconditions for a new Fronde that Ranum found before August 1648: provincial disorder, economic depression, and high taxation. In addition, the war against Spain still raged with the outcome seriously in doubt. Would the impact of Retz's escape stir the regime's enemies to take decisive action? First reports seemed encouraging to those who still identified with the heady period of 1648 to 1652. Now it was the clergy, the ecclesiastical frondeurs, who proved the most serious threat to governmental stability, assuming the role of instigators earlier played by the magistrates. Like those parlementaires, these clerics sheltered their disobedience under a legalistic umbrella. Curés, and for a while canons, shook the foundations of stability in the name of Church privileges. The doctrine of ecclesiastical immunities and the principle that spiritual affairs must not be dominated by the secular arm served as rallying points for clerical resistance immediately subsequent to the liberation of Retz.

The inclusion of the First Estate among the rebels should have increased the possibility of a Paris in arms. Why, then, did provincial sparks not ignite Paris in 1654? No doubt decisive action by the court in Paris and in the provinces frustrated opposition. In the beginning of September, Mazarin momentarily defused the resistance to Fouquet's handling of the *rentes* by agreeing to the Parlement's demands. Retz thus lost potentially valuable allies, as his supporters had been attempting to utilize the financial crisis and parlementary opposition on his behalf.[71] Because of the discontent, the king interrupted the military campaign and returned to Paris. He was therefore unable to exploit the triumph at Arras, but his stay in the capital, combined with a decision to abolish recently imposed taxes, may have calmed his subjects. The crown wanted to disprove the idea that the success of French arms depended on high taxes.[72]

Mazarin's absence from Paris may have deprived frondeurs of a personal focus for that animosity which so characterized 1648. On the other hand, the failure of a leader like Retz to appear, one around whom defiance could be transposed into sedition, could have been significant. Certainly by his imprisonment and by the abuse he suffered from the government, Retz presented a martyr image similar to that formerly enjoyed by the parlementaire Pierre Broussel, whose arrest in 1648 had provoked the uprising known as the Days of Barricades. What does seem probable is that Retz's presence in the capital had great potential as a catalyst for rebellion, and that his failure to assert himself at the crucial moment blunted the Religious Fronde. But perhaps the curés realized that even if Condé's Spanish army had triumphed and Retz had returned to Paris, the curés and their interests might have been ignored. Although the curés ardently supported him, they could have speculated that the crafty Retz might not continue to tolerate their independent tendencies once he was in power.

The hypersensibility of the populace and the inclination to revolt among stable and well-placed social and professional groups are difficult to gauge. One can only conclude that the reasons, precipitants, and factors which explain the raising of barricades are elusive and sometimes seemingly fortuitous. "There is no strict determinism in the matter of revolt and revolution, no logical sequence, no direct link between the set of circumstances explaining and justifying revolt and the act of revolt itself. The link is a psychological one, a very complex psychological one, and in most cases the historian is unable to enter into the psychology, conscious or subconscious, of the men he studies."[73] As one scholar has noted, the effort to "establish a clear causal connection between the preconditions of revolution and the events triggering it presents an almost insoluble problem, not only in historical psychology but also in logic."[74] Historians have tended to study the "successes" rather than those periods (1654, for example) during which high levels of discontent failed to culminate in armed rebellion.

The news of Retz's escape sent shock waves through Paris and rallied the clergy to his support. The chapter, in open defiance of the government, sang a Te Deum attended by more than six hundred persons, while the curés joined in the celebrations along with the populace. On the very day of his escape, Retz formally recanted his resignation of the archbishopric, which he had tendered at Vincennes, and sent letters to the chapter and curés of Paris expressing his resolve to stand with his clergy.[75] The chapter's response to Retz signified its joy at his safety and informed him of the Te Deum and prayers offered on his behalf.[76]

Séguier was both alarmed and furious. His letters to Mazarin and the latter's replies before the lifting of the siege of Arras reveal the ministers' desperate efforts to crush clerical resistance. In fact, the government's harsh suppression of ecclesiastical protest in Paris during August, while setting an example that would intimidate future defiance to a degree, cast the government in the role of tyrant, oppressing the liberties and immunities of the First Estate. None in the government suggested moderation in dealing with the recalcitrant clerics, although Marca, for one, recognized what problems would arise from the violation of Church rights.[77]

Government reaction, then, was swift and severe. The court interpreted the public prayers and the Te Deum as a condemnation of the king's justice and as a blow to his authority that could not be tolerated. It was necessary to remove "the most seditious" from Paris.[78] A garrison was stationed in the archiepiscopal palace and all suspect persons evicted. Five canons of Notre-Dame, including Ladvocat and Chevalier, were ordered to the court at Péronne to answer for their disobedience. A royal ordinance of 20 August called for the arrest of Retz and accused him of fomenting rebellion. Two days later the crown issued five letters, ordinances, and *arrêts* designed to end the incipient Fronde. Letters sent to the governor of Paris and to the *prévôt des marchands* (the head of the municipal administration) cautioned them that Retz might return to Paris and commanded them to repress seditious behavior and rebellion. An ordinance of the same day demanded that all domestics and agents of Retz leave Paris within twenty-four hours. Moreover, an *arrêt* from the *Conseil d'état* required the chapter to turn over the register of its deliberations and its correspondence with Retz. Lastly, another *arrêt* declared the archbishopric vacant and forbade Chevalier and Ladvocat to exercise the charge of vicar-general.[79]

Mazarin was delighted with these resolutions, which, coupled with reprisals taken in the provinces, might yet forestall a revolt in Paris.[80] But resistance was not over. Chevalier and Ladvocat issued an episcopal letter prohibiting recognition, under penalty of excommunication, of any jurisdiction other than theirs.[81] The chapter also would not obey the court's demand. Séguier, shaken, suggested that recourse be made to the primate of Lyon to appoint new vicars-general even, he added, if the curés would not recognize them. The week of Ember days approached; the chancellor feared that with Retz's vicars-general sent by *lettres de cachet* to the king, ordinations would be impossible and the government would be exposed to public accusations that it had left the Paris Church without spiritual direction.[82]

The lifting of the siege of Arras relieved the pressure on the government. The clerical revolt in Paris was temporarily without hope of receiving armed assistance from outside. Writing to Mazarin, Séguier expressed satisfaction: "I do not doubt that obedience will be forthcoming after the news of the fortunate success of the king's arms . . . Paris will certainly change her mood. The Fronde is mortally wounded, and we will have peace in the state. . . . Never was a victory so advantageous for this crown."[83] Fortified by the news that the Spanish would not reach Paris, the court delivered a second *arrêt* to the chapter, even more stringent than the first, enjoining it to deliver to the government its recent capitulary deliberations and its correspondence with Retz. And, by "an unprecedented usurpation," the court ordered the chapter to appoint new vicars-general for the administration of the "vacant" archdiocese.[84] Paradoxically, these measures, intended to preserve the state from a recurrence of the Frondes and successful in the short run, stoked the fires of ecclesiastical disobedience throughout the 1650s. The wholesale violation of Church privileges, commencing with Retz's incarceration in 1652 and climaxing with the plethora of government edicts and the liberal utilization of *lettres de cachet* in August 1654, provided a future rallying point for religious frondeurs. This highhanded action by the court moved the General Assembly of 1655–57 to support Retz and guaranteed continued defiance on the part of the curés, although they were momentarily cowed in early September 1654.

The chapter yielded to the new *arrêt*, although not completely. It provided for the spiritual administration of the diocese by naming four canons as vicars-general, but it did this by reason of Retz's absence, not because of a vacancy as the government had insisted.[85] The religious frondeurs were incensed. Ladvocat at once declared that he would excommunicate those vicars-general appointed by the chapter, but he was prevented by Chevalier and Loisel, who advised that Retz should choose new ones from among "the most zealous ecclesiastics of Paris" such as Rousse, Loisel, Mazure, Duhamel, Jean-Baptiste Chassebras (curé of La Madeleine), etc. Furthermore, Retz should prepare to excommunicate all those who dared to recognize the vicars-general appointed by the chapter. "In the present state of affairs, it is necessary to defend the Church by the arms of the Church."[86]

The court saw that the chapter, in stipulating the absence of Retz, effectively recognized that he was the legitimate archbishop. However, the fact that Retz's vicars-general were dispossessed seemed a victory for the government.[87] Nor was this all. On 3 September the chapter met with Séguier to signal its submission to the government and later handed over all the acts and letters it had received from Retz.[88] Though not achieving everything it desired—the acknowledgment that Retz was not archbishop—the court could feel satisfied that Notre-Dame was no longer actively proselytizing disobedience and that it had consented to follow the government's commands. The frondeurs felt betrayed. One Mazarinade declared that the first minister had compelled the canons to usurp the diocesan administration: they were threatened with the loss of their privileges and promised rewards if they obeyed the government. Those who proved incorruptible were exiled. The pamphlet exposed the chapter's ploy of stating that Retz was merely absent; for the archbishop's presence was manifested in his vicars-general, who were duly recognized in Paris and who were performing their duties. There was then no valid reason for the chapter to arrogate their powers.[89] The chapter had conceded its role in the Religious Fronde, the University of Paris did not make a whimper after Retz's escape,[90] but what of the curés?

The special tie between the curés and their pastor was enunciated by Retz in his letter to the curés on 8 August. It was not without reason that Retz signified, on the day of his escape, his thanks for their support and his hope that they would continue to aid him.[91] On 13 August the curés convoked an extraordinary assembly to deal with the aftermath of Retz's escape. The letter from the cardinal-archbishop was immediately read. The assembly then made four resolutions. The curés thanked God for the deliverance of Retz and for the miraculous conservation of his person during his escape. Secondly, it was decided to exhort the people to pray for Retz's happy and prompt return to Paris. Next, it was resolved to await the orders of the vicars-general before singing a Te Deum. And, finally, Rousse was asked to thank Retz by letter and to assure him of the company's continuing sacrifices and prayers.[92]

Séguier wrote to Mazarin the following day to warn of the effects of public prayers and the Te Deum in the parishes and to recommend exiling the most disobedient curés.[93] On the fifteenth, the chancellor reported that as a result of the assembly of the curés he had admonished the vicars-general not to authorize the curés to deliver public prayers or even to speak of Retz's escape in their sermons. Later in the day, Séguier learned from an informant, André Du Saussay (who was both the *official* and curé of Saint-Leu-Saint-Gilles), that Chevalier and Ladvocat were to send extraordinary episcopal letters to the curés to be promulgated from the pulpit. Séguier immediately issued an *arrêt* prohibiting the vicars-general from taking such action.[94] In this way, the chancellor sought to dampen the power of the pulpit.

The court respected and feared the ability of the sermon to move the population. The government had benefited from the neutrality of the parish priests during the first Frondes. Consequently, preaching was not a weapon to be found in the frondeur arsenal, with but one great exception. Inflammatory and seditious, Retz's sermons brought him notoriety. And, now, the government was confronted with ecclesiastics—curés—who had regular and legal access to the pulpit and who had "great power over all their parishioners." The curés did indeed unleash seditious sermons in support of their archbishop.[95] Mazarin, much concerned with propaganda and the value of the press, was very conscious of the sermon's influence in this religious society.[96]

The "licentious preaching" of the curés after Retz's escape aroused the government to action. While five canons were exiled for the Te Deum sung by the chapter, three curés, Loisel, Mazure, and Nicolas de Bry, curé of Saint-Cosme, received *lettres de cachet* commanding them to appear at court. According to one contemporary, the government had correctly gauged the danger presented by the curés' sermons. "It is true, and it must be said to the shame of our century, that license was still so great in Paris, even among the preachers, that they did not fear to make note in their sermons of their aversion for the minister [Mazarin] and their old inclination for the Fronde."[97]

Mazarin and those in Paris agreed upon the need to set an example by exiling the most unruly clerics.[98] In fact, the *lettres de cachet* had been forwarded from Péronne to the ministers in the capital, who then filled in the names of those to be exiled in the blank spaces. Those sent to the court were later dispersed throughout France: Loisel, for example, was ordered to Bourges and later transferred to Compiègne under the watchful eye of the government.[99] Loisel was considered especially dangerous—so much so that Servien advised sending him to lower Brittany, while trusting that Mazure and Bry could be reprimanded and restored to their cures.[100] Mazarin concurred and permitted Mazure to return. Although the cardinal-minister knew that Mazure had "very bad intentions," that he was a Jansenist, and that he had worked against the king's interests, Mazarin accepted the curé's promise to behave in the future.[101] More important, Mazarin no doubt remembered the popular outburst over a previous exiling of the curé of Saint-Paul in April 1654.

Duhamel, however, blatantly manifested his support for Retz in his sermons. On the Sunday following Retz's escape this curé of Saint-Merry quoted the lines of the prophet: "You have broken my bonds, O Lord, and in gratitude I will sacrifice to you an offering of praise." Continuing, Duhamel commiserated with the archbishop's plight. "We will see again this beloved and kind prelate. I myself will go to find him on your behalf and embrace his knees." In order better to excite the people to desire Retz's presence, Duhamel evoked the example of Absalom who, having been deprived for several years of his father David, asked to see him or to die. All of Paris, thundered Duhamel, and particularly the parishioners of Saint-Merry to whom Retz had never refused anything, should feel the same sentiments toward their archbishop. Furthermore, the curé compared Retz to Joseph, who had been imprisoned and sold by his brothers. Joseph had become a great minister of state only after much tribulation; like him, Retz would raise himself from his captivity greater and more glorious than before. The tenderness and devotion expressed by Duhamel toward the archbishop moved the people of Saint-Merry for the rest of the day. To Rapin, the boldness of this speech was linked to the current siege of Arras, as news of that battle reached Paris the same time as that of Retz's escape.[102]

On 22 August, in response to the exiling of their colleagues and of the vicars-general, the Parisian curés held their second extraordinary assembly of the month, and one of the most defiant of the Religious Fronde. The curés reiterated their position that they assembled under the archbishop's authority, not to debate political affairs, but only to provide for the needs of their individual churches. Thus, after acknowledging that they had come together to remonstrate against the treatment accorded their fellows—who had been banished for seditious behavior—the curés insisted that their company did not concern itself with politics and so expressed the hope that the court would not take action against the assemblies. If this were not enough the curés declared that they could not recognize anyone but Retz as archbishop, nor receive orders from any but Retz's vicars-general. Moreover, having been informed that the king wanted to issue an *arrêt* attributing the spiritual administration of the archdiocese to the chapter, the curés respectfully resolved that they would rather suffer death than obey such an order so antithetical to the rules of the Church. Lastly, Jean Rousse, Pierre Colombet, curé of Saint-Germain-l'Auxerrois, and Pierre Marlin were deputed to see the latter's parishioner, Séguier. The assembly instructed these curés to point out to the chancellor that the diocese could not function very long without archbishop or vicars-general, as episcopal authority was required to resolve important matters. In a none too subtle threat, the deputies were to inform Séguier that the populace felt the absence of those who were banished, and that this situation required the return of the exiled curés and vicars-general without delay.[103]

After he had received their remonstrances, the chancellor berated the three curés, reminding them that the king had forbidden the convocation of extraordinary assemblies. The effect of such meetings, affirmed Séguier, would be to "rouse their parishioners' emotions." Finding that the curés would not concede anything, Séguier dismissed them and relayed to Mazarin his fear that if Retz were to throw an interdict on Paris, there were few curés who would not obey it.[104] Marca too noted, after preparing a detailed memorandum on policy alternatives with respect to the troubles in the archdiocese, that his plans could flounder only through the resistance of the Parisian curés.[105]

Within two weeks, however, the curés were temporarily cowed into submission. Another extraordinary assembly, of 26 August, defied the government's ban on such meetings. Though this assembly only intended to make arrangements for the celebration of the victory at Arras, the court was not about to forgive the curés' frondeur behavior. Indeed, the success at Arras allowed the government to act more forcibly and with greater confidence in suppressing internal dissent. It was not coincidental that both the chapter and the curés bowed at the same time, although for those curés who were frondeurs this was merely a momentary setback. In effect, those curés loyal to the government managed to assert themselves at the 4 September assembly. The others, perhaps depressed by the chapter's recent capitulation and by the renascent energy of both the court and its adherents, found that the corps had resolved that the chapter was correct in assuming the diocesan administration and that the curés would obey the orders of the new vicars-general. In addition, a letter addressed to the assembly from Retz was turned over to the government.[106]

Mazarin was particularly incensed at Duhamel, whom he falla-
ciously believed to have composed the curés' response to Retz's letter
of 8 August. After Duhamel's sermon on 16 August, Mazarin wrote
that the curé of Saint-Merry "is assuredly the most guilty of all. There
is nothing more seditious or more contemptuous of the king than what
he said in his sermon. It is all the more so since he had the insolence to
do this after the king's prohibitions."[107] The first minister was certainly justified in his reaction. Duhamel's appeal to the populace to
work for Retz's return constituted "the threat of a new Fronde."[108]

Nor did this curé cease his audacity. In the assembly of 22 August,
he endeavored to incite his fellows to revolt by a seditious speech in
which he declared that it was imperative to expose one's head for the
liberty of Retz and for the defense of his vicars-general. "The Church
of Paris is in ruin by the sad marks of a disastrous widowhood, and we
are not touched! Let us at least go and throw ourselves at the feet of
the chancellor or of the keeper of the seals in order to show them the
state to which the clergy has been reduced. Moreover, we know that
our strength lies in our union. Let us be united and no one will be able
to do anything to us."[109] In his sermon of Sunday, 30 August, Duhamel said it was necessary to ask God to bless the king in order that
Louis not pride himself on his successes, and "to place in his heart a
kindness toward his subjects so that he will recall our pastor to his
flock." According to Rapin, Duhamel's audience was easily swayed by
such talk.[110]

In the curés' assembly of 4 September, Duhamel vehemently defended the reading of Retz's letter against the efforts of such loyalists
as Pierre Chapelas, curé of Saint-Jacques-de-la-Boucherie, and Roullé.
Two days later, as a Te Deum for the raising of the siege of Arras was
sung amid public rejoicing, a *lettre de cachet* ordered Duhamal to
depart from Paris within twenty-four hours. The conjuncture of public
celebration and Duhamel's exile was not coincidental: the court
thought this the most opportune time to avoid antigovernment out-
bursts. Hermant caustically noted that "according to a style which has
become quite common, these public rejoicings could be fatal to some
persons."[111]

Even at this late date the government sought to convince Duhamel
to break his attachment to Retz. When this failed, the court indicated
that it would be satisfied if Duhamel would simply agree to abstain
from actively serving the disgraced cardinal. The curé asserted he

could not comply—his conscience obliged him to attend the assemblies of the curés, and he could not promise anything with respect to matters treated there. Duhamel believed in a perfect submission to the Church and so to his archbishop. Because of this outspoken support for Retz, Duhamel went into a difficult exile. Unlike previous curés, such as Mazure, Bry, or Loisel, who had been relegated either to a country home or to the itinerant court, Duhamel was ordered to Langres. From there he was moved to Quimper, in Brittany, which was, along with Auvergne, where the government at its most severe would send its exiles. In truth, exaggerating as it did the less colorful resistance of the other curés, Duhamel's behavior demanded retribution. The court had long known of Duhamel's behavior—the fact that his punishment came so late, and so reluctantly, testified to the risk involved in stirring up a parish by castigating a popular curé.[112]

Feydeau, the *vicaire* of Saint-Merry, confirmed in an audience with Mazarin that the first minister had indeed exiled Duhamel because his parish had become a center of agitation. Mazarin informed Feydeau that the clergy must inspire in the people feelings of submission and obedience toward the king. "Much sedition was heard in the parishes, which got mixed up in many things. Duhamel had preached in favor of the cardinal de Retz, who was a prisoner and in disgrace."[113] Mazarin was justified in his apprehensions: the order to exile Duhamel drew a great crowd to the curé's house to receive his blessing. The gathering frightened the court. "Emotion was nearly universal in the entire neighborhood of Saint-Merry."[114]

The curés remained relatively quiescent through the remaining months of 1654, though they still counted as the principal fund of Retz's support in Paris. In their assembly of 4 November, the curés persevered in their fidelity to Retz while affirming that they would obey the chapter's orders in regard to diocesan administration. Moreover, they resolved to continue their prayers for Retz, to express their good will to the exiled Chevalier, Ladvocat, Bry, and Loisel, and to press the ministers to learn if the king would be agreeable to receiving a remonstrance for Retz's return.[115] Meanwhile, the Retz affair shifted to the problem of his possible trial, a ferocious pamphlet war, and the entanglements caused by his reception in Rome.

The government's efforts to bring Retz to justice endured from September 1654 to April 1657, and were to be resumed under Louis' personal reign in a successful ploy to frighten Retz into resigning his archiepiscopal seat and thus to put an end to the Religious Fronde. The court's attempt to try Retz was without precedent. Never in France had a bishop been subjected to jurisdiction by the secular arm prior to his deposition by a commission of his peers. The government blundered in so blatantly violating Church immunities, as ecclesiastical frondeurs were handed a cloak of justice under which they readily leveled charges of persecution and tyranny against the ministeriat. The court's hasty actions thus had an effect antithetical to what was intended—Retz's cause remained strong as the government appeared to have put itself in the wrong.

The court was obstinate in maintaining that Retz's trial must take place in France and by Frenchmen. To begin the process the government sent the Parlement on 21 September a commission to inform against Retz, which the magistrates, ever delighted to witness the extension of their own powers, quickly registered.[116] The king's commission reiterated the accusations against Retz, which in the government's eyes clearly depicted him as an unrepentant frondeur and a serious threat to the security of the state. Retz had violated the royal amnesty; he had been advised by Condé and the latter's adherents that lifting the siege of Arras would be favorable to them; and Retz had traveled to Spain to consult with the Spanish and with Condé's agents. In addition, the commission's indictment listed the letters (to the chapter and the curés) that Retz had written after his escape; it contended that Retz had planned to come to Paris after a Condéan victory at Arras; and, lastly, it accused Retz of attempting to stir provincial nobility to rebellion.

But the court soon realized its errors. Marca had adamantly opposed sending the commission to the Parlement because he realized that clerical immunities must be respected, that only ecclesiastics could sit in judgment on Retz.[117] Marca's fears proved correct: the agents-general remonstrated against the *arrêt* of the *chambre des vacations* (the body of magistrates providing justice during the summer recess), which registered the commission. What angered the clergy were clauses in the *arrêt* which affirmed the Parlement's role in the judicial process on the grounds that Retz's crime of lese majesty nullified his exemption and immunity.[118] Now anxious to seek a solution but unable to revoke the commission without suffering undue humiliation, the government issued an *arrêt* restricting the rights granted to the Parlement while stressing the king's wish that the "authority, franchises, privileges, and immunities" of the Church would be conserved.[119]

This, however, was not sufficient. The issue of the Parlement's interference in Church affairs became a primary concern of the next General Assembly of the Clergy. Indeed, the pressure brought upon the government resulted in a substantial victory for the First Estate: an *arrêt* of the *Conseil d'état* nullified the commission of 21 September 1654. And, by recognizing their immunities and privileges, the government now agreed that cardinals and prelates accused of lese majesty would be brought before ecclesiastical judges.[120]

Retz's potential trial thus furnished an issue around which the clergy could exploit their cohesiveness in the overcharged atmosphere of the Religious Fronde into a significant triumph over the Parlement, whose sequential encroachments on the privileges of the Church provided one of the main themes of Church-state relations in early modern France. This was also a defeat for the crown, which found to its dismay that it could not easily impose its wishes upon a rebellious clerical population.

While the government floundered on the clergy's objections to a trial of Retz by laymen, it was no less rebuffed by papal refusal to accede to the court's demands that Retz be extradited to France for trial. Innocent X congratulated Retz on his deliverance in a published letter dated 30 September 1654. The pope greeted the cardinal-archbishop with expressions of friendship and esteem, conferring on Retz his cardinal's hat and presenting him with a sizable monetary gift.[121]

Although Retz had the pontiff's protection, the court sent Lionne as special ambassador to pressure Innocent to yield Retz to French justice. Lionne's instructions provided him with detailed arguments to utilize in his audiences with the pope. In addition to the specifics of the proposed trial, the instructions contained reasons why Retz's accession to the archiepiscopal see was canonically invalid and why the chapter was justified in assuming the spiritual administration.[122] Lionne's arrival was preceded by a formal letter from Louis to the pope listing Retz's crimes and asking Innocent to name commissioners to conduct the trial of the king's treasonous subject.[123] The new ambassador did not arrive in Rome until 22 January 1655, shortly after Innocent's death. However, the new pope, Alexander VII, did not prove congenial to Lionne's protracted endeavors to initiate Retz's trial. Exasperated, Lionne returned to France in 1656, having failed in his primary objective.[124]

After Retz arrived in Rome, he appealed to the French public in a series of elegantly written works. He published letters to the king and queen in which he expressed his fidelity and innocence.[125] At the same time he addressed a lengthy circular letter to the archbishops and bishops of France which had a great impact on Paris. Here, Retz complained of his arrest, imprisonment, and persecutions, while comparing his sufferings to those of certain Church Fathers and other clerics (such as Becket). Retz noted that he was not excluded from the amnesty, denied that he had made a treaty with Condé, and decried the persecution of his relatives, friends, and servants. Finally, Retz assailed the chapter's usurpation of the spiritual administration of the diocese and appealed to the episcopacy for its support.[126] Mazarin's response was to have the letter burned by the public executioner and to have his writers refute Retz in six pamphlets.

4. The Troubles of the Archdiocese (1655–1656)

This reaction typified the futility of government policy in 1655, a year that witnessed severe defeats for the court. The election of Fabio Chigi as pope Alexander VII, with the aid of Retz, was interpreted as a setback for France. Retz's partisans in Paris greeted this news with "fires of joy."[127] Indeed, the pontiff's early acts confirmed the frondeurs' expectations while they incurred Mazarin's wrath.[128] On 14 May, despite Lionne's protests, the pope conferred upon Retz the pallium, the mantle of white wool that was the symbol of his archiepiscopal authority.[129]

Government attempts to mitigate by decree Retz's influence within France continued by an ordinance of 16 April, which forbade all subjects to correspond with Retz.[130] Like so many other edicts issued during the Religious Fronde, this proved to be a dead letter. Alexander's decision to publish a bull proclaiming a jubilee—a customary act for each pope commencing his pontificate—was the occasion for wholesale disobedience to the April ordinance. The nuncio, Bagni, who supported Retz, prohibited the chapter from publishing it under pain of excommunication. Retz utilized this opportunity to exercise his authority as archbishop. On 22 May, he addressed a letter to the chapter complaining of its usurpation of the spiritual administration of the diocese and notifying it that Chevalier and Ladvocat would publish the bull. In case those two canons were prevented from discharging their duties, Retz appointed two new vicars, Chassebras and Alexandre Hodencq, curé of Saint-Severin. The Parisian curés, who had not approved of the chapter's administration, published the bull in their parishes without the chapter's orders; thus, they submitted to the new vicars-general functioning under Retz's authority.[131]

The court steadfastly sought to have the chapter retain administration of the diocese and tried to convince Bagni to withdraw or delay his orders to the chapter concerning the bull. Publicly, the government reacted to the letter of 22 March by reaffirming the act of 22 August 1654 (which had declared the archbishopric vacant), by citing precedents for the chapter's right to administer the diocese, and by once again cataloguing Retz's alleged crimes in an attempt to turn popular and clerical opinion against the forces of disorder.[132] But the arrival of Retz's letter on 14 June marked the end of the chapter's compliance with the government as well as its central role in this Fronde. Séguier, to whom the chapter communicated the letter, found the canons illdisposed to continue their defiance of Retz.[133] Two of the previous vicars-general informed the chancellor that while they would individually be willing to serve, they would face opposition from the chapter and "from the vast majority of the curés, who had always detested obeying their *vicariat*."[134]

For the remainder of the month, Séguier sought to browbeat Chassebras and Hodencq into renouncing their new offices. By accepting Retz's commission, the two curés had flagrantly violated the royal ordinance of 16 April. When threatened with *lettres de cachet*, Chassebras and Hodencq protested their duty to obey their archbishop's will.[135] It was apparent, even to those sympathetic to the government, that the Church was being persecuted. As one informant pointed out to Servien, the problem of Retz and his vicars-general could be approached in two ways. Regarded as an affair of religion, it was very delicate, for if Retz were truly the archbishop there could be no doubt that the jurisdiction of the diocese belonged to him. Considered as an affair of state, on the other hand, there was no question that Retz disrupted the public peace, and that the court therefore had to prevent the newly instituted vicars-general from functioning.[136]

But there were difficulties in separating the religious and political aspects of these altercations. It was precisely these problems which compelled the court to procrastinate before punishing the two curés. Thus, while Séguier alternately cajoled and threatened Chassebras and Hodencq, Mazarin hoped to convince the pope to recognize the vicars-general who had been selected by the chapter the previous year. The first minister had in the past experienced the errors of misjudging discontent: to repress the clergy could be dangerous.[137] If the court proceeded without caution in religious matters, it faced the possibility of causing an alignment of malcontents against the government. Certain bishops, the Parlement, and the nuncio appeared set to oppose the government. And, as Séguier noted, "The curés are the most attached to the cardinal de Retz, and secretly follow his orders."[138] Only Roullé, of all the curés, unquestionably upheld the court's position during June with respect to the problem of the vicars-general and—the real question—of Retz's status as archbishop.[139]

Séguier, faced with the defiance of Chassebras and Hodencq, was still reluctant to give them *lettres de cachet*: "They are curés, whose detention would cause a great uproar which must be avoided."[140] The possibility still existed of Retz throwing an interdict on Paris. It was indicative of the importance which the government attached to this affair that, in spite of possible repercussions, the chancellor issued *lettres de cachet* to Chassebras and Hodencq on 30 June.[141] The curé of Saint-Severin received the order and promptly traveled to the court at Soissons. Chassebras, on the other hand, went into hiding and from there administered the spiritual concerns of the diocese by himself.[142]

The court, enmeshed "in an affair which cardinal Mazarin considered the greatest of the kingdom,"[143] now had to end Chassebras' defiance, which set an example for Parisians. Above all, it was imperative to detach the curés from Retz and from Chassebras. As the curés were scheduled to assemble on 5 July, Séguier anxiously prepared to coerce them into submission and so to impede the expression of discontent at the exiling of the vicars-general.[144] On the day of the assembly, a royal *huissier* (bailiff) delivered orders to the curés specifically forbidding them to receive letters or instructions from Retz. While Séguier interpreted the curés' silence as compliance, the assembly in fact received—after the bailiff had departed—a letter addressed to it by Chassebras. The curé of la Madeleine informed his colleagues that he intended to exercise the function of vicar-general even though he was forced to remain hidden. Furthermore, he exhorted the curés to address themselves to him in matters relating to the spiritual needs of their parishes and to unite with him in order to conserve their archbishop's authority. The company resolved to recognize Chassebras as vicar-general.[145] However, perhaps because the king had recently abolished their assemblies for a three-month period (December 1654 through February 1655), the curés prudently declined to publicize this act of defiance.[146]

For the next six months, Chassebras administered the diocese from his hiding place in the towers of the Church of Saint-Jean-en-Grève. His servant, the first churchwarden of the parish, and the curé's uncle were all implored—even menaced—to aid in locating him. Seeking to obtain information about Chassebras and to acquire the original of his letter to the curés' assembly for use in his possible trial, the *lieutenant civil* interviewed twelve curés.[147] Rousse, on behalf of the curés, declined to relinquish the original. Furious, but wary of their influence, Séguier hesitated to exile these curés, even though "we truly cannot have calm in Paris if these troublesome characters are there."[148]

The *prévôt* of Paris, in light of Chassebras' disregard of the *lettre de cachet*, gave him one week to return to his duty or face persecution as one who was "refractory" and "disobedient."[149] Séguier, embarrassed by his failure to locate the curé, justified his diligence by instigating such measures. The chancellor claimed to act against Chassebras in the same way as he would against a disobedient prince of the blood. "It is important to take note of this action [Chassebras' disobedience] and treat it with severity. Otherwise, the king's commands will be little respected in the future."[150] But nowhere was Chassebras to be found, though Séguier assured Brienne that the curé must be at Port-Royal: "He is a renowned Jansenist, who acts in this occasion on their [the Jansenists at Port-Royal] advice."[151] One week later, Séguier reported that Chassebras had been with the nuncio and at Port-Royal-des-Champs, and "left only three days ago. We do not know as yet where he has gone."[152]

Those ministers outside of Paris were chagrined at Séguier's seeming impotence: "it is very strange that in a city where the king is master we cannot prevent violence and scandal."[153] Brienne warned Séguier that "the undertaking of the curé of la Madeleine has so angered the court that it will only be satisfied when he is punished."[154] Mazarin also complained of Chassebras: "It is certain that there is no greater Jansenist in the world than this so-called *vicaire* of the cardinal de Retz. He does the worst that he can, leaves no stone unturned to plot in Paris, and carries out blindly everything that is suggested to him on behalf of those among Retz's adherents who work so passionately to excite sedition."[155] It was not, then, merely the example of rebelliousness Chassebras offered which infuriated the government, but more significantly his alliance with other frondeurs and, consequently, his efforts to further discontent against the crown.

While Séguier hunted Chassebras, the curé fought back. Although he could not leave the church for fear of being discovered, he still managed to communicate with his colleagues. Chassebras left his instructions on the altar of the Church of Saint-Jean-en-Grève, from where they were taken and printed. During the night, men carried on their backs the placards, which were covered with glue; after leaning against churches, street-corners, and public places, these frondeurs simply walked on, leaving the leaflets posted behind them.[156]

On 15 August, Paris awoke to find posted an episcopal letter of Retz (dated 28 June) along with one of Chassebras. That of Retz reaffirmed Chassebras and Hodencq as vicars-general and commanded the faithful to submit to the spiritual authority of these two curés. In addition, the archbishop sought to intimidate and frighten those who dared to ignore his canonical jurisdiction:

> those who seek saving grace other than under our direction and those appointed by us, will find only their condemnation. Those who take Holy Orders will rather bind themselves before God and make themselves abominable, than place themselves in a position to absolve and sanctify others. . . . Dispensations given for marriages will not be valid, nor will religious professions be canonical. Finally, any command besides ours will be a horrible sacrilege and an odious usurpation.[157]

Chassebras' accompanying letter proclaimed his determination to retain his charge as vicar-general and not to abandon his bishop.[158] These two letters, placed on all the churches of Paris and on those of the suburbs, were timed to coincide with the festival of the Assumption, when the people would be massed in the churches during the morning and later in the streets to watch the annual solemn procession that marked this holiday.[159] The court recognized this ploy, but Séguier could soon report that the letters had caused no disturbance.[160]

Chassebras, however, was not finished. On 8 September, he posted a monition throughout Paris, in which he reviewed the violences committed against him and, through him, against the archbishop. In conclusion he demanded that those responsible for his persecution make public reparation for their sins. If this were not done, warned Chassebras, he would have recourse "to the means which the Holy Church and the canons prescribe in such circumstances." In short, the curé threatened excommunication.[161]

In reply, the government tore down and burned the offending placards, as it was to do with all of Chassebras' decrees. The *procureur-général*, Nicolas Fouquet, presented a request to the Parlement against the monition which, he said, had been promulgated in order to incite the populace to sedition. The magistrates immediately issued an *arrêt* authorizing prosecution of writers and printers of subversive libels and placards. The Châtelet sentenced Chassebras, for rebellion and disobedience, to perpetual banishment from the kingdom. Moreover, his property was confiscated and his benefices declared vacant.[162]

But the more the crown pursued Chassebras, the greater his image as a persecuted cleric became. Hermant eloquently summed up the feelings of those malcontents who suffered (and gloried) in the treatment accorded the frondeur vicar-general. "It was a sad spectacle to see . . . a celebrated Parisian curé, doctor of the Sorbonne, treated as a criminal without his having committed any other crime than that of acquitting himself in a purely spiritual affair of the obedience which he promised his archbishop the day of his ordination."[163]

The see-saw battle continued, as Chassebras successfully exercised his jurisdictional and canonical authority. In October he forbade the provincial assembly of Paris, which had been convoked by Dominique Séguier, bishop of Meaux and the chancellor's brother, to meet without the archbishop's authorization. This assembly, composed of the suffragan bishops of Paris, had intended to appoint delegates to the upcoming General Assembly of the Clergy. Thwarted, the bishops had to disperse without deciding anything. Chassebras' action was one factor in postponing the opening of the General Assembly.[164]

On 18 October, Chassebras peppered the capital with proclamations, including an episcopal letter from Retz barring Antoine-Denis

Cohon, bishop of Saint-Pol (and former bishop of Dol), and Claude Auvry, bishop of Coutances, from exercising any ecclesiastical functions in Paris. These two bishops, in violation of canon law, had conferred ordinations in the Church of Paris, neglecting to seek permission from Retz's vicars-general. The actions of these two bishops—creatures of Mazarin—produced a scandal and a schism. The diocese divided into two camps. The first consisted of clerics loyal to the government; these men upheld the chapter's jurisdiction upon which Cohon and Auvry had based their actions. The second was composed of frondeurs and others who sympathized with those suffering from the violation of customary ecclesiastical and canonical privileges. In the latter camp were the curés of Paris and of the countryside, supported by the nuncio.[165]

While the crown defended the chapter's decision to ask the two bishops to confer orders, maintaining that it was necessary to save the diocese,[166] the frondeurs convincingly portrayed the action as but one more example of a tyrannical government persecuting the Church. Furthermore, those who recognized the recently ordained risked damnation. The faithful were told that sacraments performed by those priests were sacrileges, that their absolutions were invalid, and that marriages so performed had condemned the spouses to concubinage.[167]

Guy Joly declared that the time was opportune for an interdict, which would have had a great impact in Paris, particularly as most of the curés and the diocese could be counted upon to obey it. But, as Joly recounted, Retz could never decide to take this step, which seemed even more propitious because of Chassebras' resolute actions. Unfortunately for the frondeurs, the steadfastness of the curé was not equaled by the archbishop.[168] In fact, Retz's episcopal letter had been occasioned by open defiance of the court from another locus of discontent, the prelacy.

François d'Harlay, archbishop of Rouen, forbade the bishop of Coutances to attend the provincial assembly of Normandy. Because Auvry had ordained priests in the diocese of Paris without Retz's consent, Harlay declared the bishop of Coutances to be unworthy of participating in any episcopal gathering. In addition, Harlay's ordinance suspended Auvry from all ecclesiastical functions.[169] Since other Norman bishops sided with Auvry, there appeared the spectacle of two provincial assemblies, each choosing its own delegates to the General Assembly.

The government was appalled. Harlay's dismissal and excommunication of Auvry not only assailed a client whom Mazarin wanted elected deputy to the General Assembly but also implicitly denied the validity of the chapter's jurisdiction and thus recognized the authority of Chassebras and Retz. Although he had received support from the nuncio and the pope, Harlay, along with his suffragan, the bishop of Evreux, was ordered by *lettre de cachet* to the court.[170] Harlay refused to renounce his interdiction of a bishop whom he considered "a usurper of others' functions."[171] The king then commanded the archbishop to return to his diocese while an *arrêt* of the *Conseil d'en haut* rendered Harlay's ordinance nugatory. The Assembly of the Clergy, which opened on 25 October, the day following the *arrêt*, chose not to commence by defying the government. The assembled episcopacy permitted Auvry to take his seat but declared that the archbishopric of Paris was not vacant and declined to approve the chapter's authority. In effect, the prelates had condemned the court and recognized Retz's claims.[172]

Mazarin had hoped that the General Assembly would not side with the ecclesiastical frondeurs. Yet, besides now having to contend with a body which was to prove increasingly defiant, the cardinal-minister could not seem to rid the capital of that curé who blatantly challenged the crown from his nesting place in the towers of Loisel's church. Along with Retz's episcopal letter, Chassebras issued his own, which enjoined Auvry and Cohon from performing ecclesiastical functions in the diocese of Paris and publicly notified them of their interdiction. The chapter and curés were also informed of the vicar-general's decision. In his second monition, Chassebras listed the most recent crimes perpetrated by the secular arm on the body of the Church and advised the guilty to do penance.[173] The curé appeared ready to throw his interdict. Supported by his fellows, "this invisible man, one of the less important Parisian curés, by his courage and perseverance," held the court in check.[174] In response to the second monition, the crown proclaimed a second sentence, which renewed the ineffectual prohibitions against anyone communicating with Chassebras or deferring to his orders.[175]

Unable to repress the sedition exemplified by Chassebras, Mazarin had to seek another method to defuse the volatile situation in Paris. The excommunications of Cohon and Auvry might be duplicated with respect to other ecclesiastics; an interdict might also be forthcoming.

Unsuccessful in promoting the authority of a submissive chapter, Mazarin turned to the pope. If the papacy could be persuaded to aid in the solution of the Jansenist problem, might not Alexander finally be brought over to the government's position in the matter of the administration of the diocese of Paris? Séguier could not rid Paris of the vexatious Chassebras, but Rome could. Something had to be done to break the impasse. The problem of the convocation of the provincial assembly of Paris remained, while the General Assembly dared not conduct its traditional opening Mass because the curé of Saint-Severin, as vicar-general, refused his permission.

The pope, pressed by Lionne, listening more closely to Jesuit reports linking Retz to Jansenism, and sincerely desirous of creating order in the diocesan administration of Paris, selected the expedient of asking a suffragan bishop to govern Retz's diocese. The papal letter arrived on 26 November with the space for the recipient left blank. Mazarin was ecstatic and ordered that the bishop of Meaux be instructed to execute the commission.[176]

But the papal brief aroused the Gallican sensibilities of the episcopacy, and of the Parlement as well. Even "the most well-behaved and loyal" prelates opposed the pope's procedure.[177] The bishop of Meaux disdained to accept the charge. He maintained that the brief must have been promulgated without Retz's consent and, lacking that, no prelate could undertake the direction of the diocese.[178] Even more astonishing to the court, the General Assembly persisted in asking Hodencq for permission to hold the opening Mass. It was unprecedented, fumed Servien, to request permission from a simple curé.[179] For the crown to accede to this would imply recognition of Retz as the legitimate archbishop.

Nonetheless, Mazarin was forced to yield. Roullé, who felt that the government should once more exile the curé of Saint-Severin for his audacity and compel the chapter to take up again the diocesan administration, was overruled. Mazarin was powerless to pursue such a course of action. There was a certain amount of pathos in the appeal of the curé of Saint-Barthélemy to the first minister urging him not to compromise: "Your Eminence is too triumphant and victorious everywhere not to be so in Paris."[180]

Mazarin therefore recognized Hodencq as vicar-general (and, by doing so, Retz as archbishop) in order that the General Assembly could officially convene and proceed to its business of granting subsidies. The first minister was understandably bitter—his eighteen-month fight to deny the legality of Retz's succession to the archiepis-copal see had failed. In the cardinal-minister's opinion, the papal brief had been suggested to Alexander by Retz in a clever maneuver to further his goal of causing disorder in Paris. Retz had, insisted Maza-rin, cautioned his Parisian adherents to feign disapproval of the brief.[181] Support for Retz and what he represented was demonstrated to be strong in the capital. But for Retz's struggle to succeed completely— that is, for changes in the high offices of government to occur—he had still to overcome those forces that impeded his return to his base of power.

To solve definitively the problem of the spiritual administration, the crown proposed that Retz select a vicar-general from the list presented by the court. Although all on the list were favorable to the government, Retz agreed, as this process would formally validate his right to be arch-bishop. On 2 January 1656, Retz expedited a commission to Du Saus-say, curé of Saint-Leu-Saint-Gilles, appointing him vicar-general.[182]

It now appeared that some measure of peace might be restored to the diocese: the crown, after the intercession of the General Assembly, permitted several of the exiled canons, including Chevalier and Lad-vocat, to return to Paris. However, Du Saussay's defiance of his eccle-siastical superior and Retz's own inopportune actions led to a renewal of government repression and, more significantly, precipitated a rup-ture between the embattled archbishop and the pope.

The immediate cause for these developments was Retz's renewed attempt to turn the people and clergy against Mazarin. On 13 March, the cardinal-archbishop relayed an episcopal letter to his flock, exhort-ing them to pray for an end to the raging international war.[183] One week later, Alexander VII sent a brief to the French clergy imploring them to urge the king to conclude peace.[184] There was little doubt that the pope blamed Mazarin for pursuing a policy of war. Even at this date, Alexander felt that Mazarin would pass from power. It was not surprising that the pontiff executed the brief in concert with Retz, the man whom he considered to be the future first minister of France. Both Alexander and his predecessor firmly believed that the Fronde had only momentarily failed, that the revolt would flare up once more. A second rebellion would remove Mazarin, the one man responsible for impeding Rome's desire not to see France defeat Spain.[185]

To the court, the papal brief was nothing less than an attack on the rights of royalty.[186] The pope himself aided and sheltered the cardinal de Retz, criminal of lese majesty, who publicly preached sedition and revolt. In fact, claimed Séguier in a speech, the papal brief had been fabricated by the state's enemies (Retz) in cooperation with Spain.[187] The Gallicanism of the clergy was aroused: Retz's plan to foment disorder backfired. In its response to the pope, the General Assembly praised Mazarin, defended the king's efforts to ensure peace, and suggested instead that the pope obtain Spain's agreement to a treaty.[188]

The clergy's rebuttal signaled failure for the pope. Alexander now possessed conclusive proof that Mazarin was firmly entrenched in power. Disillusioned with his previous policy, His Holiness ceased protection of Retz.[189] Retz made the break final when, on 15 May, he revoked Du Saussay's commission.

Immediately previous to that act of defiance Retz sent another eloquent appeal to the General Assembly. In this letter, Retz portrayed the outrages committed against him: the court had prohibited him from communicating with the clergy; it had burnt his episcopal letter (of 14 December 1654); it had persecuted the legitimate vicar-general, Chassebras; it had seized the revenues of the archbishopric; and it had exiled those curés and canons whose only crime was to deplore their prelate's captivity. In effect Retz urged the episcopacy to comprehend his struggle as its own and to press the king to right the grievous wrongs committed against the archbishop of Paris.[190]

Retz's act revoking Du Saussay's commission was placarded throughout Paris so as to receive maximum exposure.[191] Retz had many grievances that led him to issue this decree, but all were grounded in one fact: Du Saussay fulfilled his functions as Mazarin, not Retz, dictated. This curé was a creature of the first minister, confident that in defying his prelate he would have Mazarin's protection.[192] More specifically, Du Saussay had not taken the oath of loyalty to Retz, nor on Retz's behalf had he taken a similar oath to the king. He had adopted as his title vicar-general of the archbishopric rather than of the archbishop. He had not defended his archbishop against detractors. Also, in spite of earlier injunctions, he had allowed the bishop of Coutances to confer holy orders and to fulfill other ecclesiastical functions in the diocese. Finally, Retz had originally approved Du Saussay's nomination with the understanding that Mazarin would call back the exiled curés and nullify the sentences against Chassebras. This had not occurred.[193]

Retz then chose Chevalier and Ladvocat as his new vicars-general, with Hodencq and Chassebras as alternates if the two canons were prevented from functioning. At the same time, Retz appointed Claude Joly as *official* and Nicolas Porcher as *vice-gérant* (the *official*'s assistant). These actions were reinforced when the Parisian curés, who had never ceased to press for the return of their exiled colleagues, met and in opposition to the court agreed that they recognized only Retz's authority.[194]

The government interpreted Retz's letter of 8 May and his revocation of Du Saussay as an appeal for revolt. Had Retz not purposely promulgated the revocation when the king was on the frontier in order to be more easily able to cause trouble in Paris? Was Retz not working in concert with Spain?[195] Mazarin wrote: "the king is persuaded that his dignity does not permit him to suffer such crimes, all the more as his [Retz's] dissembling, far from preventing turmoil and disorder, contributes to it. This is so because the men [Chevalier, Ladvocat, Hodencq, and Chassebras] he has nominated, when they do not act according to his instructions, are themselves inclined to sedition."[196]

In addition to the content of Retz's letter, which exposed government policies to the public, and the act of revocation, which again plunged the diocese under the control of disobedient clerics, the court resented Retz's very daring to communicate with the king's subjects. As recently as 28 March the crown had promulgated yet another ordinance enjoining anyone from corresponding with the disgraced archbishop.[197] Now the government was treated to the spectacle of an anonymous ecclesiastic, who identified himself as the abbé de Saint-Jean, appearing at the 19 June session of the General Assembly. The abbé, in reality Jean-Jacques Dorat, was an agent of Retz who had intended to deliver Retz's letter to the assembled prelates and so draw them into a defense of his master's cause.[198]

Retz's ploy to involve the episcopacy in his struggle succeeded because of the justness of his claim to nominate vicars-general responsible to him and because of new government blunders. On 20 June, armed soldiers appeared at the General Assembly to arrest the abbé de Saint-Jean if he reappeared. The prelates regarded this intrusion as an insult and protested to the king. Then, refusing to accede to disloyal clerics in positions of power, the government once again resorted to the *lettre de cachet*. Ladvocat escaped from Paris, but Chevalier was incarcerated in the Bastille. The canon's room was searched and evidence found which confirmed the goverment's belief in a network of ecclesiastical frondeurs intriguing to foment disorder in Paris: among the papers of Chevalier were letters and memoranda from Dorat and Chassebras.[199]

The diocese now lacked spiritual direction: it was inconceivable that the General Assembly would not be drawn into the problem. To forestall this, the court issued still one more ordinance against Retz and his adherents on 2 July. On the same day, Louis dispatched a letter to the General Assembly in which he reiterated his anathemas against Retz while affirming that the crown would not suffer that criminal to exercise authority, whether personally or through a subordinate, in Paris.[200] But Ladvocat formally notified the Assembly of the arrest of Chevalier and asked it to remonstrate in his favor, claiming that Chevalier's only crime was to submit to his archbishop's orders.[201] The episcopacy had to defend the principle of ecclesiastical immunities and so pleaded with the court on Chevalier's behalf.

It was not until the end of the summer that the problem of the spiritual administration of the archdiocese was resolved. In September, following his informants' advice and the supplications of the General Assembly, Mazarin allowed Hodencq to function as interim vicar-general. Also because of the intervention of the episcopacy, the court released Chevalier after receiving assurances that he would cease his obstinate behavior and leave Paris. Despite these concessions the government instructed Du Saussay to appeal his revocation to the archbishop of Lyon, primate of the Gauls. The sentence from the *officialité* of Lyon overturned Retz's dismissal of Du Saussay.

Once again the General Assembly supported Retz, this time by asserting that the ecclesiastical court of Lyon had no authority to judge the decision of the archbishop of Paris. The role of the General Assembly now proved crucial. It convinced Retz to appoint new vicars-general in return for a promise to aid him in the recovery of his revenues, which the government had sequestered. At the same time, the episcopacy demonstrated to Mazarin that it was in his best interests to provide for a speedy resolution to the affairs of the diocese. The spiritual anarchy was scandalous and threatened to disturb the calm of the capital. Already, the curé of Saint-Roch had made an impassioned speech on behalf of the Parisian curés in the General Assembly categorizing the chaos that prevailed in Paris. Rousse had enumerated the consequences of the crown's actions. Cures could not be conferred without the authority of Retz or of his vicars-general. Sacramental life was in complete disorder and the system of ecclesiastical justice had ceased to function. "Besides these diocesan evils, the cardinal de Retz archbishop, his four vicars-general, and his exiled curés suffered in their persons and dignities, in their charges and honors, [and] in their benefices and revenues, afflictions which everyone was aware of. These were all the more notorious because those who suffered them were removed . . . to the great harm of the parishes."[202]

The government dared not ignore the religious concerns of the population. Moreover, the prelacy itself posed a threat to the government, which dreaded the incorporation of this powerful group into the Religious Fronde. Besides providing a sounding board for Retz and his adherents, the General Assembly opposed the court on issues arising from Retz's persecution, such as the inviolability of clerics and the privileges of the Church. The court was embarrassed by this recalcitrance seemingly run rampant and met with no success in its attempts to bring the sessions to a speedy conclusion.[203] With all factions desirous of an end to the deplorable state of affairs that persisted in the summer of 1656, Retz finally appointed as new vicars-general—the last of the Religious Fronde—Hodencq and the dean of Notre-Dame, Jean-Baptiste de Contes.

While discontent over the affair of the vicars-general became manifest in the General Assembly and in Paris, the crown feared armed rebellion. As was the case in August 1654, the ecclesiastical situation in Paris dovetailed with other events to provide a situation in which unruly clerics could again hope for a quick solution to their problems.

July was particularly crucial. On 16 July Condé raised the siege of Valenciennes, thus inflicting a severe defeat on the French while ensuring that peace between France and Spain would not be quickly concluded.[204] In Paris, and in the General Assembly, the partisans of Retz and Condé waited for the effects the battle could produce.[205] Mazarin did not believe that the failure at Valenciennes would ignite rebellion in Paris but he had expressed this same optimism many times in the past, even in 1648. He confided to abbé Fouquet: "You cannot prevent the riffraff and the partisans of the prince de Condé and of the cardinal de Retz from inappropriately starting up; but they will soon discover that they are mistaken in their calculations." Nevertheless, the first minister cautioned abbé Fouquet, the head of Mazarin's network of spies and agents, to continue the war of libels, to arrest certain seditious clerics, and to maintain surveillance over Retz's partisans.[206]

The raising of the siege of Valenciennes had another important effect: it encouraged Retz to pursue his intrigues. The vision appeared to Retz of Condé advancing toward a Paris whose inhabitants yearned for the opportunity to overthrow their Italian master in favor of their beloved archbishop. This vision was not to be realized. Although the break with the pope (after the debacle of the brief for peace and after Alexander's opposition to the revocation of Du Saussay) might not have been decisive in Retz's defeat, it weakened his cause by depriving him of a support that had great moral and psychological value. But he still menaced the government. As Retz departed from Rome to commence six years of wanderings, the crown was stirred to action. Mazarin "feared that the cardinal de Retz would come straight back to France, that he would be received with open arms by the inhabitants of his diocese, and that the [General] Assembly would make some resolutions in his favor."[207] Hermant claimed that Retz was feared more than ever after he left Italy.[208] In Rome, Retz could be watched; now, he could be anywhere, even in France—and perhaps in Paris.

A flurry of government activity marked the serious concern about Retz's possible intentions. Nicolas Fouquet cautioned his fellow ministers not to exhibit undue apprehension, which would only encourage the *malintentionnés*. Instead, Fouquet urged the crown to pretend that the archbishop would never dare return.[209] Mazarin could not feign indifference, although he was confident that the royal armies could repel Condé's forces. The first minister wrote Colbert that he had learned that "the emissaries of the cardinal de Retz and of the prince de Condé have fashioned a great cabal in Paris. We are beginning to see its effects. The principal reason for causing trouble is the fear that the malevolent have of peace [between France and Spain]."[210]

On 13 September, Mazarin informed Colbert that sources whose veracity he did not doubt had indicated that Retz was coming incognito to Paris. Already Mazarin had given orders in Provence and elsewhere to watch for Retz.

> We must not doubt that the said cardinal has a great cabal in
> Paris, because the malevolent and the adherents of the prince de
> Condé are always for the one who will put himself at the head of
> a disturbance. It is easy to see that those who had a great part in

the last enterprise of the Parlement, and those who have worked
to create a division in the last [General] Assembly of the Clergy
and to support the Parisian curés, assuredly act in concert with
the said cardinal, or by his orders.

Mazarin continued to say that he could not believe that Retz would
come back to Paris, but that precautions must be taken. Included
among these was the necessity of discovering what the curés would do
if Retz returned.[211]

A new royal ordinance, which was immediately dispatched to provincial governors, ordered Retz's arrest and forbade any subject from
giving him aid.[212] Colbert advised Mazarin to send spies to all suspect
houses in the provinces as well as to the cloister of Notre-Dame, and
subsequently related that Retz was on his way to Paris intending to
take advantage of the opportunity afforded by the siege of Valenciennes.[213]

These rumors were false, but on 23 September an even more serious
threat appeared when a letter from Retz arrived at the General Assembly. This was the most vituperative of Retz's public statements; in
it he threatened an interdict if his demands were not met. That is, Retz
required the reestablishment of those curés who had been exiled for
upholding his authority, the release from captivity and exile of his
vicars-general, the freedom to communicate with his flock, and the
restitution of his revenues. The letter left little doubt that government
persecution had exhausted Retz's patience. "I recognize, Sirs [the
deputies of the General Assembly], and without a doubt you recognize
with me, that I should, according to all the rules of the Church, use my
authority to repel such great outrages which have been perpetrated
against it for so long. . . . So, Sirs . . . I cannot bear much longer the
disorders in my diocese without working to repress them with all the
legitimate ways of spiritual authority God has given me."[214]

The government and its adherents recognized the import of Retz's
words. The bishop of Aire, recounting to Mazarin the reception of
Retz's message by the General Assembly, exclaimed: "behold the mask
raised." Retz must be dealt with as "a declared rebel . . . because these
are threats which are insolent for a subject dealing with his king."[215]
The bishop of Séez feared that the interdict would soon be forthcoming. He warned the first minister of the effect this would have in
Paris because of the curés, who were devoted to Retz and who would

sustain an interdict: "Most [of the curés] seek grounds for a disturbance; for they have a blind obedience [for Retz] and few of the others
will oppose them. So, with the exception of the regular clergy, we
should suppose that the interdict will be almost universally obeyed in
the parishes."[216] Retz's demands to reestablish those vicars-general
who had proved unacceptable to the king and to return the exiled
curés were intended to incite a new disturbance in Paris.[217]

Colbert considered the menace of an interdict to be one of the most
important affairs of state; since the General Assembly would be im-
potent in face of an interdict, remedies must be found elsewhere.
Colbert found that bulls had been issued to Saint Louis and Philip III
which exempted them from excommunication and interdict unless the
pope's permission had first been obtained. These bulls had been registered by the Parlement of Paris. Colbert therefore suggested that if
Retz promulgated an interdict, curés loyal to the government might be
persuaded to interject an *appel comme d'abus*.[218]

Throughout the remaining months of 1656, the court awaited an
interdict and possibly the king's excommunication. Learned arguments were prepared for public consumption irrefutably demonstrating that Retz had no legitimate cause to fulminate an interdict, and
relating a history of interdicts in an attempt both to portray them as a
recent innovation and to undermine Retz's authority to issue one.[219]

The government's fears proved groundless. Despite his threats and
subsequent letters to the General Assembly which ceaselessly bela-
bored the clergy to support him, Retz did nothing. The closing of the
General Assembly in 1657 found Retz unwilling to act decisively for
his own cause and unable to prod the prelacy into revolt against the
crown. However, Retz succeeded on some points. His vicars-general
administered the diocese, and their functioning was clear acknowledgment that he was the legitimate archbishop. The 26 April 1657
arrêt removed the threat of a secular court judging Retz, recognized
that the government had overstepped its rights while pursuing him,
and preserved episcopal immunities. Indeed, the prelacy supported
certain claims of Retz in order to secure its own independence from
the government. And, when the government admitted it had violated
Church privileges, the quarrel between court and clergy died down.

The General Assembly did not resolve Retz's personal affairs—the
archbishopric remained in *régale* while Retz's other income continued
to be sequestered. On the most important issue, Mazarin emerged

victorious: he had prevented Retz from returning to Paris. Divorced from the pope, bereft of aid from the episcopate, and frightened by the prospect of arrest, Retz journeyed from city to city in the Rhineland and the Low Countries. In Paris, his only locus of support remained the curés; outside of France, Condé's army seemed the sole lever by which Retz might propel himself to his archiepiscopal seat.

5. The End of the Religious Fronde

Irresolute and dissolute, Retz displayed after 1657 little of the vigor that had characterized his decisive participation in the first years of the Religious Fronde. In the five years preceding his resignation as archbishop in 1662, Retz devoted more time to his amusements than to his role as political leader. Except for occasional bursts of activity, the cardinal-archbishop served principally as a figurehead to those ecclesiastical forces unreconciled to Mazarin's rule.

The Parisian curés never failed to worry the court both by their support of Retz and by their contestations with those clerical bodies and individuals protected by the government. The significant role assumed by the curés within the ecclesiastical nexus of Paris itself angered a government unaccustomed to seeing a change in the behavior of a traditionally submissive professional group. We shall discuss elsewhere the curés' activities within the Church. For the purposes of this chapter it is necessary to emphasize their role as adherents of Retz and their position as political opponents of the government.

Although the curés' support for Retz was not always overt during the period between Retz's arrest and his resignation, it was ever-present. Several factors ensured that this would be so. As Jansenists, the curés realized that they would suffer if the government were to choose a successor to Retz as archbishop. It was believed—correctly so, as events proved—that the virulently anti-Jansenist archbishop of Toulouse, Pierre Marca, would be appointed next to the see of Paris. Also, the curés themselves required at least Retz's indifference if they were to implement successfully their claims of curial autonomy and jurisdiction. Their major adversaries in this regard were the Jesuits, and Retz was a notorious opponent of those militant fathers. In addition to these self-interested motivations there was the real belief that Retz was the legitimate archbishop, that he had been unjustly persecuted along with many of his followers, and that Church privileges and immunities had been violated by a tyrannical government controlled by a foreign minister.

The attacks of the Parisian curés on the Society of Jesus were perennially linked to the curés' support of Retz and of his cause. After the entreaties of Father Annat, Nicolas Fouquet explained in early 1658 that the court could not compel the curés to end their campaign against the Jesuits, because if the government attempted to do so, "the curés could rouse the cardinal de Retz."[220] During this time Rousse implored the king to pardon those curés exiled in 1654,[221] while Antoine Dupuys, curé of Saints-Innocents, published a speech in which he had lauded Retz. After assailing the Jesuits' lax morality, Dupuys commented that the "cardinal de Retz, our very worthy archbishop, who is absent in body but not in spirit from his flock, could receive no sweeter consolation than to be informed of the zeal and faithful ministry of his pastors for the honor of his Church and for the spiritual guardianship of those whom he has always loved and considered as his children."[222]

To the government, the ties between the Jansenist curés and Retz were always apparent. Roullé, the court's best source of information about the curés, constantly lambasted his fellows for their support of the frondeur archbishop. The curé of Saint-Barthélemy informed Mazarin that the curés "have always acted and still act on behalf of the cardinal de Retz against the state, the king, and Your Eminence. They would willingly destroy all three for Retz's return."[223]

The court finally dealt conclusively with the problem of the curés when it suppressed their regular assemblies in July 1659. No longer could the curés depend upon a forum for the common discussion of their grievances; no more did the crown have to contend with a continuous stream of defiant activity by upstart curés. The curés only occasionally opposed the government after this time. On the political plane, the court crushed the curés because of their ability to cause trouble or to make some disturbance that might have propelled Retz to power. The government also interpreted politically the theological disputes of the curés with the Jesuits as pretexts to foment discontent.[224]

Besides the danger posed by the curés, other factors threatened the government. The location of Retz, as well as the impact his pamphlets could have, still caused anxiety. It remained conceivable that Retz might yet return to Paris, so the court took necessary precautions, which included preventing him from communicating with his partisans in the capital.[225]

In short, conditions that could lead to a new day of barricades still existed. To calm the common people, Nicolas Fouquet diminished the *taille* (the principal royal tax) and suppressed certain other taxes. The war against Spain required taxes, but the nobility, sovereign courts, and clergy resisted payment.[226] Then in July 1658, the government passed through a crisis as Louis became sick on campaign and hovered on the brink of death. Plots immediately formed around the king's brother; members of the earlier Frondes publicly rejoiced at the news of the king's illness, as did the supporters in Paris of Retz and Condé. Mazarin was alarmed: he ordered Colbert to strengthen the garrisons at the Bastille and at Vincennes, and, after the king had recovered, the first minister commanded punishment for the intrigants.[227]

Also ominous to the government was the possibility that the forces of Retz and Condé would unite, a merger that never did materialize. Retz met with Condé in Brussels in 1658 but refused to align himself with that prince. The only positive result was an agreement stipulating that Condé would not make peace nor Retz resign his archbishopric without one first consulting the other. Guy Joly described the conference as a missed opportunity, one in which Retz betrayed his friends by failing to take the decisive steps that would have provoked disorder in the state. According to Joly, Retz "refrained from informing Condé of the resources which remained with his spiritual authority. An interdict issued in concert with Condé and with the Spanish could have brought about the pope's protection. No doubt this would have caused very great disorder in Paris and given to the malcontents a beautiful opportunity to undertake something considerable."[228]

There occurred a second meeting between Retz and Condé that year concerning the revolt of the Norman nobility. Here a plan was devised, although its contents are murky. By one account the marshal d'Hocquincourt, who was at Brussels with Retz and Condé, was to lead four thousand cavalry into Normandy. This army would then join with Condé's for a march on Paris. Another version held that Condé was prepared to help the Normans only if peace between Spain and France, which was to include him, did not eventuate. In any case, the defeat of the Spanish army at the Battle of the Dunes, in which the marshal was killed and his army dissipated, nullified the frondeurs' plans.[229]

The crown faced agitation at this time from the nobility of several provinces, of which that in Normandy was the most extensive. The origins of this rebellion date back to 1651 when more than one thousand nobles converged on Paris in anticipation of the convocation of the Estates-General. But Gaston d'Orléans persuaded the nobles to disperse by offering them assurances that the government would satisfy their demands when the perils of the times had passed. By 1657, the Norman nobility began to demonstrate, utilizing Gaston's promise as a pretext to legitimate new assemblies in preparation of an Estates-General. The levying of new taxes by the court increased the discontent. Retz, Condé, and other former participants in the Fronde of the Princes hastened to join in and take advantage of the revolt. The king's sickness animated the hopes of the nobles, who convened a provincial assembly, with representatives from the nobility of Orléans and Berry, in July 1658. The resolutions adopted were audacious; the court hastened to repress the agitation. Mazarin realized the danger posed by the provincial nobility and by their correspondence with Retz and Condé. It was not until the end of 1659, however, that the government was able to quell the disturbances and punish those who were most guilty. The conclusion of this insurrection marked the end of the Fronde in the provinces.[230]

The Treaty of the Pyrenees, signed on 7 November 1659, stipulated the pardoning of Condé and his return to France. The year 1659, then, was a watershed in the crown's efforts to stabilize its rule against both foreign and internal opponents. Spain had been defeated; international war no longer demanded the attention and resources of the state. By seeming to renounce his previous behavior, Condé had contributed to the discrediting of any future opposition to the crown.[231] The provincial nobility had been forced to submit, preparatory to their emasculation as a political power under the personal aegis of Louis XIV. In Paris, the curés had been quashed as a corporate force and their significance correspondingly decreased as court successes multiplied. No longer could the curés take advantage of a weakened government, although they still hoped for a reversal of their archbishop's fortunes. Thus, by 1660, Retz was nearly alone.

Ironically, Retz then shook off his lethargy and engaged in a new flurry of activity. Shortly after Hodencq proposed that the government accede to the reestablishment of the cardinal-archbishop and to the return of the exiled curés,[232] Retz addressed a circular letter to the "bishops, priests, and children" of the Church. This work, which has been called "the last reverberation of the Fronde,"[233] recounted the entire history of the affair of Retz, including his persecution, the seizure of his revenues, the attacks on his vicars-general, his oppression in France and Rome, and the attempts to compel him to abdicate his archiepiscopal seat. Taking advantage of Mazarin's sickness, this letter—perhaps the strongest and most eloquent of Retz's works during the Religious Fronde—threw the diocese into confusion. Again Retz had threatened an interdict.[234]

And again Retz declined to implement his threats. Although Retz's agents informed him that his recent letter had not had the desired effects and that an interdict might yet stir up the populace, Retz preferred to await the death of his antagonist, Mazarin.[235] Indeed, Retz's letter to the clergy, along with two others sent at the same time to the king and the vicars-general, merely increased the court's resolve never to tolerate an accommodation with the archbishop. The General Assembly of 1660 declined to question the government's treatment of Retz: "episcopal magnanimity was then a virtue of the old days; the interests of individuals made them very willingly forget those of the Church."[236]

Haunted by the fear that Retz might follow him as first minister, Mazarin in early 1661 made Louis and Anne promise that they would neither appoint Retz as his successor nor allow the traitor to regain his see. Mazarin's incorrigible hatred of Retz combined with a belief that Retz was dangerous to France because of his inclination to place his personal interests above those of the state. In deference to Mazarin, the king issued an ordinance which repeated the strictures of earlier edicts: it was forbidden to communicate with Retz or to offer him assistance. On 9 March, Mazarin died. The following day, in the first session of the *Conseil privé,* Louis declared that he would be his own first minister and that he would never permit Retz to return to France.[237]

The drama of Retz was nearly at an end. Government strategy was twofold: to expose Retz as head of the Jansenists and to renew pressure on the pope for his consent to a trial of the archbishop of Paris. The Jansenist episcopal letter of the vicars-general, which resisted the Formulary and which was backed by the curés, proved Retz's undoing. If he did nothing or if he approved the episcopal letter, Retz would confirm the court's warnings that he was Jansenist and would alienate the pope. If he repudiated the episcopal letter, Retz would in fact cut his ties to his Jansenist supporters. Retz chose to betray his allies.[238]

Nevertheless, it appeared that the pope would finally yield to the king's demands and agree to Retz's trial. Throughout 1661, Retz had sought through intermediaries to return to the king's good graces. Now, in the face of the crown's impending success in Rome and in light of Louis' resolve that Retz be dispossessed, the archbishop of Paris decided to retain his dignity by resigning. In February 1662, Retz officially gave up his archdiocese and went to live on his estate at Commercy, in Lorraine. The government then permitted the exiled canons and curés to return to Paris. Though Louis would in the future face enormous difficulties with the Church, he had brought to a close the last manifestations of the Frondes. The king turned his back on the capital, preferring other habitations, but he first ensured that Paris would be free of that ecclesiastical revolt which had so often shaken and nearly toppled the government.

In one way, and in the manner understood by such nineteenth-century historians as Chantelauze and Gazier, the Religious Fronde was a personal battle bitterly and persistently waged between Mazarin and Retz. Only superficially was this the case because that struggle was not divorced from other developments. Condé's defiance, the war with Spain, provincial revolt, and popular unrest all figured in the turmoil of the 1650s, all endangered the preservation of Mazarin's government. Even the Parlement of Paris, once thought to have been drummed into obedience by 1652, has now come to be regarded as an important source of opposition throughout the decade.[239] More often ignored are the Parisian curés, clerics of the second order, who in spite of the infrequency with which they walked the corridors of high politics, yet provided the pillars of support upon which Retz's individual Fronde was based. More significantly, while clinging to their archbishop's robes, the curés attempted what can only be considered an ecclesiastical revolution. Drawing on the Richerist corpus and seeking to exclude both their arch-rivals, the Jesuits and the episcopate, from parochial affairs, the curés sought to form a new order within the Church. This order, conceived both in corporate terms and in the sense of a stratum within the clergy directly below that of prelates, was innovative, and, to regulars and bishops, revolutionary. For the curés, the Religious Fronde was nothing less than the formation of a corps and the claim that they exercised sole and complete authority within the territory of their parishes.

CHAPTER TWO

A NEW ORDER IN THE CHURCH

1. The Curés' Richerism

He wants to make pass for a constant truth,
and one which cannot be doubted,
that curés have the same rank and
the same degree of jurisdiction as have popes and
bishops because all receive their jurisdiction directly
from Jesus Christ. According to him, the curé
in his parish is a little bishop.
Bagot, *Défense du droict épiscopal*, p. 14

In his critique of Nicolas Mazure's *L'Obligation des fidèles de se confesser à leur curé* (published anonymously in 1653), the Jesuit Jean Bagot underscored the precept behind the attempts of the Parisian curés to form a new order within the Church during the Religious Fronde. The curés' plea for a reassessed equality of status within the Church rested on an argument from analogy, namely, that what the pope was to Christendom, and the bishop was to his diocese, so was the curé to his parish. This recognition of the theme of Mazure's work and of the curés' aims represented a widening of what had previously been a local conflict between the curés and Jesuits of Paris. Mazure, curé of Saint-Paul from 1633 to 1664, was, along with the overwhelming majority of his colleagues, an inveterate opponent of the Jesuits. Because the parish of Saint-Paul bordered on the Jesuits' *maison professe* (headed by Bagot from 1655 to 1657), Mazure squabbled constantly with the Society over its right to administer the sacraments to his parishioners and with the churchwardens over their habit of inviting Jesuits to preach at Saint-Paul. *L'Obligation des fidèles* was Mazure's theoretical justification for the curés' daily struggle to achieve supremacy over the parish.[1]

In speaking of the curés' efforts both to elevate themselves within the Church hierarchy and to increase their dominion within the parish, Bagot effectively brought the matter before the public and, more importantly, before the episcopacy. It was not accidental that Bagot entitled his refutation of the curés' position a *Défense du droict épiscopal*. Although this title could not mitigate the ultramontanist tenor of the work nor prevent its condemnation, it did succeed in provoking the censure of *L'Obligation* and, ultimately, of the curés. Bagot's politics could not effect an alliance between the Jesuits and the episcopacy, but it could prevent the traditional enemies of the regulars—the bishops and curés—from uniting. And, given the social, political, and religious ties that Mazarin's government maintained with both the episcopacy and the Jesuits, the curés' hopes of becoming bishops in their parishes were slim indeed.

The curés based their position on two fundamental propositions: first, that they had been established directly by Christ, and second, that they were the direct descendants of the seventy-two disciples (Luke 10:1–16). Rousse, who represented the curés of Paris as syndic, elaborated this interpretation of curial origins in the course of clarifying Mazure's *L'Obligation des fidèles*. The curés' power, as described by Rousse, must originate directly from Christ, not from the institution of the Church, nor by the Church. Commenting on Mazure's statement that "curés hold the power of jurisdiction directly from Jesus Christ," Rousse contended that Christ instituted the cure of souls and the jurisdiction of parishes with the intention that bishops delegate these powers to the curés. Rousse explained this in the following manner. Christ established the apostles and in their persons the bishops, their successors. By so instituting them, Christ made the bishops "priests par excellence" and "major and superior pastors." Christ bestowed on the prelates, as "priests par excellence," the authority merely to ordain priests rather than to institute the priesthood. As "superior pastors," the bishops were not endowed by Christ with the ability to establish the "subordinate cure," but only to confer it on the "subordinate pastor." Therefore, "the priesthood comes directly from Jesus Christ with regard to its institution and from bishops with regard to its ordination." And because simple priests hold immediately from Christ the prerogative of consecrating his real body, the curés possess directly from him the right to govern his mystical body—that is, the portion of the Church committed to them by the prelates. In short, the curés' authority and jurisdiction stem directly from Christ, both through divine succession from the seventy-two disciples and by being inherent in the cure and charge of souls. These powers are inherent in that when the cure is conferred, the authority and jurisdiction ensue. They are irrevocable because neither pope nor bishop can prevent the curé from exercising his jurisdiction. In returning to Christ for justification and legitimacy and by denying the right of bishop and pope to interfere in curial functions, Rousse and the curés of Paris formulated a radical and unorthodox religious doctrine. Never before this time had the lower clergy developed so thoroughly and boldly such a doctrine. Now sufficiently armed with an elaborate conception of their own dignity, the curés could face with equanimity all those who sought to oppose the justice of their claims to organize as a corporate body, separate from and on the margin of the episcopacy.[2]

The attendant debate assumed the pattern of seventeenth-century theological controversies—each side mustered the sources of tradition. Councils, Church Fathers, popes, and theologians—all were called upon to ratify or denounce the curés' aspirations. It hardly mattered that the curés were wrong in their statements about their divine origin, their descent from the seventy-two disciples, and in their assertion of forming a niche in the Church hierarchy directly below that of the episcopacy. The decisive factor in this debate was not the inherent truth of any particular contention[3] but whether or not the material interests of other groups converged with the curés' claims. The tragedy of the curés was that their supporters—other Jansenists, Retz, his vicars-general, and a vocal minority of the episcopate—were not strong enough to counterbalance the animosity of the government, the regulars, and the overwhelming majority of bishops.

The curés opened their challenge in 1653 with *L'Obligation des fidèles*, which contended that the curé alone was the "proper priest," and that, therefore, other ecclesiastical authorities must withdraw from his legitimate sphere of action. "It is clear that by 'proper priest,' Saint Peter means the curé alone."[4] The following year, another work confirmed the dictum that the "proper priest" can be neither a regular nor a bishop, but only the curé.[5]

The curés also published a sermon by Jean Gerson, the fifteenth-century chancellor of the University of Paris. His belief in the divine right of curés and his Gallican insistence on a limitation to papal supremacy were still relevant in the seventeenth century. Gerson had defended the right of the curé to his proper jurisdiction by depicting any intrusion upon it as a violation of the correct, eternal hierarchical order of the Church. Appealing to the authority of Saint Paul, Gerson had proclaimed this order as an apostolic legacy: there is a pope vicar of Christ, cardinals, archbishops, bishops successors of the apostles, and curés, who have descended from the seventy-two disciples. Furthermore, Gerson had contended that the curés "are established directly by Jesus Christ in order to have the most important authority in the Church and to govern the people who are submitted to them."[6] The Jesuits continually refuted these views and eventually so did the episcopacy, who ordered the curés to renounce their extremist opinions before the General Assembly of the Clergy in 1656 and 1657. For although the debate raged around the issues of the curés' origins, it was apparent to all that the crux of the struggle—and, from the curés' point of view, of the entire Religious Fronde—centered on the dogma that the jurisdiction of the curé within his parish was analogous to that of the bishop within the diocese and that of the pope within the entire Church.[7]

This was indeed an attempted revolution within the Church. The curés aimed at nothing less than dominion over their parishes, while at the same time seeking to exclude other segments of the Church—papacy, episcopacy, and regulars—which for centuries had claimed the right to intercede in parochial affairs. The genesis of this challenge to the episcopacy and to the papacy, to Episcopal Gallicanism and to ultramontanism, remains to be examined.

Historians of French religion of the Old Regime have tended to equate any movement by the lower clergy with Richerism, the term applied to the doctrines of the early seventeenth-century theologian, Edmond Richer. Because Richerism seems to have been the only systematic body of religious and political thought that affirmed the significance of the lower clergy, and because the demands of clerics of the second order coincided with statements of Richer himself, historians have linked the original ideology directly to the attainment of a sense of self-importance on the part of the second order of the First Estate. But in fact Richerism was an "eclectic compromise" among episcopalism, parlementary Gallicanism, a type of Erastianism, and doctrines that elevated the authority of the lower clergy. According to Richer, the government of the Church, while in appearance a monarchy, was in reality an aristocracy. Legislative power belonged to the synod on the local level and to a general council for all of Christendom. This council was superior to the pope, who wielded executive power. Acting as an effective president, the pontiff could see his power modified by the Church. Nevertheless, the pope had primacy of honor and jurisdiction by divine right. Richer maintained that Christ had given infallibility not to Peter but to the Church. To administer ecclesiastical jurisdiction, which belonged to the entire Church, Christ had established a hierarchy consisting of bishops, successors of the apostles, and priests, descendants of the seventy-two disciples. Bishops must be elected by the clergy and confirmed by the populace or by the king. The priest—that is, the curé, charged with the care of souls in a particular territory—had been instituted by Christ himself and exercised penitential discipline throughout the parish. Only the priest could permit a regular to hear confession and grant absolution. Gathered in synods under the guidance of the bishop, the priests collaborated in the government of the Church. Called to the general councils, the priests possessed the decisive votes.[8] Depending on which of the layers of Richer's thought are emphasized, supporters of Richerism could belong to any section of the First Estate. Further complications arise from the use of the word *Richériste*. In the seventeenth century *Richériste* had a pejorative connotation, much like *Janséniste*. And just as Jansenists continually denied that they were Jansenists, asserting instead that they were "Disciples of Saint Augustine," those who espoused controversial elements in Richer's thought did not necessarily label themselves *Richéristes*.

Moreover, the emergence of Richerism among the lower clergy has traditionally been dated at the end of the seventeenth century and linked to Jansenism. Préclin, whose work on the lower clergy remains authoritative, maintains that between 1620 and 1675 the Jansenists did not adopt Richerism out of fear of offending the bishops, their possible allies in the struggle against the Society of Jesus. Rather, the Jansenists sustained a moderate Gallicanism, unwilling to endanger their ties either with the episcopacy or with the papacy.[9] Préclin's mistake was to make Port-Royal synonymous with Jansenism, thus looking for Richerism only in the major figures (such as Saint-Cyran, Singlin, and the Arnauld family). Other historians have followed Préclin, attributing the spread of the democratic elements of Richerism among the Jansenists to Pierre Quesnel. According to this view a "New Jansenism" appeared around 1670, one that deemphasized theological debates and championed the clergy of the second order, who only then espoused Richerist ideas.[10]

But this "New Jansenism" was not new in its sustaining of the lower clergy. During the Religious Fronde, the Parisian curés professed a Jansenism tinged with Richerism as a vehicle for asserting their own aspirations. Although never explicitly using Richer's name, the curés nonetheless advanced positions consistent with those in the Richer corpus. Both the Parisian curés and Richer drew inspiration from the Gallican Gerson; both viewed the curés as having been instituted by Christ and as successors of the seventy-two disciples; both claimed that the curé exercised complete penitential jurisdiction over the parish; and both recognized that the episcopacy was superior to the second order of the clergy.[11] In short, the curés perceived themselves as an independent corps with a significant role in the Church and therefore deserving of power. Accordingly, the curés meant to institute a "New Order" in the First Estate. The clergy, the *premier ordre* of the kingdom, included a series of degrees, very unequal in dignity. The curés wanted to increase their own authority and rank, thus removing themselves from and placing themselves clearly above the rest of the lower clergy and the religious. Also, the effort to raise the curés' status served to bring them closer to the rank of the prelacy while at the same time restricting the power of bishops over curés. A heightened sense of their own separate position and of the powers which arose from their particular dignity characterized the curés' new order.

The creation of this new order in the 1650s was possible because an ecclesiastical vacuum existed in Paris. The archbishop stood accused of lese majesty and remained in exile from France for eight years. By supporting their archbishop and, in so doing, by posing as the champions of the immunities of the Church against a tyrannical government, the curés had a legalistic umbrella under which they could satisfy their own ambitions.[12] Confident that their ecclesiastical superior—Retz— would not oppose those who were his staunchest adherents in his struggle to maintain control over the archdiocese, the curés pursued a course of action that was revolutionary within the context of the First Estate. And by openly advocating the cause of Retz, who in his person continued the Fronde through the 1650s, the curés became frondeurs themselves. As religious frondeurs, acting as a new order, the curés needed a means by which to organize, to resolve a common strategy, and to implement their Richerist ideas. The curés' assemblies served this purpose.

2. The Assemblies of the Curés

The curés' success in forming a new order, in increasing their power vis-à-vis the episcopate and the regulars, and in opposing the government through their obedience to their archbishop and his vicars-general, depended on their assemblies. The assemblies were the means by which the curés endeavored to implement their ecclesiastic revolution—that is, to achieve the transfer of all parochial authority to the curés. The periodic meetings of the assemblies confirmed their dignity as a corps and gave them the status with which to treat with other bodies in the corporate society of Paris. Also, the assemblies endowed the curés with the strength of numbers acting in concert. Were it not for the assemblies, the curés would have been individuals acting alone, with little hope of success in resolving their conflicts with others. Realizing the supreme importance of their assemblies, the curés did everything they could to formalize their procedures and to keep them functioning. On the other hand, the government, episcopate, and regulars attempted to undermine the influence of the curés by denying the legitimacy of their assemblies. It was apparent that the " 'right of assembly,' an essential right . . . gave them the means to protect all the others."[13]

Paul Beurrier, curé of Saint-Etienne-du-Mont, described in his memoirs the curés' assemblies, to which he was admitted on 4 November 1653.[14] Beurrier found that the Parisian curés formed a considerable corps. They elected a syndic whose function was to conserve the hierarchical and other rights of the curés while acting in the name of the entire company in every common and public matter that reflected on the government of their parishes. The eldest curé presided as dean over the assembly, which was usually held in the residence of one of the older curés. The dean opened each assembly by invoking the Holy Spirit. After each member had taken his seat according to the length of time he had been a curé in Paris,[15] the greffier (recorder) read the results of the previous assembly. The company then debated cases of conscience, the curés stating their opinions before a plurality of voices determined the issue. Finally, the curés discussed the general business of their corps. If these problems proved to be difficult, the assembly appointed deputies to examine them and to report back at the subsequent assembly.[16]

Beurrier was inexact in stating that the curés had one syndic and one *greffier*. In reality, there were two syndics, the second serving as recorder. Rousse, a syndic throughout the Religious Fronde, explained that, "According to the statutes, the senior syndic's function is to designate the common business, as is done in all chapters of cathedral and collegiate churches. The second syndic records the judgments and the deliberations, which are ended by the presiding officer. We have never had a *greffier*."[17]

There were two types of assemblies: ordinary assemblies met on the first Monday of the month, while extraordinary assemblies convened to deal with unexpected problems whose resolution could not await the next ordinary assembly. For example, after their archbishop had escaped from prison on 8 August 1654, the curés held three extraordinary assemblies within a two-week period.[18]

Attendance in the assemblies, although varying from a high of thirty to a low of seven, remained steady throughout the Religious Fronde (figure 1). There were only seven curés at the 26 August 1654 assembly because it had been convoked suddenly, without the knowledge of many of the curés. Relatively high attendance accompanied crises. For example, a large number were present on 4 May 1654 to discuss Mazure's exile and his struggles with the Jesuits. Similarly, the assembly of 4 September 1654 climaxed the repercussions caused by Retz's escape. The average number of curés attending the assemblies for which records are extant during the period 1653–59 is 20.45. The average from 29 April 1653 to 1 March 1655 is 20.47, and that from 5 June 1658 through 7 July 1659 is 20.42. Thus, the curés' ardor did not diminish over time. Thirty-four of the thirty-nine curés of Paris were represented at various times in the assemblies, along with twelve neighboring parishes in the environs. The total number of individual curés who attended at one time or another during the Religious Fronde was over fifty.

Publicly, the curés maintained that their assemblies dealt only with ecclesiastical matters directly related to the conduct of parish affairs. The syndics Dupuys and Rousse, in presenting a petition to the General Assembly of the Clergy on 24 November 1656, which requested a

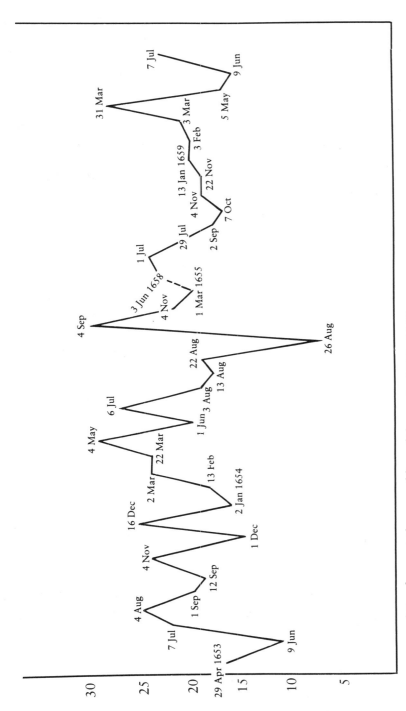

FIGURE 1. *Attendance at the assemblies of the curés, 1653–1659*

condemnation of certain propositions of the Jesuits' moral theology, included this brief defense of the curés' assemblies: "It is known that in the assemblies where we have habitually met, and which are authorized not only by custom and by the approval of our archbishop, but also by the letters which it has pleased His Majesty to send, we never discuss anything that concerns public affairs. It is not our place to do so. We treat only what relates to the needs of our parishes and the spiritual well-being of the souls entrusted to us, because that is the duty of our charge."[19] On another occasion, in protesting the treatment of Retz, the curés did not think it incongruous to affirm that they held their assemblies "not to treat with any political matter, but only to provide for the needs of their individual churches. And because they came together for purely ecclesiastical affairs, they hoped that His Majesty's council would see nothing wrong with their assemblies."[20]

Such protestations of noninvolvement in the world outside their parishes were simply not true. The curés' desire to elevate their status within the First Estate and the support—or at least benevolent neutrality—of Retz, which they believed essential for their success, precluded any withdrawal from affairs beyond the parish. Their ambitions necessitated contact with both the episcopacy and the government. The register of their assemblies clearly reflects the broad scope of the curés' activities. Besides their debates on ethical and moral questions relative to their duties as confessors, their concern with jurisdictional disputes among certain curés, and their conflicts with the Jesuits and others over the exercise of curial functions, the curés judged books, opposed the government both as frondeurs and as a corporation whose legality was denied, and, of course, confronted the bishops. The curés' enemies attacked the assemblies precisely because their activities seemed to perceive no limits.

On the basis of the Jesuit Rapin's *Mémoires*, a nineteenth-century historian contended that the majority of Parisian curés abused the credit that the faith of the people bestowed upon them. The curés assembled under pretext of deliberating parochial affairs, but in reality they fomented opposition to the pope, appealed to the Parlement, and intrigued among the magistrates so as to prevent the publication of papal bulls. Far from restricting themselves to the discussion of parish problems, the assemblies were a means by which the curés could propagate Jansenism and, in so doing, obstruct the influence both of the papacy and of the Jesuits.[21]

In addition to protesting the involvement of the assemblies in religious affairs beyond those relevant simply to the conduct of souls, Rapin blasted the assemblies for the important political role they played through their links to Retz. "It was by his [Retz's] charge that these frequent assemblies of curés, which were held in Paris at that time, were aroused. These curés took it into their heads to form a corporation in the capital of the kingdom, to elect a syndic and other officers, and to render themselves formidable to both magistrate and minister by their union and by the secret intrigue of their deliberations on affairs which did not concern their functions."[22]

The existence of the assemblies themselves as well as the curés' behavior became a source of antagonism in the 1650s. The curés recognized that "the general and extraordinary assemblies are not acceptable to the court, which perceives them as odious and not obedient to the King's will. The court does not agree that the curés of the city and suburbs of Paris form a corporation or assemble in that capacity."[23] Even the chapter of Notre-Dame which at times allied with the curés during this period, particularly in regard to the spiritual administration of the archdiocese, challenged the lawfulness of the assemblies. In a conflict between the chapter and Pierre Marlin, curé of Saint-Eustache, over the performance of curial functions in Paris,[24] the chapter went beyond the immediate issues in contention and directly attacked the curés' assemblies.

> The plaintiffs [the dean and canons of the chapter] challenge in this encounter the Parisian curés and ask them under what authority they come together in order to present petitions for intervention, since they have not always enjoyed this right. The court has never suffered it and its consequence is dangerous. The curés do not have the power to assemble except by episcopal authority. The curés advance themselves when they are limited to their territory and in the same process want to create a small diocese within another one. This is to raise altar against altar. The synods are their legitimate assemblies where they should account for their actions before the archdeacons of the Church of Paris. This is why the plaintiffs . . . hope that the court . . . will forbid the curés to assemble any longer and to have syndics.[25]

Thus, to other ecclesiastical bodies in Paris, the curés' assemblies were a basis from which the curés could behave as a corporation and could exert more power within the First Estate. But any such movement within a church structure conceived as fixed by the seventeenth-century French mind necessitated confrontation and opposition from every vested interest that saw its own role menaced. The corporate actions of the curés invited resistance and ultimately brought about the suppression of their assemblies.

3. Corporate Behavior and Government Suppression

The curés' opponents rejected the curés' right to function as a corporate body just as they had denied the legality of their assemblies. Seemingly harmless collective activities incensed the curés' antagonists precisely because it was this type of comportment that gave the curés the cohesion requisite for a significant role in the Religious Fronde. The curés, then, took advantage of every opportunity to act as a corporation. Often it was not the action itself that was important but the occasion afforded the curés to present themselves as a corps. For example, the curés publicly complimented Pomponne de Bellièvre on his promotion to the office of *premier président* of the Parlement of Paris; they congratulated Retz on his elevation to the cardinalate; they welcomed the queen of Sweden to Paris; and their representative delivered the funeral oration of the archbishop of Paris, Jean François de Gondi. All of these activities were later published in an endeavor to achieve public recognition of the curés' status.[26] Moreover, it became obvious during the 1650s that any attack on an individual curé must be considered as an affront to the entire company. The government, episcopacy, and Jesuits could no longer proceed with impunity against any one curé.

To enhance this sense of cohesion the curés marched together in processions, sent delegations to visit their sick colleagues, and held funeral services for those deceased. In addition, they required that every new curé admitted into their company take an oath "not to say or reveal anything, either in the present or in the future, about what will be said and done in the company, and to keep inviolably this secret."[27] Such a demand for secrecy could not fail to antagonize a government inclined to believe in conspiracies. Those curés who violated their pledge were ostracized. Roullé functioned as a spy for Mazarin in the curés' assemblies at the same time as he held the office of syndic. The curés expelled him from his charge because of this breach of confidentiality.[28] Roullé never again achieved his colleagues' trust. He begged Mazarin for a benefice outside of Paris where he could be safe from abuse by the other curés.[29] Nor was Roullé the only curé removed from the corps. Edmond Amyot, curé of Saint-Merry, like Roullé an adversary of Jansenism and Retz's authority, was also ejected.[30] Supporting each other in their myriad problems, bound together by an oath of secrecy, cleansing themselves through purges, the curés further provoked other power blocs through their bypassing of the episcopate's jurisdictional authority, their union with curés in major provincial cities, their opposition to the assemblies of the bishops, and their campaign against the Jesuits' moral theology.

These specific actions, which demonstrated the application of the curés' Richerist mentality and which crystallized the hostility against this new order of curés, began after the success of Pascal's *Lettres provinciales*. This work publicized views already disseminated on the parish level by the curés and galvanized sentiment against their inveterate enemies, the Jesuits. The curés capitalized on this opportunity by attempting to implement their jurisdictional claims and by strengthening their corporate identity. As early as 12 May 1656, Rousse had proposed in an assembly of the curés that they examine the propositions of the new casuists.[31]

At the same time the curés of Rouen, led by Charles du Four, curé of Saint-Maclou, assailed the Jesuits. In the synod of Rouen on 30 May, du Four harangued those present on the propositions of the casuists. Offended, the Jesuits appealed, through their spokesman Jean Brisacier, rector of the Jesuit *collège* of Rouen, to the archbishop for satisfaction. But the curés of Rouen did not recognize the archbishop's jurisdiction and wrote to the Parisian curés "to request their union."[32]

The letter from the curés of Rouen was presented to the assembly of the curés of Paris on 7 August. The Parisian curés resolved to answer their colleagues, expressing sympathy for their cause and asking for copies of their reports on the dangerous propositions of the Jesuits.[33] Twenty-eight curés of Paris assembled on 4 September when a deputy of the curés of Rouen spoke on the affair at Rouen. The deputy presented copies of Brisacier's appeal to the archbishop and of the 28 August request of the curés of Rouen to the archbishop for the censure of the maxims of the casuists.[34] The curés then determined to join

with their fellows of Rouen and to publish a circular letter to curés of
the provinces inviting them to unite with those in Paris for the purpose
of obtaining the condemnation of the casuists' moral theology. "It is
in the same spirit of peace, of concord, and charity, and in the same
wish to benefit the souls entrusted to all of us, that you should join
together with us as several of the curés of other dioceses have already
offered to do, and send for that purpose your procurations to the
syndics of our company."[35]

The resolutions of the assembly of 4 September had a great effect on
the General Assembly of the Clergy, which the episcopacy dominated.
The prelates, already confronted with the challenge to Episcopal Gallicanism posed by the curés' Richerist writings, now faced the prospect
of the curés implementing their extremist religious ideas through this
circular letter. The specter of a league among the curés of France
materialized before the episcopacy. According to Hermant, "The union
of the Parisian curés with those of Rouen against the Jesuits' moral
theology was so important a matter that it aroused at last the prelates'
vigilance."[36] The bishops, many of whom shared the curés' attitude in
regard to the casuistic propositions denounced in the circular letter,
believed that the initiative in such doctrinal matters belonged to the
episcopacy.

The affair first came before the sessions of the General Assembly on
28 September, as the archbishop of Rouen asked the Assembly to
adjudicate the conflict between the Jesuits and curés of Rouen. Commissioners were then appointed to study the incident.[37] On 10 October, the archbishop of Narbonne, presiding at the General Assembly,
reported that the curés of Paris had come to see him for permission to
appear before the Assembly. The bishops at once complained that "the
curés advised all the other curés in the kingdom of everything that
happened in the affair of their colleagues at Rouen because they requested their union through a type of circular letter." The bishop of
Meaux fumed that the circular letter was the product "of a plot and a
usurpation of the authority of the bishops." He wanted the letter
suppressed because "the Parisian curés have no right to assemble.
Since they do not constitute a body within the Church, they cannot
legitimately have syndics, nor can they write, as they did, circular
letters."[38] Although several prelates defended the curés, stating that
they assembled by permission of their archbishop and that their circular letter reflected their zeal to protect the faithful from the poison of a

pernicious doctrine, the General Assembly approved the sentiments of the bishop of Meaux and summoned Rousse and Dupuys to appear. This would lead to the first instance of decisive action by the episcopacy against the curés and their assemblies. For years the Jesuits had warned that the Parisian curés had joined together to form "a type of corporation" with officers, statutes, and regular assemblies.[39] In this way the Parisian curés served as a model for the curés of Rouen and for those of many other French cities.

On 13 October, the archbishop of Narbonne informed Rousse and Dupuys that the General Assembly found it very strange that the curés of Paris claimed to be a corps distinct from the other ecclesiastics of the archdiocese. The Assembly had learned of the circular letter and wanted to know why the Parisian curés had written to curés of other dioceses without the participation of the episcopacy. It appeared to the prelates that the Parisian curés hoped to unite with those in the provinces in order to remove them from their dependence on their bishops.[40]

Rousse replied that the Parisian curés had never had any intention to create a league among the curés of France, nor to detach those curés from dependence on their bishops. Containing an account of the request presented by the curés of Rouen to their archbishop, the circular letter served only to convince provincial curés to demand the same censure of this pernicious morality from their bishop. The curés of Paris recognized that the bishop alone could judge doctrine in his diocese and that curés must seek and receive this judgment from him. As for their ordinary and extraordinary assemblies, Rousse asserted that they were legitimate, both because of their age and because they have always been held with the permission of the bishops, and later archbishops, of Paris. To mollify the General Assembly, Rousse promised that the curés would desist from pursuing the censure of lax casuistry if the General Assembly so ordered and that the curés would send a second circular letter advising their colleagues in the provinces not to act in this matter without the permission of their bishops. In addition, the syndics of the curés would forward to the episcopacy any actions undertaken by provincial curés without the consent of local bishops.[41] The General Assembly then voted to require Rousse to submit a summary of his speech. This résumé should contain those submissions that he had made before the assembly, including his statements that the assemblies of the curés met only with the consent of the archbishop of Paris and were dependent upon him in all things.[42]

Although the subservience of Rousse and the curés satisfied the majority of the General Assembly, those bishops tied to the government were less pleased. For example, the bishop of Séez, an informant of Mazarin in the assembly, wrote that frondeurs were preventing the General Assembly from taking stronger measures to counteract the effects of the curés' circular letter. "Your Eminence might recall that I pointed out that the union of curés was capable of setting the state on fire."[43] Mazarin, however, needed no convincing that the curés were seditious. His fear of all assemblies that he could not control and his displeasure at the curés for their support of Retz had already made him anxious to move against the curés. But he had to secure the support of the episcopacy before proceeding on a course of action that involved secular interference within the First Estate.

A delegation of curés, led by Rousse, returned to the General Assembly on 27 October in order to comply with the resolutions of 13 October. Rousse again protested that the Parisian curés had no plan to form a union with those of other dioceses and that they recognized the bishops as sole judges of doctrine. Then Rousse presented the summary which had been demanded, affirming that he would alter this résumé as the assembly desired. He also submitted a second circular letter addressed to the curés of France, which revoked the first one.[44] Lastly, Rousse furnished a copy of the curés' request to the vicar-general of the archdiocese of Paris for the condemnation of maxims of the casuists, along with a similar request to the General Assembly. The prelacy was satisfied with these documents and with the curés' submission. The General Assembly soon issued its own circular letter stating that the curés' procedures were new and extraordinary, and not to be suffered. Only bishops were competent to authorize communications among dioceses. Each bishop was advised to prevent his diocesan curés from deferring to letters of the Parisian curés, from forming any assembly, and from deliberating on these matters except by episcopal authority.[45]

Having complied with the episcopate's injunctions, the curés had no recourse but to seek the censure of lax casuistry before the General Assembly. Rousse and Dupuys returned on 24 November to press again for the condemnation of laxism. While attacking the doctrine of

probable opinions and certain propositions extracted from the casuists, the curés took pains to protest their inviolable submission to
episcopal authority.[46] The General Assembly examined the extracts
tendered by the curés but, instead of issuing a condemnation of the
propositions, merely ordered on 1 February that the *Instructions* of
Saint Charles Borromeo be reprinted for the benefit of confessors.

Although hardly satisfied by this decision, the curés obeyed the
strictures of the General Assembly. For ten months the curés took little
action against the casuists. This changed in January 1658 when the
curés of Paris, in launching a national campaign against a Jesuit book,
reneged on their submission to the General Assembly and reverted to
the course of action they had followed in their first circular letter. By
joining with curés throughout France, by holding the Jesuits up to
international ridicule, and by deliberately opposing the wishes and
orders of the episcopacy and government, the curés set in motion the
events that resulted in the suppression of their regular assemblies in
July 1659.

The direct cause of these unprecedented steps on the part of the
curés was the appearance in December 1657 of the Jesuit Georges
Pirot's *L'Apologie pour les casuistes contre les calomnies des jansénistes*. Pirot's work was part of a broader but largely futile effort by
the Jesuits to refute Pascal's *Lettres provinciales*. Unlike previous
apologists, Pirot did not claim that the doctrine of the casuists had
been falsified. Instead he defended their maxims, maintaining that
even the least probable could be followed with a safe conscience.

The curés' response was immediate. In their assembly of 7 January
1658, they voted to take the steps necessary to secure the censure of
the *Apologie* by the vicars-general, the Faculty of Theology, and the
government.[47] While in 1656 the curés' strategy consisted in assailing
the Jesuits through the proscription of specific precepts, in 1658 and
1659 the offensive revolved around the total condemnation of one
book. The degree of success achieved by the curés against the *Apologie* was a measure of their success in elevating their own prerogatives
within the Church. Traditional ecclesiastical bodies did not take the
initiative against this book, which so clearly outraged the clerical and
lay public of that time. The Sorbonne, torn by internal faction, vacil-
lated for six months before censuring the *Apologie* on 16 July. The
episcopacy, save for those prelates who responded to the curés, did
nothing. The pope also wavered until 21 August 1659, when he finally

succumbed to the overwhelming revulsion expressed against the *Apologie* and its defenders.

In contrast to this inaction, the curés actively pressed for the condemnation of the *Apologie*. They lobbied within Paris, published the famous *Ecrits des curés de Paris* elaborating their theological position, and corresponded with curés in other cities and with prelates throughout the kingdom.[48] Eventually, the Parisian curés managed to have the *Apologie* censured by the archbishops of Sens, Rouen, and Bourges; the vicars-general of the archbishop of Paris; and by the bishops of Nevers, Angers, Beauvais, Aleth, Tulle, Soissons, Pamiers, Comminges, Bazas, Conserans, Cahors, Orléans, Evreux, Lisieux, Châlons-sur-Marne, Digne, Dijon, and Vence. These episcopal censures were often petitioned by those curés of provincial cities who had aligned with their colleagues in Paris. These included the curés of Sens, Reims, Evreux, Rouen, Angers, Beauvais, Nevers, Lisieux, and Amiens.[49]

The curés' publication of their *Premier écrit* in January 1658 was so strange and unforeseen—neither canons nor custom appeared to sanction such a procedure by the lower clergy—that the curés' enemies did not fail to exploit this apparent innovation.[50] This *Premier écrit* outlined the reasons why the curés had sought the condemnation of the *Apologie*. As pastors, they had a duty to warn their parishioners of these abominations. Moreover, the *Apologie* was not an anonymous work without authority but was sustained and approved by "a very important society." The struggle over the *Apologie* was that between the curés and the Jesuits, because what the curés preached in the parishes was antithetical to the teachings of the Jesuit *collège* of Clermont (where the *Apologie* was sold and where Pirot was a professor).[51]

On 4 February, in their next ordinary assembly, the curés resolved to present two requests against the *Apologie* to the Parlement and to the vicars-general. In the first, they asked that this libel be publicly burned by the executioner; and, in the second request, they supplicated the vicars-general to censure the *Apologie* and to prohibit its sale and possession. Although warned that the *Conseil du roi* would not suffer the Parlement's involvement in this affair, every curé in the assembly signed both requests.[52]

Two days later the king ordered Rousse and Mazure to come to the Louvre and explain what had occurred in the curés' assembly and why they had determined to obtain a condemnation of the *Apologie* from the Parlement. Mazarin indicated that they must content themselves with appealing to the vicars-general. The two curés responded that the *Apologie*, in addition to violating the principles of the Christian religion, proved dangerous to the state and therefore should be condemned by those whose responsibility it was to defend the civil law. After heated discussion, the king, through Séguier, prohibited the curés from prosecuting the *Apologie* before the Parlement, restricting them to the Faculty of Theology, the vicars-general, and the *official*.

On 7 February, Rousse was asked to see the *lieutenant civil*, who demanded to know why the curés had not addressed themselves to the Châtelet for the suppression of the *Apologie*. Again Rousse defended the curés' actions, this time with success, as the *lieutenant civil* issued a prohibition of the *Apologie* the next day.

On 9 February, the curés' request was submitted to the Parlement, whereupon the *procureur-général*, Nicolas Fouquet, sent for Mazure. Fouquet angrily informed him that if Mazarin had not been told that the request to the Parlement had been presented by someone who had not known of the king's injunction, Mazure and Rousse would have been exiled by *lettres de cachet*. At the same time, however, Fouquet ordered them to appear before Mazarin. Furious, the first minister questioned the two curés on this violation of the king's express order not to seek justice in this affair from the Parlement. Rousse temporarily soothed Mazarin by denying the curés' complicity in this action, affirming instead that one of the laymen who were charged with the prosecution of the curés' affairs must have inadvertently failed to inform the Parlement of the government's disposition.

Not at all placated by Rousse's explanation, Mazarin raised the subject of the curés' disobedience at an assembly of bishops on 15 February. Afraid that the curés might issue another circular letter to all the curés of the kingdom, Mazarin asked the prelates for advice on the problems caused by the ill-timed *Apologie*. The assembly resolved to allow the Faculty of Theology to examine the book; but, if its course of action did not prove satisfactory to the government, the bishops would then handle the affair.[53]

In their assembly on 11 March, the curés reaffirmed their intention of pressing the vicars-general for the condemnation of the *Apologie*. During Easter, the curés delivered sermons castigating the Jesuits' relaxed morality. Meanwhile, the Jesuits engaged the Parisian curés in a pamphlet war revolving around the *Ecrits*; the Faculty of Theology proceeded to debate the *Apologie*; and, throughout France, curés and

Jesuits became embroiled in the scenario of condemnation and defense of the *Apologie*.

Once more, in their April assembly, the Parisian curés discussed their campaign against the *Apologie*. Convinced of the righteousness of their cause and of the necessity for remaining united as a corps, they resolved that those of their colleagues who refused to sign the request to the vicars-general for the condemnation of the *Apologie* would be expelled from the assembly.[54]

As the curés' campaign persisted through 1658 and into 1659, the government and episcopacy, probably intimidated by the force of public opinion, gradually began to assert themselves against the curés. Mazarin's latent fear of assemblies received new impetus from the revolt of the Norman nobility during the summer of 1658. Linked to Retz and to Condé's Spanish army, the rebellion in Normandy posed a very real threat to the government. The crown viewed the treason of the nobles as a direct consequence of their participation in illicit assemblies. For this reason, the king issued an *arrêt* in June forbidding such assemblies.[55]

While the Jesuits ceaselessly proclaimed that the curés were trying to start an uprising in Paris and that they were hopeful of the success of the Norman revolt, the court now saw the curés' actions against the *Apologie* as having serious political implications. Already aware of the curés' adherence to the cause of Retz, the government interpreted their astonishing success against the *Apologie* as a further expression of political involvement. The curés extended their influence beyond clerics, beyond the parish, and out of Paris to much of the kingdom. Their immersion in all types of affairs, both political and religious, was, as Colbert indicated to Mazarin, "a very dangerous introduction."[56]

The tension between the government and the curés increased dramatically when the Faculty of Theology censured the *Apologie*. But immediately before the publication of the censure was to be confirmed, a representative of the chancellor entered the Sorbonne and asked that promulgation of the censure be delayed until the king returned to Paris. Disturbed by this unexpected request, the Faculty delegated four doctors, including Mazure and Marlin, to impress upon the chancellor the need to issue the censure promptly. Séguier, however, proved inflexible. He informed the deputies that the censure might cause an uproar and that "the King's presence would check the disturbances that could come from it."[57]

Although angry at the mitigation of their success in the Faculty, the curés accepted Séguier's excuse and took no decisive action in their next assembly (on 29 July). The curés did resolve to go to greet the king, who had just returned to Paris from the army in Picardy.[58] But the chancellor informed Marlin that, as the Parisian curés did not form a corporation, it was not necessary for them to pay their respects to the king.[59]

Stung by this rebuke, the curés correctly interpreted the excuse of the king's return as a deliberate deception. Their suspicion was confirmed when Louis left Paris for Fontainebleau without having regulated the affairs of the Church. The curés then resolved to complain as a corps, but Fouquet forbade this action, permitting them only to act individually.[60] Frustrated, Mazure wrote to Mazarin on behalf of the curés, asking that the Sorbonne's censure be promulgated. Mazure pointed out that the government had previously ordered the curés to appeal to the Faculty of Theology but not to prosecute the *Apologie* before the Parlement. Therefore, the publication of the censure of the Faculty would fulfill the king's intention.[61]

The first minister replied to the curés on 28 August, affirming that he would do everything that had been promised them as soon as he returned from Calais.[62] Again deluded, the curés interpreted this letter as a pledge to publish the censure. To ensure this, the assembly of 3 September empowered Mazure to see Mazarin.[63]

The failure of Mazure's visit to Mazarin was assured three days prior to their meeting. On 13 September, an assembly of bishops loyal to the government convened at Fontainebleau. The prelates recommended to Mazarin that the publication of the Sorbonne's censure be suspended indefinitely, as judgment over ecclesiastical doctrine belonged to the episcopacy. Moreover, a diversity of opinion among the bishops—the vast majority of whom had not proscribed the *Apologie*—and the Faculty of Theology had to be avoided in order not to disturb the faithful. And in a direct slap at those bishops who had supported the curés' initiatives, the assembly defined according to canon law the correct procedures by which the prelacy must determine doctrinal matters. The government was also advised to issue two *lettres de cachet* to the Sorbonne and to the vicars-general of Paris prohibiting them from publishing censures of the *Apologie*.[64]

On 16 September, Mazure greeted Mazarin as deputy of the Parisian curés. The cardinal responded abruptly that he would not listen

to talk of a deputation, that the bishops had informed him that the
curés were not a corporation. Mazure replied that the company of
curés had always been a corporation. They possessed syndics, and
when there were syndics there was always a corporation. Furthermore, Richelieu as well as the kings of France had invariably honored
the curés' deputations. Mazure then argued for the publication of the
censure. Utilizing the opinions of the assembly of bishops, Mazarin
retorted that the proclamation of individual censures would cause a
schism. In refuting this, Mazure enunciated opinions of the curés that
were so blatantly antiepiscopal as to solidify the determination of
those bishops at court to quash the curés' pretensions.[65]

The import of Mazure's remarks can only be understood in the
context of the crisis facing the court prelates at this time. On 30 July
1658, the Parlement of Paris had issued an *arrêt* ordering those bishops who resided in Paris to withdraw to their dioceses within one
month under threat of seizure of their revenues. As diocesan residency
was one precept of the seventeenth-century French Catholic Reformation, the Parlement's demand was consistent with earlier episcopal
proclamations. Nonetheless, the prelates at court, led by Marca, vehemently defended both their right to assemble and their obligation to
remain in Paris.[66]

Consequently, Mazure, realizing the precarious situation of the
court bishops, refuted Mazarin's declaration that individual censures
of the *Apologie* might cause a schism. On the contrary, Mazure contended that a schism could result if the bishops issued a censure in
their assembly. He argued that the court prelates had no power to hold
an assembly without the consent of the ecclesiastical provinces of
France. For this reason any circular letter issued by such an assembly
would be rejected as null and impertinent. Finally, Mazure proclaimed
that the Parisian curés would protest against these episcopal assemblies and would never recognize their legitimacy. Bishops, asserted
Mazure, had neither power nor jurisdiction outside of their own dioceses; they assembled in Paris so as to have an excuse to remain in
Paris. Mazure warned Mazarin that he would suffer the curse of God
on the kingdom if he tolerated these twenty-five indolent prelates'
residence at court.[67]

In a subsequent interview, Mazure again pleaded for the publication of the Sorbonne's censure. While indicating that a further post-

ponement was imperative, Mazarin denounced the assemblies of the curés and their vitriolic attacks on the Jesuits. Indeed, Mazarin threatened to imprison the most unruly of the curés. Undaunted, Mazure responded that the Jesuits were to blame for having published a defense of the most harmful doctrines that had ever been taught.[68]

Then, on 7 October, the assembly of the curés resolved to wait only one more month for the government to lift its restraints on the publication of the censure. If this condition were not met, every member of the company of curés would devote his sermons entirely to the condemnation of the Jesuits' relaxed morality. This campaign from the pulpit would continue until parishioners were fully instructed.[69] The curés never implemented this threat because the government yielded and advised the Sorbonne that it would no longer prevent the printing of the censure. On 30 October, three and one-half months after it had been resolved, the censure was published. On that same day the vicars-general promulgated their censure, which had been delayed since 23 August.[70]

This concession by the court (and episcopacy) was extraordinary; it demonstrated the weakened position of the ministeriat in 1658 and the curés' power. But the concession did not have the desired effect, because far from remaining satisfied with their victory in Paris, the curés continued their pressure against the *Apologie* throughout the kingdom. During the next seven months, the Parisian curés maintained their correspondence with curés in provincial cities and with some bishops. As their mutual interests gradually supplanted the primary concern for the *Apologie*'s condemnation, provincial curés looked to those in Paris for leadership, asking their advice on various problems and using their assemblies as a model.[71] The curés of France were joining together to form a new order within the French Church.

Just as alarming to the government and court episcopacy as the ties among the curés were those maintained by the Parisian curés with various bishops. Nearly all of the bishops who corresponded with the Parisian curés and issued condemnations of the *Apologie* had a history of opposition to the government either as frondeurs or as Jansenists. For example, Gondrin, archbishop of Sens and closest ally of the Parisian curés among the prelates, supported Condé during the Fronde, expelled the Jesuits from his diocese for twenty-five years, and resisted Mazarin's policies in regard to Jansenism and Retz. In fact, Le Tellier exiled Gondrin to his diocese in February 1659 for his association with the curés, while Mazarin instructed abbé Fouquet to inform him of the archbishop's activities and of "cabals" among the curés.[72]

Several of the bishops who supported the curés' initiatives had gained notoriety as Jansenists, particularly after their resistance to the 1653 anti-Jansenist bull, *Cum occasione*. These included Gilbert de Choiseul, bishop of Comminges; Henri Arnauld, bishop of Angers; and Louis-François Le Fèvre de Caumartin, bishop of Beauvais. Antoine Godeau, bishop of Vence; Nicolas Pavillon, bishop of Aleth; and Etienne Caulet, bishop of Pamiers, were others who were tied both to Jansenism and to the curés. The crown could not help interpreting the corporate actions of the curés in political as well as in religious terms when the curés sought and found aid among those who had continually thwarted government policies. As soon as they had weathered the attack on their own assemblies, the court bishops were prepared to proceed against the curés. As the bishops viewed the situation, the curés had subverted episcopal jurisdiction and authority despite their protestations to the General Assembly, and now they had even successfully petitioned the most recalcitrant members of the prelacy.

The reprisals against the curés began on 7 June 1659, when an *arrêt* of the *Conseil d'état* suppressed the *Septième écrit*, their first work censured by the government. While the previous six *Ecrits* had postulated a moral theology antithetical to that propagated by the Jesuits, the *Septième écrit* was an accurate historical record of the curés' activities. As a journal of what the curés had done as a corporate body, the *Septième écrit* publicly flaunted the curés' disobedience to the episcopacy and government. The publication of this work was a mark of bravura, a sign that the curés had risen in the seemingly static order of the First Estate. The censure of this work was an indication that the traditional forces in French society were prepared to reassert themselves against the upstart curés.

In an assembly of bishops on 22 June, Mazarin, as was his custom, appealed to those prelates loyal to him for advice and for ecclesiastical approval of his policies. At this time, Mazarin wanted to rid the state of the vexatious problem of the Parisian curés. The first minister informed the bishops that the king had learned

that the Parisian curés dealt with matters in their assemblies which they must not take cognizance of. Because they intended to form a new corporation in the clergy of the diocese of Paris, the curés have appointed syndics. . . . Moreover, they have debated questions and taken resolutions that are contrary to episcopal dignity and jurisdiction, and to ecclesiastical discipline. If a remedy is not applied, these actions could disturb the peace of the Church.[73]

The agent of the clergy next reviewed the curés' offenses.[74] The agent cited their assemblies, their attempts to form a union with other curés of the kingdom, and their disobedience to the 1656 General Assembly. The assembled bishops then resolved to ask the king to issue a letter to the vicars-general ordering them to stop the curés' assemblies and to eliminate their offices. If the curés wished to confer together in the future "on the good government of their parishes," they could do so only with the permission and in the presence of one or both of the vicars-general.[75]

On 27 June, Séguier, staunch anti-Jansenist and supporter of the Jesuits, denounced the curés before the king's council. The chancellor maintained that curés did not form a corporation, that they discussed dangerous matters in their assemblies, and that their *Ecrits* were filled with lies. After Séguier had presented the bishops' recommendation for the suppression of the curés' assemblies, the ministers concurred with the chancellor's opinions. There remained only to issue the edict.[76]

Mindful of the possible repercussions of an action taken against the curés' assemblies, the government adopted the stratagem of having the vicars-general deliver the ordinance to the curés. As was pointed out to Mazarin, the charge that Church immunities had been violated would be less credible if the order for suppression came from within the Church. In addition, Retz would not be able to appeal to the public that his archiepiscopal authority had been usurped, for it would be his vicars-general—responsible for diocesan affairs during his absence—who had abolished the assemblies. Thus, the court sought to avoid giving either the clergy or Retz a pretext for creating a disturbance in Paris.[77]

The vicars-general received the ordinance for suppression on 6 July in order that they might present it to the ordinary assembly of the curés scheduled for the next day. In a letter accompanying the ordi-

nance, Le Tellier reminded the vicars-general that although the king's
desire was for the regular assemblies to be abolished, he had taken this
step only on the advice of the archbishops and bishops at court.[78]

The ordinance itself—primarily an elaboration of Mazarin's speech
of 22 June—consisted of two portions: an indictment of the curés'
Richerist claims and activities and a precise description of how the
curés would be allowed to meet in the future. Among the accusations
leveled at the curés was the complaint that, while ostensibly assembling to deal with spiritual affairs which concerned the administration
of their parishes, they had in fact deliberated on matters well beyond
the responsibilities of their charge. The curés had attempted to create a
new order that disrupted the Church hierarchy. They had subverted
ecclesiastical discipline and episcopal dignity and jurisdiction. They
had elected syndics and kept a register as if they were a corporation;
and they had published without the permission of their superiors.[79]

If, in the future, the curés petitioned the vicars-general for permission to assemble, the latter could grant permission only if they were
certain that the matters to be discussed concerned the conduct of souls
and the spiritual administration of the parishes. A vicar-general must
be present at every assembly, which could be convened only in the
archbishop's palace. The register of such assemblies would be closely
supervised by the vicars-general.[80] In short, this ordinance forbade the
holding of regular assemblies by the curés, abolished the office of
syndic, and ended the independence of future assemblies while limiting
their frequency and points of discussion.

On 7 July, the vicars-general carried out their commission before
the assembled curés. The curés protested the accusations against them,
affirming their submission to both king and episcopacy. While promis-
ing to obey the ordinance, the curés sought clarification in an attempt
to circumvent its provisions. Thus, they agreed to the abolition of the
charge of syndic but requested that the functions be transferred to
another officer.[81]

The syndics led the curés in this vain effort to preserve their corporate identity. Rousse wrote to Mazarin in July and August and
submitted a memorandum in defense of the assemblies. In his letters,
Rousse misrepresented the assemblies by depicting them as little more
than a debating society. It was the function of the syndic, said Rousse,
to prepare and study cases of conscience, which the subsequent assembly discussed. Since these assemblies were only "simple confer-

ences of study and doctrine," there would be no harm in their continuing to meet once a month with their officers.[82] Marlin, the other syndic, besides refuting the contents of the ordinance during the 7 July assembly, worked to convince the court prelates of the curés' innocence.[83]

The government proved inflexible. Le Tellier, relaying the curés' request to elect another officer comparable to the syndic, urged Mazarin to reject this artifice.[84] Séguier, on the other hand, proposed an even harsher measure—the curés should not be permitted to assemble at all. Even if they held their assemblies sporadically, argued Séguier, they would consequently be able to claim that they were a corporation. It would be better to force them to act individually in all matters.[85]

Mazarin accepted Le Tellier's advice, refusing the curés' request and demanding strict compliance with the ordinance.[86] In response to Mazarin, Le Tellier issued a new ordinance on 18 July that prohibited the curés from choosing anyone to take charge of their affairs.[87] This effectively eliminated the curés' ability to function as a corporate body.

Although the curés assembled intermittently for the next few years, their assemblies never again seriously threatened the government or the episcopacy. The curés' major role in the Religious Fronde had ended. The court prelates and government ministers were elated at the curés' submission and filled their correspondence to Mazarin with accounts of the curés' obedience.[88]

Never again in the seventeenth century would the Parisian curés achieve such national importance. Their primacy and ability to lead curés of provincial cities had ended. It would be at least another generation before the second order of the First Estate received any new ideological justification for its significance, and not until the eighteenth century would curés again become a major political-religious force.

Those few writers who have noted the suppression of the curés' assemblies have interpreted the act as a consequence of the curés' attacks on the Jesuits. According to this view, the Jesuits reacted to the *Ecrits des curés de Paris* and to the censures of the *Apologie* by causing the regular assemblies to be dissolved.[89] This is only a partial explanation. Though the Jesuits did contribute to the curés' downfall, only the episcopacy and government could have supplied the force requisite for the suppression. Seen in this light, the national campaign against the *Apologie* would have remained as another example of the recurrent infighting between Jesuits and curés had it not solidified the enmity of bishops and court toward the curés.

By forcing the curés to repudiate their first circular letter in October 1656 and by censuring in April 1657 those Richerist works—Mazure's *L'Obligation des fidèles* and Rousse's *Sommaire* of Mazure's book—which postulated scriptural and canonical justification for the curés' authority, the episcopacy believed it had eliminated this attack on the Church hierarchy. However, the prelacy construed the later junction of the Parisian curés with those throughout France and their initiation of doctrinal judgment in the affair of the *Apologie* as a very real threat to the tenets of Episcopal Gallicanism. The curés' opposition to the court assemblies of bishops further determined the episcopacy to take decisive action against the curés.

If the prelates interpreted the union of curés throughout the kingdom in religious terms, the government viewed it as having serious political ramifications. Already mistrustful of the curés as supporters of Retz, the court did not desire to see these frondeurs extend their relationships to curés in provincial cities. Wary of Retz's possible return to France, the government sought to reduce the strength of those who would welcome his reestablishment as archbishop. To dissipate the curés' strength, the court opposed their acting collectively. Denying that the curés could be a corporation, the government eventually suppressed the means by which the curés behaved corporately. Nevertheless, even without their allegiance to Retz, the curés no doubt would have been persecuted. Mazarin would have opposed any assembly that attempted to conduct its affairs secretly and whose business intruded into areas previously dominated by groups loyal to the government.[90]

The common denominator of these reasons for the crushing of the curés as a new order in the Church was the fact that every assertion of their authority was seen by each other group as a lessening of its own powers. Similar to his acceptance of mercantilist theories of a fixed quantity of goods and resources, the seventeenth-century Frenchman believed there was a static amount of power in society. The increase of the power of one group necessarily resulted in a diminution in that of another. Consequently, given the impossibility of creating a new order within the First Estate without antagonizing more powerful interests, the curés were foredoomed to failure.

CHAPTER THREE

THE FOUNDATIONS OF OPPOSITION: THE STRUGGLE FOR POWER IN THE PARISHES OF PARIS DURING THE RELIGIOUS FRONDE

> Animosity against the Jesuits was a great quality
> . . . in a cabal which was formed solely because of aversion
> to their company. It was especially this consideration which
> attached part of the curés of Paris and of neighboring
> villages to the new opinion [Jansenism]. Because the
> interests of the hierarchy had aroused the curés to revolt
> against this Society, they were the first to join a league
> which was created for the purpose of destroying the Jesuits.
> Rapin, *Mémoires*, 1: 114

The Jesuit Rapin, though often maligned for his biases, astutely recognized the motivations of those who wished to destroy his company. As Rapin pointed out, the curés' aversion for the Society of Jesus stemmed from what they considered to be their legitimate interests within the Church hierarchy. To defend those interests against the regulars and to establish supremacy over all parish affairs, the curés adopted their intellectual and doctrinal positions—as well as their political allies—of the Religious Fronde.

At the heart of the Religious Fronde lay the struggle for control of the parishes of Paris. The curés wanted exclusive authority over their parishioners' religious practices, while the Jesuits proclaimed their right to administer to the spiritual needs of anyone who came to them. Jurisdictional power as well as additional revenues would accrue to the side that triumphed. The curés and Jesuits argued their respective positions in the Church hierarchy and the problem of the privileges of regulars. This type of conflict was not peculiar to the 1650s but was part of a whole tradition of regular-secular controversies that had originated in the Middle Ages. On the other hand, the battle between curés and Jesuits became particularly significant in the 1650s, as seemingly innocuous issues of daily religious life reverberated beyond the parish to involve the government and the principal religious bodies of the French Church, to determine the ecclesiastical-political alignments of the Religious Fronde, and to occasion the formation of extremist religious thought. An examination of this struggle between curés and Jesuits—the issues involved and the particular quarrels themselves— is therefore requisite for an understanding of the Religious Fronde.

1. *The Regular-Secular Conflict in the French Church*

With the papal creation in the early thirteenth century of the first mendicant orders, the Franciscans and the Dominicans, the regular-secular conflict emerged in Paris. The ensuing battle was both jurisdictional and theological: jurisdictional in the question of alleged exemptions accorded to the regulars and in the problem of the composition of the Church hierarchy; and theological in the discussion over the origin, nature, and excellence of the religious life. The first incidents in this recurring struggle centered in the University of Paris, where secular doctors, led by William of Saint-Amour, sought both to restrict the numbers and privileges of regulars in the university and at the same time to challenge the mendicants' conception of their role in the Church. Bonaventure and Aquinas, among others, refuted the works of the seculars.

William argued in his polemic, *Tractatus de periculis novissimorum temporum* (1255), that the friars usurped the functions of secular priests and that they should be prohibited from pastoral work, teaching, and preaching. Indeed, the mendicants should be denied all privileges. Ultimately, William and his followers attributed ecclesiastical perfection to the secular clergy as the concomitant of their pastoral duties. By renouncing temporal goods, the mendicants made the cure of souls infeasible and charity impossible. The apologists of the regulars resisted these charges by asserting the perfection of the life of poverty and the right of regulars to assist in pastoral life.[1]

Two significant factors led to the unusual vehemence of the conflict in the seventeenth century: the continued development of Gallicanism and the increasing power of the Jesuits. Their strength and cohesion, their alleged influence within the Curia, and their role as confessors to the Bourbon kings made the Jesuits the focus of the antiregulars' hatred in France. To those who supported the monarchy against decentralizing forces, the Society of Jesus was forever linked to the party of the League. Both the Parisian curés and the Sorbonne had opposed the Jesuits in the 1580s and had aided in the temporary expulsion of this order from France in 1594.

Their power and their staunch ultramontanism thus made the Jesuits anathema to Gallican churchmen. Ardently Gallican, the Faculty of Theology (which included many of the Parisian curés) struggled against the Jesuits and ultramontanism in the *Guerre de plumes* following the assassination of Henry IV, in the Santarelli affair of 1626, and in numerous other encounters. In 1630 the regulars presented to the Faculty propositions resembling those against which William of Saint-Amour had protested in the thirteenth century: the regulars were the wisest and the favored part of the ecclesiastical hierarchy; the superiors of the regulars were more worthy than bishops; the papacy could not revoke the privileges of regulars; regulars were the true— and the only—pastors; regulars could administer all of the sacraments, even against the will of the curé; parishioners were not obligated to take communion in their own parish during Easter.[2] From such propositions, the antagonism of secular doctors, curés, and bishops toward the Jesuits would inevitably arise.

These quarrels within the Faculty dragged on continuously through the 1630s and 1640s, into the period of the Religious Fronde and beyond. After 1640 the Jesuits played an even more important role in the regular-secular conflicts within the Faculty, just as they seriously challenged the curés on the parish level after 1653. By this time the conflict had widened to involve the Jansenist question, as the Jesuits, already ultramontane, became the major adversaries of Jansenism. By equating the regulars' cause with both ultramontanism and anti-Jansenism, the Jesuits had driven the staunchly Gallican secular doctors of the Faculty, if not to Jansenism, then at least to a position whereby their Gallicanism became tenable only by siding with Jansenists. This situation, forming in the 1640s, was solidified in the 1650s when those who were most anti-Jesuit could be identified as antiregular, Gallican, Jansenist, and frondeur.

Of the quarrels in the Faculty during this period,[3] it is important to note only that the Parisian curés led the secular members of the Faculty in opposing the regulars and ultramontanism and in defending Gallicanism and Jansenism. What the curés initiated in their assemblies against the Jesuits they invariably carried before the Faculty. The most obvious examples were those two *causes célèbres* of the 1650s, the Bagot-Mazure controversy and the affair of Pirot's *Apologie*. In short, possessing a tradition of antiregular activities, the Faculty, or at least part of the Faculty, was available as a platform from which the curés could decry their inveterate enemies, the Jesuits. Though the curés' frequent utilization of the Faculty coincided with the Religious Fronde, the squabbles between regulars and seculars within the Faculty persisted unabated throughout the Old Regime.

Along with the Faculty of Theology, the episcopate constantly quarreled with the regulars, and, until the Religious Fronde, the curés' cause was subsumed in that of the prelates. The episcopal-regular conflict, while similar to that between the University of Paris and the regulars in regard to the problem of ultramontanism-Gallicanism and the claim of the regulars for privileged status and certain exemptions, centered on issues germane to episcopal authority and jurisdiction. The bishops viewed the regulars as foreigners to the diocese, as maintaining subordination to superiors in Rome, and as defending exemptions that inhibited the prelate from satisfactorily performing his diocesan functions.[4]

To these interminable points of contention, new problems arose in the seventeenth century. The French Catholic Reformation, manifesting itself to a significant degree in monastic reform, saw the regulars resist that reform led by the prelacy by claiming a violation of their exemptions and by subsequently appealing to Rome. Salesian doctrine further complicated the idea of religious perfection. Seeking to reconcile the worldly and the Christian life, François de Sales blurred the distinction between layman and regular. Now *dévot* as well as regular could affirm that he lived a life of virtue. Lastly, Richerism, though used by the lower clergy against the episcopacy, condemned the privileges of regulars and bequeathed to the prelates the doctrine that they were the equals of the popes.[5] This doctrine—that the episcopacy, forming what was in effect an oligarchical government within the Church, could legitimately assert its own rights against the papacy—was the cornerstone of Episcopal Gallicanism. These rights included jurisdiction over all within the diocese; the final authority for granting permission to confess and to preach; and the recognition, on the theological level, that generals and provincials of regulars were not equal in rank to the episcopacy.

Issues like these exacerbated relations between the bishops and regulars and caused disputes throughout the seventeenth century. A brief listing of some of these quarrels clearly demonstrates their high incidence. Toward 1625, prelates at Bordeaux, Langres, Léon, and Poitiers quarreled with their regulars; in the 1630s, it was the turn of the dioceses of Blois, Rouen, Tréguier, Béziers, and Narbonne; during the next decade the archbishop of Paris clashed with the abbé of Saint-Germain-des-Prés, while the archbishop of Bordeaux confronted five regular orders.[6] During the Religious Fronde, the most spectacular conflicts between the episcopacy and regulars occurred. The archbishop of Sens, who had struggled against the Jesuits since the beginning of his episcopate, brought his campaign against them to a climax—his archdiocese became "the purgatory of the Jesuits." Even more notorious was the conflict between Henri Arnauld, bishop of Angers, and the Jacobins, Carmes, Augustinians, Recollets, and Cordeliers of his diocese.

The Angers conflict, beginning in 1653, quickly spread as the participants appealed to the General Assembly of the Clergy, the pope, and the public. After being defended by the General Assembly in 1656,[7] Bishop Arnauld allowed Father François Bonichon to publish a book supportive of the prelate's claims.[8] This book broadened the struggle beyond the original issues (the extent of the powers of the bishop in relation to the regulars within the diocese of Angers) to the question of the limits of episcopal authority within the Catholic Church—that is, to the problems of Episcopal Gallicanism and papal infallibility. Bonichon's book prompted a response by Jacques de Vernant, which the Faculty of Theology censured as "insulting to the King, seditious, and contrary to the true liberties of the Gallican Church."[9] Pope Alexander VII immediately wrote to the king and issued a bull against the Sorbonne's censure. Predictably, the Parlement of Paris issued an *arrêt* against the bull, and the General Assembly of 1665 reopened discussions of this affair, which it had considered solved in 1656. The Angers conflict, then, reflected how local, diocesan disputes between regulars and seculars could engulf the entire Church.[10]

Such struggles were relatively normal occurrences. Both the Faculty of Theology and the episcopate ceaselessly battled regulars. In the

1650s, however, the conflict between curés and Jesuits achieved central importance, as religious issues masking the fight for local power in the parishes determined the intellectual and political composition of the Religious Fronde.

2. The Issues Contested

The conflict between curés and Jesuits for jurisdictional authority and economic benefits centered around several crucial issues: the problem of confession, particularly of annual confession and the right to hear death confessions; the location of burial; the question of parishioners' obligation to attend parish Mass; and the position of curés and Jesuits within the ecclesiastical hierarchy, and the privileges attendant upon their respective ranks. These seemingly mundane considerations were in fact all-important for the curés; the battle over these issues was no less than a struggle to control local religious life in Paris. The determination to win these controversies led the curés to posit the heretical doctrine that they possessed jurisdictional control and autonomy within the parish, to adopt the moral theology of Jansenism so as to discredit the apparent laxism of the Society of Jesus, and to back the frondeur Retz in order that the curés' positions might be grounded in archiepiscopal consent. Accordingly, the struggle with the Jesuits over the problems of confession, burial, and so on, was the foundation of the curés' opposition to both the government and the episcopacy. The curés' actions during the Religious Fronde cannot be understood apart from the backdrop of constant clashes with the Jesuits.

Contemporaries well understood the reasons for the curés' aversion to the Society of Jesus. These reasons were quite obvious: the presence of Jesuits within a parish resulted in many parishioners abandoning their curé to confess to the Jesuits, to listen to their sermons, and, most significantly, to be financially generous to the Jesuits at the expense of their own curé.

Thus, a 1654 pamphlet of the Jesuits charged the curés with being motivated by greed in contesting the right of regulars to hear confessions of those who were dying; the curés simply desired the money that dying persons gave to the Jesuits.[11] The curés denied this motive of greed, defending in general the *droits* and *dîmes* owed by parishioners to their curés and specifically rejecting the accusation that they claimed sole right to hear death confessions because of a wish to influence wills.[12] Instead, the curés denounced the Jesuits for influencing the best families in France to bequeath money to their Society and for appropriating funds which rightfully belonged to widows and orphans of the deceased.[13] In fact, both sides accurately stated the motivations of their foes. Power—seen as the control of the population and territory of the parish and as the financial rewards which followed that control—was the matter contended.

The obligation of annual confession and paschal communion has been an accepted part of religious practice since the thirteenth century, and all of the synodal statutes of Parisian bishops emphasized that the faithful acquit themselves of this obligation before the parish priest. By the seventeenth century, performance of the paschal duty had become nearly universal among Catholics in most of the dioceses of France.[14] Canon law, as well as custom, sanctioned this practice. The Fourth Lateran Council in 1215 had declared that "Every *fidelis* of either sex shall after the attainment of years of discretion separately confess his sins with all fidelity to his own priest at least once in the year: and shall endeavour to fulfil the penance imposed upon him to the best of his ability, reverently receiving the sacrament of the Eucharist at least at Easter."[15] The Council of Trent reaffirmed this decree and strengthened the parochial unit and the pastor at the expense of the regular clergy.[16] This did not prevent the Jesuits from encroaching on the curés' prerogative, as the right to hear the annual confession became a burning issue in the 1650s.

Although Bagot recognized in his *Défense du droict épiscopal* that paschal communion must be made in the parish, he assailed the alleged right of the curés to hear annual confession by including it in a broader denunciation of their powers. Thus, while denying the curés' claim to administer all sacraments to the exclusion of bishops and the pope, Bagot hoped to subsume the problem of annual confession within a general condemnation of the totality of the curés' pretensions. Bagot asserted that bishops could dispense parishioners from the obligation to confess annually to their curé and that the curé did not hold his jurisdiction independently (i.e., from Christ) from the bishop. More specifically, Bagot posited that popes had validly commissioned regulars to hear confessions, without the necessity of the curés' consent. Consequently, the faithful could confess—even against the wish of the curé—to the pope, bishop, or to someone delegated by them. Writing in 1655, Bagot maintained that the curés' insistence on absolute control over confessions dated from an assembly of the curés held two years earlier. The curés' position, then, was an innovation and hence indefensible.[17]

Later, in order to mollify the General Assembly of the Clergy, Bagot restated his opinion on confession. At that time, he said that even an ecclesiastic deputed by the pope to hear confessions could not do so without the bishop's approval. Nevertheless, Bagot was adamant in maintaining that the canon of the Fourth Lateran Council could be satisfied by confessing either to a regular or to a secular priest.[18]

Although Bagot's position on annual confession clearly violated the canons of both the Fourth Lateran Council and the Council of Trent, it did not lack defenders. One line of argumentation held that, in addition to the curé, the pope and the local bishop were the parishioner's priest. Furthermore, both pope and bishop could legitimately delegate to regulars the right to hear confessions.[19] Similarly, some contended that any priest who had cure of souls—not only the curé—could hear the annual confession.[20] In short, the Jesuits professed that it was as meritorious to confess to a delegate—whether regular or secular—of the bishop or pope, as it was to confess to the curé.[21]

The curés based their arguments on the decrees of the Fourth Lateran Council and of the Council of Trent.[22] However, the curés sometimes took an extreme position, affirming that the annual confession had to be made to the curé or to someone delegated by him. No one could hear confession in the parish without the curé's permission. This claim to exercise sole right of confessing was a corollary of the curés' attempt during the Religious Fronde to form a new order within the First Estate: the curé was the "proper priest," and the bishops, pope, and regulars could not interfere with his functions.[23]

Even when the curés mitigated their views concerning the power of bishops and pope with respect to confession, they never admitted that regulars had any canonical role in the administration of that sacrament. Rousse, in the process of tempering Mazure's emphasis on the responsibility of the "curé alone" to regulate annual confession, added that the phrase "curé alone" applied only to the exclusion of regulars. The penitent was not free to choose any confessor, whether secular or regular, without the permission of his curé or bishop.[24]

More subtle, but no less antiregular, was a conference held by Duhamel at Saint-Merry on 4 April 1652, which debated the question: "Whether the penitent who has been bound by one confessor can be released by another." The conference resolved that once tied to a confessor, the penitent could sever those ties only with the permission of that priest.[25] The implication for one's annual confession was clear—the penitent, confessing to the curé throughout the year, was not at liberty to confess to anyone else during Easter.

The episcopacy rejected both the arguments of the Jesuits and the curés' extremist position. However, the prelates did favor the curés over the regulars by citing both the canons of the Fourth Lateran Council and the Council of Trent and by affirming that the parishioner could confess outside of his parish only with the consent of his curé or bishop. Thus, the moderate view of the curés prevailed in the General Assembly of the Clergy.[26] The Faculty of Theology decided this issue even more favorably for the curés. In addition to ruling that it was more proper to confess to one's curé, the Faculty declared that the faithful must fulfill the duty of annual confession at the parish and could confess elsewhere only with the curé's authorization.[27]

Enmeshed in this controversy over confession was the specific question of who had the authority to hear confession from a dying person. This power was especially significant for economic reasons, for it was believed that he who was in a position to grant final absolution could at the same time influence the dying person to alter his will as a prerequisite for that absolution.

The curés' view was explicit. In an assembly, the curés resolved a case of conscience: if a sick person confessed to a regular without the curé's consent, was the confession invalid? The conclusion was that the confession was null and would have to be made again.[28] The Jesuits' position was also clear: as delegates of the bishop or pope, they had a right to hear all confessions, including those of sick and dying persons.[29] At one point, the curés' assembly pressed for a settlement with the Jesuits. The curés proposed that parishioners could make paschal confession to the regulars and receive from them the last sacrament if the regulars agreed that parishioners needed their curé's permission to do so. The Jesuits in Paris found this proposal unacceptable.[30]

The episcopacy attempted to arbitrate this problem along with the broader issue of confession. For example, among Bagot's other propositions, the commission on regulars of the General Assembly of the

Clergy examined his statement that "the popes have said so clearly that one can always confess to the regulars, even during Easter and during sickness, that they have condemned as mistaken those who held a contrary opinion. It is an error to think otherwise, even in matters of faith."[31] The commission included in its report presented to the General Assembly in March 1657 the episcopal judgment "On confession during illness." Although the Church had not established the same obligation of confessing to one's curé in time of sickness as during Easter, the commissioners recommended giving confession to the curé. Nonetheless, if a dying person were not attended by his curé, he could in extreme necessity confess to a priest—whether regular or secular—approved by the bishop. This priest had then to attest to the curé, with the proof of a letter written and signed by the sick person, that he had indeed heard the confession of that person. Therefore, as was the case with the issue of annual confession, the episcopate again sided with the curés, preferring to support the secular clergy against the regulars.[32]

The third major issue which came between the curés and Jesuits was burial. Did the parishioner have the liberty to choose his own place of burial? The curés responded negatively, asserting that the parishioner was obligated to be interred in his own parish. Here, again, economic and jurisdictional motives predominated. As with the sacraments of baptism, matrimony, penance, and communion, extreme unction and burial were not free in the seventeenth century. Also, the rich often bestowed gifts on those churches in which they and their families were buried and, of course, paid for masses to be said for their souls.[33]

In one dispute over the right of parishioners to select their own place of burial, the priests of Saint-Paul physically contested possession of a body in what amounted to a small battle against the Jesuits on the steps of the church.[34] So important was this issue to the curés that they engaged the chapter of Notre-Dame in a three-year lawsuit on the eve of the Religious Fronde. The curés saw their right to control the interment of their parishioners as crucial to the maintenance of all of their curial prerogatives. Thus, while the immediate burial of one canon was the subject of the protracted suit, the curés' defense rested upon their total control of ecclesiastical functions within the parish. Their printed statements against the chapter listed the curés' rights so as to demonstrate that control over burial was consistent with the institution of curé: the curé administered the sacraments; there was only one curé in a parish—i.e., canons (and Jesuits) were responsible to the curé; and the curé administered to canons and regulars within the parish.[35] The curés' assertion of these rights was the crux of parish politics.

Another point of contention between curés and Jesuits concerned the obligation of the faithful to attend parish Mass. The duty to hear Sunday Mass dated from the earliest days of the Church and was codified in the fourth century. In 638, the Council of Nantes stipulated that this Mass was to be heard at the parish. Although the mendicants and Jesuits obtained some exceptions to this during the sixteenth century, the Council of Trent proposed that one attend the parish Mass at least on Sundays and festivals.[36]

The curés insisted on this attendance. A conference at Saint-Merry resolved that the Church, through its councils, had indeed required the faithful to go to the Mass of the parish. It was against the order of the Church for a parishioner to go to another church to hear Mass. In this way, the curés were protected against the encroachments of the regulars.[37]

This concern to keep their parishioners away from the churches of the regulars (and from private chapels) was not peculiar to the Parisian curés. After receiving a letter from the curés of Angers warning that the regulars were trying to obtain a bull from the pope declaring that parish Mass, parish communion, and annual confession were not obligatory, the assembly of the curés resolved to uncover the truth of this matter and to seek suggestions as to what could be done.[38] In their *Septième écrit*, the Parisian curés publicized the charge that the Jesuits led the people to believe that parishioners would be granted pardons able to deliver souls from purgatory if they communed at the churches of the Jesuits, even on Sundays and festivals.[39]

The Jesuits maintained that the faithful satisfied the commandment to attend Mass on festivals and Sundays in churches of the regulars. The obligation to hear Mass during holy days and on Sundays was not to be confused with the particular obligation to hear the parish Mass at some time.[40] Bagot concluded this subject by affirming that "the faithful have never been obligated under pain of mortal sin to hear Mass on Sundays and holy days in parish churches as these gentlemen the antiregulars claim. One could always hear in good conscience the Mass of obligation in individual oratories and in domestic chapels provided that one had the permission of bishops or of the pope."[41]

Echoing this Jesuit position, Vernant's book was "the claim of liberty for the faithful with respect to annual confession, paschal communion, [and] the hearing of Sunday mass."[42]

On the question of attendance at Mass, both the Faculty of Theology and the episcopacy rejected the Jesuits' presumptions. The Faculty censured Vernant's work and, in regard to Bagot's statements, affirmed that according to the Council of Trent "the faithful are obliged to attend the parish church on Sundays and on the principal festivals, or at least on one of every three Sundays."[43] The General Assembly utilized this same phraseology, adding that Trent had exhorted the prelates to warn the people of their duty to go to the parish Mass and had charged the curés with preaching this doctrine.[44]

The last of the major issues separating the curés and Jesuits concerned their respective positions within the Church hierarchy. Similar to the theological quarrel involving William of Saint-Amour in the thirteenth century, the problem assumed new significance during the Religious Fronde when the curés attempted to create a new order in the First Estate. Basing their assertions on canon law and elements of Richerism, the curés enunciated their prerogatives at the expense of the regulars by claiming to exercise sovereignty over all parish affairs and parishioners. The corollary of this right was the curés' authority to enforce their interpretation of confession, burial, and attendance at parish Mass.

Since the struggle for power in the Parisian parishes revolved around these basic religious issues, and as control over these matters was directly related to one's rank in the hierarchy, the curés elaborated their radical doctrine of curial origins and preeminence in order to combat the Jesuits' encroachments. In this way, the conflict with the Jesuits was a major causal factor in the curés becoming frondeurs in that it conditioned the curés to form their new order and to seek for their cause the sanction of their archbishop, renowned for his hatred of the Jesuits. This in turn angered both the episcopate and government, the former because it saw its own theories of Episcopal Gallicanism and jurisdiction threatened, and the latter because of its fear of any union with the frondeur Retz and because of its close ties with the Jesuits.

The Jesuits refuted the curés' Richerism and instead maintained "that the regulars who are called mendicants and the other privileged [religious] are as much and more summoned by God to the hierarchi-

cal functions than secular priests."[45] Bagot, for example, denied that
the curés' power was independent or absolute and therefore affirmed
that those more elevated in the hierarchy could delegate the administration of sacraments and other curial duties.[46] This question of hierarchy, containing, as it were, the answer to the other points of contention between the curés and Jesuits, dominated many of their conflicts
during the 1650s. It was these conflicts which reflected the hatred of
curés and Jesuits and which determined alignments during the Religious Fronde.

3. The Succession of Conflicts

Though the struggles between the curés and Jesuits were continuous
throughout the 1650s, three of the more prominent conflicts merit
scrutiny, because they demonstrate how the disputes over local religious issues could grow during this period of upheaval to become
matters of national or even international concern.

The first of these altercations occurred in April 1654. On 30 March
the Jesuit Claude de Lingendes, whom Rapin in his enthusiasm called
the greatest preacher of the century, delivered a sermon at the end of
Lent at the Church of Saint-Paul. Lingendes postulated in his sermon
that a parishioner could choose at the time of death any confessor
whom he considered "a right-thinking man." Furthermore, Lingendes
added that the pope, as sovereign head of the Church, could delegate
confessional authority to regulars. The curé Mazure—later supported
by the corps of Parisian curés—was furious at what he understood to
be an attempt to remove the people from their obligations to their
legitimate pastors. To the curés, the remarks by Lingendes prejudiced
the establishment that Christ had made in the Church; regulars were
to be called upon by the curés when the latter had need of their
assistance, and the regular clergy did not belong in the Church hierarchy. On the other hand, the Jesuits interpreted the ferocity of the
curés' opposition to Lingendes' sermon as evidence of the "parish
spirit" that infected the curés with "this air of pride and of empire
which carried their authority beyond limits."[47]

Despite the reaction to his assertions, Lingendes repeated his attack
on the curés in his subsequent sermon on 12 April. Just as one might
not be content with one's ordinary doctor and call another who was

more capable, so, Lingendes held, one could at the time of death turn to a more capable confessor.[48] Lingendes then decried the curés' conception of the hierarchy and enunciated the privileges of the regulars at the expense of both bishops and curés. Enraged, Mazure interrupted Lingendes by ordering the ecclesiastics of his parish who were in the choir to chant vespers. The choir sang at the top of their voices, Lingendes shouted his sermon, and the faithful were scandalized. Only when Lingendes could no longer be heard did he leave the pulpit.[49] An account of the incident by Christophe Petit, *prêtre habitué* of Saint-Paul, reflected the intense hatred felt by the curés and their priests toward the Jesuits. Mazure, said Petit, "had nones begun and then vespers. As a result the Jesuits and their supporters created an unprecedented disturbance in the church, saying that it was necessary to beat unmercifully the curé and his priests. . . . Behold the times we have arrived at when a foreigner, who does not belong to the Church hierarchy, is preferred over one's own and very worthy pastor. This is a true sign of the immediate coming of the antichrist."[50]

Infuriated by the treatment accorded Lingendes, the Jesuits complained to the court and especially to Séguier. To the Jesuits and their friends in the government, this affair appeared as an opportunity to dispose of Mazure, whose tenure as curé was replete with contestations—both theological and in daily religious affairs—against the Jesuits. Mazure was later characterized to the government as a "man of intrigue . . . , hating the Jesuits and the court of Rome. Using well what he knows, he wore out the Jesuits with persecutions."[51]

Receptive to the Jesuit request, Séguier ordered Mazure to come to court. Séguier informed the curé that the king desired Lingendes to preach again at Saint-Paul on 19 April. Mazure refused to consent, asserting that he himself would preach the next Sunday and that he would disgrace his ministry if he permitted Lingendes to preach without the Jesuit first offering a public apology and retraction, especially for advancing that people possessed the liberty of selecting their confessor. After Séguier had repeated the king's wish that the affair be terminated in the manner proposed, Mazure replied that although the king was master over his life and property, he could dishonor neither his conscience nor God by submitting to the king's will in this matter.[52]

Although they held no assembly in April because of the meeting of the diocesan synod and because of Easter, the company of curés begged the king not to persist in his demand, for this infringed on the prerogative of the curé to preach in his own parish. The curés of Saint-Roch, Saint-Germain-l'Auxerrois, Saint-Eustache, Saint-Barthélemy, and Saint-Paul made several visits to the king's ministers, pleaded with various court prelates to intervene on their behalf, and submitted remonstrances to the king and queen. Notwithstanding the intense lobbying, the king banished Mazure by *lettre de cachet* to his country home on 18 April.[53]

The government had blundered. Mazure's parishioners protested the king's order, claiming that their father was being removed and blaming the Jesuits for this great evil. According to Hermant, Mazure with difficulty resisted the attempts of the poor to prevent his departure. Afterwards, it was only the priests of Saint-Paul who were able to forestall a popular uprising. These same priests went into mourning, discontinued all High Masses within the church, performed only a few Low Masses, and refused to celebrate the festival of Saint-Marc.[54]

The Jesuits regarded these actions as seditious, and, along with the churchwardens (who were consistently opposed to Mazure), they protested to the court. In vain did Séguier threaten the priests, ordering them to conduct church functions. Finally, as a result of the hostility of the populace, the Jesuits asked for Mazure's recall.[55]

Concomitant with these developments were the efforts of the Parisian curés to secure Mazure's return. They preferred not to hold an extraordinary assembly because their assemblies were suspect to the government, which refused to recognize the curés as a corporation and which opposed their assembling in that quality. Instead, the curés decided to trust their syndics to pursue the affair with the aid of a small number of their colleagues. Thus, seven curés met on 20 April to discuss strategy. They resolved to accomplish Mazure's reinstatement by peaceful means, and so persistently solicited the queen, ministers, and certain court bishops.[56] These curés were successful in reaching an accommodation. In consideration for Mazure's return, the priests of Saint-Paul agreed to renew their religious services and preaching.[57]

The sudden change on the part of the court did not result from the curés' efforts alone; prominent parishioners also worked for the return of their curé. And, most importantly, the government feared a demonstration in support of Mazure. The continual complaints of the poor—especially the porters and boatmen of the port of Saint-Paul—were seen by the government as a possible disposition to revolt.[58] The Mazure affair occurred only one month after the turmoil resulting

from the archbishop's death and Retz's accession to the see, and while
Paris remained under threat of an interdict. Therefore, the court
deemed it prudent to give in to the curés and so prevent possible
popular disturbances.

Mazure's homecoming on 2 May was a triumph for the curés and
demonstrated their strength at the beginning of the Religious Fronde.
The press of parishioners to see Mazure on his return was so great that
he had to change from his carriage to his horse; the bells were sounded
and the Te Deum was sung. Although they continued to denounce
Mazure and to defend Lingendes in print,[59] the Jesuits were defeated
in this instance and ceased their efforts to have Lingendes preach again
at Saint-Paul.

In their assembly of 4 May, the curés reviewed the April events and
resolved to pursue at the next General Assembly of the Clergy the
issues raised during this controversy, namely the curés' prerogative to
hear the confession of the sick and the curés' authority to regulate
preaching in the parish church. In a direct affront to the court, the
company decided to thank not the king, queen, and ministers, but
rather only four of the court bishops for the successful conclusion of
the Lingendes affair.[60] And, to propagate their interpretation of that
affair, the curés issued a circular letter praising Mazure's actions,
castigating Lingendes' sermon and the Jesuits' libels, and, in general,
denouncing "the odious usurpations that the Jesuits continually make
of the authority of pastors."[61]

Most indicative of the importance of the local religious conflict
between the curés and Jesuits was the Bagot-Mazure controversy, in
which the debate over such questions as annual confession and attendance at parish Mass grew to involve the Faculty of Theology, the
General Assembly of the Clergy, the government, and the papacy. As
part of the defense of their contentions, Mazure and the curés invoked
elements of Richerism, extreme Gallicanism, and canon law to postu-
late their sovereignty within the parish.[62] On the other hand, to ward
off both the curés' radical doctrine as well as the Jesuits' position
(which was based on ultramontanism as a guarantee of their alleged
privileges), the bishops enunciated tenets of Episcopal Gallicanism
totally unacceptable to the pope. The resultant clash between the prelates and Rome aroused Mazarin, who in a dramatic appearance at the
General Assembly on 7 April 1657 ensured that the resolution of the

Bagot-Mazure quarrel would not endanger France's relations with the Holy See.

During the Religious Fronde, then, the discussion of ordinary religious practice had tremendous repercussions. A brief description of how these local religious issues treated earlier in this chapter affected the sessions of the General Assembly will illustrate that the struggle for power between the curés and Jesuits underlay the ecclesiastical politics of the Religious Fronde.[63]

In his journal, the abbé de Beaubrun judiciously reported the reasons for the Jesuits' alarm at the publication of Mazure's *L'Obligation des fidèles*. According to Beaubrun, the Jesuits saw that the work established maxims which undercut their privileges and immunities, as well as their conception of their role in the Church hierarchy. Moreover, they feared that acceptance of the proposition that the faithful had to confess to their curé would lead to desertion of the Jesuit churches and confessionals and so result in the Society's losing its authority over consciences.[64] Indeed, Mazure's work posited three theses which reflected the curés' concern to eliminate the Jesuits as competitors in Parisian religious life. These themes were that the flock had to confess to their curé during illness and at the point of death, that each parishioner was obligated to go to his curé for annual confession, and that the curé alone was the "proper priest" of the parish and consequently exercised exclusive authority within the parish.

Bagot's refutation of Mazure advanced the traditional views of the regulars with respect to confession, attendance at parish Mass, and papal sanction for their privileges, and rejected the curés' radical claims for exclusive control over parish affairs. Bagot defined four major issues in his *Défense du droict épiscopal*: confession, parish Mass, the power of curés, and the power of bishops and pope. Already, the ingredients were present to develop what had originated as a squabble over interpretations of canon law into a concern for ecclesiastical bodies—episcopacy and papacy—which had considered themselves to be the legitimate interpretaters of Church doctrine.

On 19 May 1656, Rousse led a deputation of curés to the General Assembly and formally asked for the censure of the *Défense du droict épiscopal*. As for *L'Obligation des fidèles*, which had been published anonymously and attributed to the curés, Rousse requested an extract of those articles to which the prelates objected and promised that the curés would submit to the episcopacy. Bagot also informed the General Assembly of his willingness to accede to its decision in regard to his book.[65]

From 17 through 23 October, the commission on regulars delivered its report as the General Assembly prepared to formulate its decision on the two books. On 24 October, however, Bagot informed the assembly of his submission to the articles it had extracted from his book. Two days later an extraordinary assembly of the curés resolved not to abandon *L'Obligation des fidèles* and to defend and explain the eleven propositions extracted from that book by the General Assembly's commission on regulars. So instructed by his fellows, Rousse delivered a declaration on the eleven propositions[66] to the General Assembly on 27 October. These explanations by the curés, still espousing their interpretation of sacramental authority, were deemed unsatisfactory. The printed *Sommaire* of the curés' statements was later included in the General Assembly's suppression of the works of Bagot and Mazure. Meanwhile the curés' declaration—and the publication by Rousse of the *Sommaire* authorized by an assembly of the curés on 8 January 1657—intensified the pamphlet war.[67]

The explanations tendered by Bagot in October on the objectionable propositions of his *Défense du droict épiscopal* were also considered intolerable by the episcopacy, which asked him to prepare a second retraction. In his first retraction, Bagot had continued to denounce the curés, denying, for example, their power to command parishioners to give confession to their curés; at the same time, Bagot simply elaborated and defended what he had sustained in his book.[68] The commissioners considered Bagot's second response, offered at the beginning of December, somewhat better than the first. Here, Bagot mollified the episcopacy by tempering his ultramontanism with a recognition of the privileges of the Gallican Church. Moreover, he agreed to the special status of the secular clergy in his article on the power of curés: "Curés, who are called by a canonical mission, must by the obligation of their charge guide souls in the Christian way of life. The curés have more right to do this and are aided by more free grace and sanctity than those who without this mission and obligation want to conduct souls."[69]

Other Jesuits aided Bagot in his efforts to avoid censure without repudiating the cause of the regulars. Both Josselin Des Déserts and François Annat (confessor to the king)[70] disputed the allegedly heretical maxims of *L'Obligation des fidèles* on the subjects of annual confession, parish Mass, and the power of bishops.[71] Des Déserts also published a detailed defense of one statement from Bagot's book, that "One must not be persuaded that the curé's charge *precisely* gives him more right or free grace and benediction for the direction of his parishioners in the spiritual and Christian life."[72] Bagot's design, claimed Des Déserts, was only to maintain the rights of bishops, the pope, and their delegates against the heretical *L'Obligation des fidèles*, which asserted that the curé, being more closely bound to his parishioners than the bishop, was therefore due more grace.[73] Another Jesuit pamphlet was entirely devoted to the problem of annual confession, sustaining Bagot's affirmation that the canon of the Fourth Lateran Council did not, as Mazure claimed it did, require that one confess only to his curé.[74] Bagot himself appealed to the public, publishing a version of one of the explanations he had given to the General Assembly, as well as what amounted to another book refuting the attacks on his *Défense du droict épiscopal*.[75] Bagot referred to the authors of *L'Obligation des fidèles* as Jansenists, the "new antiregulars."[76]

Nor were the curés silent. As early as one year after the appearance of Mazure's book, they published an extract approving Mazure's contentions that the curé was the "proper priest" and that regulars could not legitimately hear the confession of parishioners.[77] Later, for the benefit of the General Assembly, the curés promulgated a significantly different interpretation of *L'Obligation des fidèles* by assuring the episcopacy of the subordination of their curés while still maintaining a stringent position vis-à-vis the Jesuits.[78]

In conjunction with the defense of Mazure was the curés' campaign against Bagot. On one occasion, the curés simply published a long list of quotations from the *Défense du droict épiscopal*, labeling those statements "insulting," "calumnious," "presumptuous," or "false."[79] Furthermore, Rousse issued another set of propositions extracted from Bagot's work grouped under such topics as curés, bishops, the term "proper priest," parish, the Church hierarchy, annual confession, and parish Mass.[80] This work asked that the episcopal examiners of Bagot recognize that, under the pretext of protecting the bishops from the curés, he had actually increased the pope's authority over the bishops and, under the excuse of defending the liberty of the faithful, he had delivered them to libertinage and to invalid confessions.[81]

In an effort to settle the affair, Marca and Pierre de Bertier, bishop of Montauban, presented twelve articles on the powers and rights of pope, bishops, curés, and regulars. This plan reserved final control over the administration of sacraments to the episcopacy. To mollify the curés, it was admitted that the parishioner was obliged to confess annually to his curé and that the curés' interpretation of attendance at parish Mass was correct. Nevertheless, the project for accommodation stipulated that one could confess to regulars approved by the bishop. The act of confessing to a curé while sick or about to die was merely termed praiseworthy.[82]

The curés held an extraordinary assembly on 29 January 1657 to discuss this claim of the bishops to delegate regulars in the parish without including in their letters the phrase *cum consensu parochorum*. Rousse, who had previously assured the prelates that the project of accommodation would be acceptable to his colleagues, found to his surprise that more than thirty of them voted to reject it.[83]

The following day, the curés entered the General Assembly to protest the settlement of Marca and Bertier. A great tumult occurred as bishops berated the curés for their lack of obedience. For their part, the curés firmly argued their position, asserting that they exercised their functions by divine right; that bishops, having once ordained curés, could not interfere in their ministry. Thomas Fortin, curé of Saint-Christophe, at one point replied to the prelates' admonishments: "Sirs, when you treat us as your children, we will obey and honor you as our fathers. But when you treat us as slaves, we will say that you are hard and troublesome masters."[84] This contestation between curés and bishops was so agitated that the General Assembly erased all mention of it from the journal of the proceedings.

Despite the curés' complaints at their treatment, the General Assembly resolved on 1 February to prepare articles contrary to the objectionable propositions contained in the works under examination. In accordance with this instruction, the commission on regulars drew up twenty-six articles on the following subjects: the pope, bishops, curés, annual confession, confession of the sick, parish Mass, and the privileges of regulars. This report, delivered to the General Assembly on 17 March, was in fact only an elaboration of the twelve articles submitted by Marca and Bertier in January. Again, while sustaining the rights of the curés vis-à-vis the regulars on the problems of annual confession and parish Mass, the episcopacy affirmed its jurisdictional authority over curés in all ecclesiastical functions.[85]

On 22 March, the General Assembly resolved to receive the articles of the commissioners without prohibiting contrary doctrines from being taught, and to suppress the works of Bagot and Mazure, and the *Sommaire*. However, because the nuncio objected to Mazarin that the contention in those articles—that bishops received their jurisdiction immediately from Christ—was injurious to the pope, the controversy was not yet settled.

The drama continued when Mazarin unexpectedly arrived at the General Assembly on 7 April, a day, according to Hermant, that was "fatal to the entire Church hierarchy. He made a wound so deep in the liberty of the French clergy that it will be difficult to heal it without leaving a shameful scar."[86] Mazarin informed the prelates of the king's wish that they defer their examination and publication of the articles. After heated debate, the General Assembly bent to the government's pressure by resolving to suppress the three works as "containing evil propositions contrary to episcopal authority, the hierarchy, and to ecclesiastical discipline and policy, and as capable of disturbing the peace and tranquillity of the Church. As for the articles and the report which have been read in the assembly, they will be given to the agents in order that they might be discussed at a more proper time."[87]

Successful here, Mazarin suffered a temporary setback 17 April, when Bertier contrived to convince the prelates to approve a circular letter he had prepared which included the same contents as the suppressed articles. The archbishop of Sens, presiding at the time, issued the letter and had it inserted into the minutes of 25 April.[88] Mazarin, however, emerged victorious by commanding the agents of the clergy on 6 August 1657 to withdraw the offensive letter from the official record.[89]

Thus, the apparently inconsequential issues of parish life—annual confession, Mass, and so on—evolved into affairs of state in the Bagot-Mazure controversy. What had begun as just another episode in the recurring battle between the curés and Jesuits soon developed in the volatile atmosphere of the Religious Fronde into extremist theories of the degree of power wielded in the Church by curés, regulars, bishops, and pope. Religious questions determined political alignments: the curés saw themselves isolated from all other religious bodies and more fully realized that their only possible basis of support lay in their rebellious archbishop; the Jesuits, although not able to prevent the condemnation of Bagot's book, were able to circumvent a total repu-

diation of their theories through their support of the papacy, their ties
to the government, and Mazarin's need to maintain amiable relations
with His Holiness; the episcopacy asserted its prerogatives against
both curés and regulars and was only temporarily estranged from the
government.

The last great conflict between the curés and Jesuits occurred immediately after both groups had suffered severe setbacks. Occasioned
by sermons that Louis Maimbourg delivered at the Jesuit Church of
Saint-Paul on 31 July and 3 August 1659, this quarrel followed by less
than a month the suppression of the curés' assemblies and came in the
wake of the national humiliation of the Jesuits through Pascal's *Lettres provinciales* and through the curés' successful campaign against
Pirot's *Apologie pour les casuistes*.

In his first sermon, Maimbourg complained of the persecution that
the Jesuits suffered from the Parisian curés and their *Ecrits*. Preaching
on 3 August, Maimbourg assailed the curés as being the new money-
changers of the temple, comparable to those castigated by Christ. The
curés were furious, reproaching Maimbourg for "publicly accusing us
of robbing our parishioners by selling the sacraments and by conduct-
ing an infamous traffic in all holy things."[90]

Maimbourg had indeed accused the curés of trafficking in the administration of sacraments:

> But what will we speak of those who say that this burial will cost
> so much and this marriage so much, and who demand payment in
> advance? Does this not horrify everyone and draw tears from the
> eyes of all good Catholics? Because of this a newborn child is
> compelled to cry two times, once because it enters the world,
> which is a vale of misery, and then because in order to become an
> adopted child of God, money is necessary. In funeral processions
> we must cry two times, once because our relations and friends are
> dead, and also because their burial exhausts our purse. We are
> constrained to satisfy the intolerable avarice of these base mer-
> chants of God's temple. What is all of this? Simony! What is all of
> this? Robbery! Instead of seeing these ministers of the Church full
> of charity, opening their hands, their houses, and their purses to
> their wretched flock and to the needy poor of a parish, we see
> them swollen with good living and pride, and traveling in great
> pomp with a carriage and attendants. They behave this way even
> though they are lowborn.[91]

So labeled, the curés promptly appealed to the *officialité* for satisfaction. In an assembly held on 26 August, they strongly urged the vicars-general to forbid Maimbourg to preach in Paris. At the same time, Degraves, curé of Saint-Louis-en-l'Ile, led the others in using this opportunity to implore the vicars-general to reinstate the ordinary assemblies of the curés on a fixed day every month.[92]

Angered at the curés' procedures against Maimbourg and at their efforts to avoid the restrictions placed on their assemblies, Séguier, with the concurrence of Fouquet, issued an *arrêt* removing the suit from the jurisdiction of the *officialité* and placing it in the *Conseil du roi*.[93] This in turn caused the curés to complain once again to the vicars-general and directly to Mazarin.

Writing on the curés' behalf, Mazure professed their loyalty to the cardinal-minister and disabused him of the charge that the curés maintained ties to Retz or that they had disobeyed the king's order for the suppression of their assemblies. Mazure then reviewed the outrages committed by Maimbourg against both the charges and persons of the curés and concluded by beseeching Mazarin to break Séguier's *arrêt* in order to return the case to the justice of the *officialité*.[94]

The bishop of Coutances, an informant and advisor of Mazarin in ecclesiastical affairs, forwarded Mazure's letter to the cardinal. This bishop supported the curés' plea, recommending that they not be pushed further. Moreover, Séguier and Fouquet had promulgated the *arrêt* because of their friendship and political ties with the Jesuits. In sum, the bishop believed it preferable to conclude this affair as quickly as possible.[95]

Soon afterwards, Rousse and Mazure had the promoter of justice (whose function was to defend the integrity of the bishop's jurisdiction) of the *officialité* appeal the case to the Parlement. With this violation of the *arrêt*, Séguier exhorted Le Tellier—also tied to the Jesuits—to exile the two curés and to compel the Parlement not to interfere in the Maimbourg affair.[96] Séguier's efforts failed. On 12 September, the *premier président* of the Parlement indicated that legal procedures should be discontinued; instead, in view of the uproar emanating from the contestation, an accommodation between the curés and Jesuits should be reached. In addition, the court ordered Séguier to reassign the case to the vicars-general, while Mazarin asked that a final settlement be postponed until the king's return to Paris.[97]

Throughout September and October, the vicars-general, Séguier, and the bishop of Coutances mediated a possible conciliation. The late-September news in Paris that Pirot's *Apologie* had been placed on the Index of Prohibited Books weakened the Jesuits' ability to sustain accusations of simony and ecclesiastical misconduct while their own authors were being denounced on these same issues.[98]

Nevertheless, this did not prevent Maimbourg from continuing to berate the curés. On 26 October, he delivered a sermon in which he compared himself to the prophet Jeremiah, who had railed against those mercenary priests who trafficked in their ministerial duties. Jeremiah's words had drawn on him the hatred of those priests who had proceeded against him before the judges. In keeping with his gentle disposition, Jeremiah had, asserted Maimbourg, proposed an accommodation. Yet the priests would never forgive him, especially Phassur (Mazure), the most stubborn of all, who had persisted in greeting each offer of satisfaction with the words "I will never pardon him." Finally, these priests had demanded that the prophet be banished from Jerusalem, but one of the principal magistrates had opposed them and had saved Jeremiah from his enemies.[99]

Maimbourg's drama did not unfold as Jeremiah's had. On 14 November, in the presence of the vicars-general, Maimbourg signed a declaration stating that he had not intended in his sermons to offend either the curés or the episcopacy, that he would not say anything in the future against the persons or the ministry of the curés, and that he desired the curés' affection.[100]

Though seemingly humiliated, Maimbourg retained the right of preaching. The declaration was certainly not harsh enough for the curés, who complained uselessly of what they considered to be lenient treatment. On the other hand, taking into account the relative impotency of the curés after the suppression of their assemblies, it was surprising that they had any success at all. As the bishop of Coutances informed Mazarin, the charges against Maimbourg were not substantial—the *officialité* would probably have acquitted him.[101] The court placated the curés on this occasion only because Retz was still at large, a situation that made their tranquillity or neutrality highly desirable.[102]

A volatile situation prevailed in the parishes of Paris during the Religious Fronde as curés and Jesuits battled for sacramental and jurisdictional control. This consistent struggle was the basic condition of parish life, as both sides fought over such problems as confession, burial, and attendance at Mass. Certainly, this confrontation with the Jesuits was the sine qua non for the curés' collective behavior, and their Jansenism, Richerism, and opposition to the government as frondeurs cannot be explained apart from the precondition of their enmity toward the Jesuits.

Who controlled the religious life of the parishioner? This was the basis for the virulent struggle between curés and Jesuits. The Jesuits affirmed the liberty of the faithful to confess, receive communion, be buried, and hear Mass in any church they wished. Consistent with this view was their moral theology, which bestowed greater freedom on the lives of penitents in the broadening of their permissible actions, and which allowed, through ethical laxity, more of the flock to enter the fold of absolution. On the other hand, the curés asserted authoritarian control over the religious lives of their parishioners, strictly regulating the performance of their sacramental duties. Not unexpectedly, the curés turned to Jansenism, both because of their enmity toward the Jesuits and because the moral theology of Jansenism, with its emphasis on the authority of the parish confessor, meshed so perfectly with the curés' desire to control parish life.

Rapin, for example, was explicit in stating that the curés during the Religious Fronde were motivated by a self-interested hatred of his company: the curés utilized Jansenism and joined against the Society of Jesus so as to promote their interests within the Church hierarchy. The curés "everywhere began to speak in praise of the hierarchy and to extol only the hierarchs. They called by this lofty name those who clung to their parish so as to follow their curé's direction. This was how the severe manner of direction, which was then practiced at Port-Royal, came into fashion."[103] In fact Rapin attributed the existence of the curés' assemblies to their desire to repel what they considered as encroachments by the Jesuits on their parishes. The curés, observed Rapin, were seduced by Jansenism because they thought it offered them a means with which to maintain their rights and to destroy the Jesuits' power.[104]

Although part of a centuries-old quarrel, this regular-secular conflict achieved added significance in the 1650s because of the political and religious situation. As a result of its recent experiences in the earlier Frondes and of the efforts of unreconstructed frondeurs to regain their former positions of preeminence, the government was exceedingly wary of any incident which might be construed as opposition to its policies or which might ignite revolt.

Also, the 1650s were unusual in the strength of the respective combatants of the parish wars. While the Jesuits had walked the corridors of power throughout the century, their loyalty during the Frondes and their personal ties to the king and such ministers as Le Tellier and Séguier had increased their influence. Moreover, the Jesuits profited by the temporary split between the curés and the episcopacy. Until the Religious Fronde, the prelates and curés had fought together against the regulars. A conjunction of certain factors at that time splintered this union of interests. Most important, the curés' attempt to form a new order within the Church hierarchy joined with their particular brand of Richerism to pose a direct threat to the bishops. In addition, the curés' Jansenism ensured a confrontation with the prelates, the overwhelming majority of whom were not Jansenist.

To combat this undiminished influence of the Jesuits, the curés began to assert what was for them a novel position of strength, a position constructed out of their opposition to the Jesuits. Richerism and the effort to form a new order in the hierarchy, though resulting in the loss of episcopal support, afforded the curés doctrinal and canonical justification for their supremacy over the Jesuits; Jansenism, when viewed in contrast to a lax moral theology which was thought to encourage libertinism, could preserve the curés' control over the direction of their parishioners' consciences; extreme Gallicanism, contrasted with the unrepentant ultramontanism of the Jesuits, could successfully be utilized to secure the aid of others concerned with preserving Gallican liberties; and support for Retz (arch-enemy of the Jesuits and Mazarin) enabled the curés to confront their opponents with the weight of archiepiscopal authority.

In this way, the defining characteristics of the ecclesiastical frondeur emerged: the rebellious curé was Richerist, Jansenist, Gallican, a frondeur through his support of Retz, and, at bottom, a determined antagonist of the Society of Jesus.

CHAPTER FOUR

THE MENTALITY OF OPPOSITION: THE JANSENISM OF THE CURÉS OF PARIS

Jansenism remains to this day one of the great problems of seventeenth-century French historiography and, consequently, has received more attention than any other religious movement of the time. While in recent decades the focus has shifted to the relationship of Jansenism to social classes, questions that arose in the seventeenth century, such as the role of Jansenism as a political ideology, or even the definition of Jansenism itself, continue to dominate historical studies. In addition to these basically theoretical categories of discussion, both contemporaries and historians have debated the practical manifestations of these problems. Were the Jansenists loyal during the Parlementary and Noble Frondes, and, later, did they actively support Retz against the government? How did the court view Jansenism?

To understand the significance of the curés' Jansenism, it is necessary to examine this phenomenon within the context of the problems enumerated above; for the adoption of Jansenism implied, besides the social and theological attitudes traditionally associated with it, a certain malaise and rebelliousness—in short, a level of discontent that other groups and powers competing in the realm of ecclesiastical politics found intolerable.

1. Toward a Definition of Jansenism

Seventeenth-century Jansenists invariably agreed that Jansenism was a myth, that it simply did not exist. Because the label "Jansenist" stigmatized its bearer, much like "Spinozist" at the end of the seventeenth century and "philosophe" in certain eighteenth-century circles, the

Jansenists called themselves the "Defenders" or "Disciples| of Saint Augustine." This view has since been adopted by some historians partial to those "Disciples." Even so notable a scholar as Augustin Gazier could assert that Jansenism was a *fantôme*.[1] But in fact one could call Jansenist those persons labeled as such by anti-Jansenists, who were certainly not imaginary.[2] Historians attempting to grapple with the problem of Jansenism have explained it according to its particular manifestations in different periods,[3] or else they have identified those groups or classes who professed its tenets or that conglomeration of attitudes and intellectual beliefs associated with it.[4]

The conception of Jansenism as a monolithic movement has been definitively refuted by a Marxist school of historians that has studied the doctrine as the ideology of a social class.[5] Although Henri Lefebvre was the first to represent Jansenism as the ideological form of the discontent of the upper-middle class, Lucien Goldmann's studies have kindled the greatest controversy. According to Goldmann, Jansenism was the religious manifestation of the robe's reaction to the economic and social crises that group was undergoing between the years 1637 and 1677. At that time, the development of Jansenism paralleled that of the absolutist monarchy and its burgeoning central bureaucracy. The utilization of *commissaires* (royal agents with temporary commissions), to whom were transferred many of the tasks and prerogatives of the *officiers* (those who had purchased an office in the judicial and financial administration), naturally caused great resentment among the latter. This malaise was manifested in two reactions: withdrawal from the world as Jansenists or active opposition to the centralizing monarchy as frondeurs. Although Goldmann admits that the majority of *officiers* remained only vaguely estranged and did not adopt a particular ideological attitude, he nonetheless emphasizes the connection between the social origins of the *officiers*—notably the barristers and members of the sovereign courts—and Jansenist ideology.

There are serious reservations to Goldmann's linking of the robe to the "tragic vision" that he sees as the heart of Jansenism. Goldmann himself recognizes—although he does not accept—several important objections raised by Roland Mousnier, who questions the historical accuracy of Goldmann's assessment of the growth of royal absolutism and who rejects the claim that a specific relationship between the nobility of the robe (men ennobled through office in the judiciary) and

Jansenism has been proven.[6] The "first Jansenism" was a religious phenomenon involving theologians, priests, and bishops—not the robe. It can be argued that before the Fronde, despite the encroachments on their powers by the *commissaires*, the *officiers* were optimistic. Their actions in 1648 reflected ambition, not despair. These *officiers* held an enviable position in a highly stratified society; united in corps, the *présidents* and *conseillers* of the sovereign courts and the *trésoriers* were honored as personal representatives of the king. Socially, the transition from trade to robe was eminently desirable; the increased difficulty of this change attested to the robe's prestige. Economically, the robe did not experience depression. Robe fortunes were constituted in the land, in *rentes* on the Hôtel de Ville, and in their offices. Income from the first was solidly based and may have actually increased; *rentes* were irregular and not certain; while offices continued to be a fruitful investment (although the revenues of an office seen as a percentage of the value of an office declined).[7]

More a philosopher than a historian, Goldmann does not explain the ties of certain parlementaires to the Jesuits, nor does he realize that the phenomenon of the appeal of Jansenism—pointed out by Sainte-Beuve—to "the upper middle class, the parlementary class, the one which, under the League, more or less sided with the *politiques* [the political moderates]," might have been owing to cultural reasons. In the context of French society, these robins constituted a group that enjoyed both leisure and a relatively high degree of education; it was not surprising that a new and intellectually difficult doctrine such as Jansenism would find adherents in such a milieu.[8] For the most part the judges of the Parlement of Paris were opposed to Jansenism but reluctantly supported it as circumstances linked the Jansenist movement with parlementary Gallicanism.[9] Goldmann could assert that Jesuit inroads among the robe merely indicated false-consciousness among some robins and that quantification of Jansenist members of the robe was not imperative to the argument that Jansenism was the ideological expression of that social class. However, without raising the question of the existence of classes in seventeenth-century society or even asking whether the robe in fact constituted a social class before the eighteenth century, it would seem that Goldmann's methodology, which identifies an ideology with a "class," implies that other classes or groups possess differing ideologies arising from dissimilar world visions—a world vision being defined by Goldmann as "this combination of aspirations, feelings, and ideas which joins together the members of a group (most often a social class) and opposes them to other groups."[10] Since there existed a popular Jansenism, a monastic Jansenism, and, as this chapter will prove, a Jansenism of the curés, it would be fallacious to maintain that Jansenism was the particular expression of one group, the robe.

More valid than Goldmann's thesis of the relationship between a Jansenist ideology and a robe social class is his analysis of various groups within Jansenism, an analysis that demolishes any lingering belief in Jansenism as a monolithic current. Goldmann depicts four forms of seventeenth-century Jansenism: (1) Distinguished by their reluctant accommodation with the evil of the world was the "third party," the moderate group represented by the bishop of Comminges and Arnauld d'Andilly. Because this group had no characteristic ideology, subsequent historians have not included it in their typology of Jansenism. (2) The second current involved a struggle for goodness and truth, which were held to have a real, albeit restricted, place in the world. This centrist or moderate group, led by Antoine Arnauld and Pierre Nicole, combined a maximum of possible justice compatible with a maximum of submission, and so sought to obtain from Rome and from the court the best compromise between compliance and defense of the truth. (3) The stream of Jansenism as practiced by Saint-Cyran, Martin de Barcos, Antoine Singlin, and Mère Angélique, rejected the world but admitted complete deference to secular and ecclesiastical authority. (4) Lastly, the Jansenism of *extrémisme intramondain* proclaimed goodness and truth in an evil world that would misunderstand and persecute them. For the abbé Le Roy and Jacqueline Pascal, this was the battle *à outrance*, the refusal of concession.[11] Namer expands Goldmann's typology to five by splitting the *extrémisme intramondain* into two separate groups, one which viewed the essential struggle as being for ecclesiastical liberties against Rome, and the other which maintained that the fight was for its interpretation of efficacious grace.[12]

Consistent with both the chronological divisions and the categorization of divergent Jansenist currents were those traits which, while differing in emphasis according to time and personage, yet distinguished Jansenists from others. These characteristics provide the most satisfactory definition of Jansenism. It was a movement, affected by the Counter Reformation, that rejected thoroughly the humanism of the Renaissance. Jansenists wanted to remove the worldly elements that humanism had brought into the Christian life. They reproached the Jesuits for accommodating themselves with humanism and so exalting man instead of placing him under God. Although Cardinal Bona's characterization, that "the Jansenists are Catholics who do not like the Jesuits," was too facile, it did indicate one significant generalization: it was possible to despise Jesuits and not be Jansenist, but it was highly improbable—if not impossible—to favor the Jesuits and remain Jansenist. On a higher level, this hatred of the Society of Jesus expressed itself in a moral rigorism opposed to the lax moral theology propagated by the Jesuits. For the morality of the *honnête homme*, Jansenists substituted that of saintliness, the necessary condition for each man whose valid participation in the sacraments depended upon a complete interior transformation. There was always a severe, self-denying tendency in Jansenism that demanded internal reform on the part of the penitent. The individual Christian was to repudiate the values of a sinful world through a rigorous penitential ethic, charity, and reform of the Church. In addition, a Jansenist was one who defended the work of Cornelius Jansenius and, with him, favored Saint Augustine's foreboding doctrine of predestination against the Molinist belief in free will. The Jansenists desired to restore the theological climate of the ancient Church and the unfailing authority of Saint Augustine. The relative homogeneity of Jansenism can also be explained in terms of the common psychological orientations of its adherents. Jansenists shared the conception of a highly demanding Christianity that disdained concession or compromise and an intense awareness of the rights of the individual—especially of his thought— in the face of authority. Finally, Jansenism sought to extend the control of the secular clergy in the Church at the expense of the regulars.[13]

2. *Jansenism as an Opposition Movement*

In the *Abrégé de l'histoire de Port-Royal*, Racine vehemently denied that Jansenism (although he would never admit this term) was a doctrine of opposition. There was no one, asserted Racine, who did not know "that it was the doctrine of Port-Royal that a subject could not, for any reason, in good conscience revolt against his legitimate prince. Even if the subject were unjustly oppressed, he had to endure the oppression and ask justice only from God. For only God has the right to make kings account for their actions. This is what has always been taught at Port-Royal."[14] In striving to convince his audience of the fidelity and righteousness of Port-Royal, Racine was not entirely accurate in his statement, especially if one considered such Jansenist firebrands as Le Roy. Even "centrists" such as Arnauld theoretically legitimized passive resistance as the proper mean between servile obedience and open revolt.[15] Racine would have us believe that the docility of Barcos was characteristic of Jansenism, that Jansenists stood united behind the concept of total acquiescence in the will of the prince.

Others, notably Saint-Simon, Montesquieu, Voltaire, and Joseph de Maistre, have interpreted Jansenism as a republican party within both Church and state. This opinion is erroneous, resulting from a judgment of the entire Jansenist current according to its later, more democratic and political character, and from a transference of Jansenist leveling ideas on the Church hierarchy to the social hierarchy.[16] Richerism in its merging with Jansenism emphasized a "democratic" conception of the ecclesiastical hierarchy only in its calling for a redistribution of power within the First Estate. The Parisian curés, for example, were democratic only in that sense; within the confines of the parish they strove for complete autocracy. The curés did not seek to share their power with other parish priests; rather they interpreted their canonical role as sanctioning their total sway over those priests. Even so limited a democratic view as this had no correlation with Jansenist attitudes toward the social structure. Jansenists accepted the existing social order without qualms; this conservatism was mirrored in a lack of hostility to luxury and to the accumulation of wealth, and in a view of the poor as an annoyance and a danger.[17] The Jansenists desired no social or democratic revolution.

To say that the Jansenists espoused no ideology of revolution does not mean that Jansenism was not an opposition movement. A recent historian of the Fronde, while seeking to explain the lack of a sense of purpose among frondeurs, posits that Jansenism could not have provided such motivation because of its pessimism regarding prospects of social change and its otherworldly character.[18] But, besides confusing social and political-religious spheres of action, this interpretation falsely generalizes from Jansenist loyalty to the monarchy in the early Frondes to the inability of Jansenism to provide opposition in other

periods. Jansenius himself inaugurated a tradition of overt opposition
to crown policies with his 1635 pamphlet, *Mars gallicus*, which confronted Richelieu's program of alliances to Protestant powers with a
Tridentine view of the unity of Catholic Europe. Richelieu's subsequent imprisonment of Saint-Cyran was politically motivated: he
feared the abbé's support of the views expressed in *Mars gallicus* and
appreciated Saint-Cyran's position of leadership in the *dévot* party
after the death of Pierre de Bérulle. Jansenism never ceased to be a
means of resistance. Although Port-Royal did not participate in the
early Frondes, it was hostile to Mazarin and established close ties with
several frondeurs, including the princesse de Guémenée, the duchesse
de Chevreuse, the duc de Luynes, the comte de Chavigny, and the duc
de Liancourt.[19] It was meaningful that certain frondeurs, such as the
archbishop of Sens and the duchesse de Longueville, turned to Jansenism after the collapse of the Noble Fronde, and so substituted for
overt political opposition one that was more religious and moral.

In a society of orders vertically structured according to ties of dependence, Jansenists advanced a type of individualism arising from
their self-proclaimed role as defenders of the autonomous conscience;
this mode of behavior was anathema to the corporate structure of the
Old Regime. Moreover, not content for the most part to advocate
their views apart from society, Jansenists committed the political sin
of appealing to the emergent forces of public opinion.

Contemporaries were well aware of the relationship between Jansenism and those who confronted both the crown and its supporters in
the Church. However, the Jansenists were often used as scapegoats by
their enemies or by those who could not cope with enigmatic problems
except in terms of a conspiracy. Rapin thus charged that the Jansenists
plotted frondeur activities from their supposed headquarters in Paris
at the Hôtel de Nevers. According to Rapin, the Jansenists worked to
foment disorder because they believed civil war to be propitious for
the dissemination of their doctrine. At one point, he asserted, the
Jansenists offered Gaston, the king's uncle, ten thousand troops maintained at their expense in order to wage war against the king.[20] Hermant's memoirs, the counterpart to those of Rapin, were replete with
denials of allegations brought by the Jesuits in what Hermant considered to be a systematic campaign to portray the Jansenists as rebels.
Hermant was particularly incensed by Jesuit claims—sustained by
François Hallier, a noted anti-Jansenist, in a speech before the king,

queen, and Mazarin—that the Jansenists had offered Cromwell six thousand soldiers if he would invade France as their protector, that they had proposed to defray the expenses of Condé's army if he would come to their aid, and that they had incited the curés to ignite a revolt in Paris in support of Retz. Although these charges were false, it is interesting that Hermant repudiated them by restricting the "Disciples of Saint Augustine" to those ten to fifteen solitary theologians at Port-Royal, while elsewhere he included among the "Disciples" all, including himself, who sympathized with those tenets associated with what we have called Jansenism.[21]

Rapin and Hallier were not alone in linking Jansenism to rebellious activity; the court and those associated with it shared this attitude. Henri d'Estampes de Valençay, French ambassador to Rome, wrote to Mazarin in 1649 that he had informed the pope "that the principal instigators of the rebellion in Paris were the persons attached to the view of this Flemish bishop [Cornelius Jansenius], sworn enemy of the monarchy."[22] Saint-Amour confirmed in several conversations with Valencay that the ambassador held the Jansenists responsible for much of the disorder in France.[23] Anne of Austria believed in the Jansenist threat. Mazarin's correspondents and informants ceaselessly bombarded him with warnings of Jansenist complicity in sedition. Fears of Jansenism, which bordered on paranoia during the earlier Frondes, were grounded in reality during the Religious Fronde, as Jansenists—both those at Port-Royal and those among the Parisian curés—sided with the cause of the frondeur archbishop of Paris. Colbert, for example, linked evidence of discontent to Jansenists and Retz. Writing to Mazarin in 1657, Colbert warned that "all these sorts of religious affairs are fought with so much ferocity in Paris that we can not doubt that the Jansenists, the friends of the cardinal de Retz . . . are deeply involved and carry along the *dévots*. The ill-intentioned join them and nearly everyone follows."[24] Séguier always considered the Jansenists to be frondeurs. He could explain the disobedience to a direct order from the king and the subsequent rebelliousness of Chassebras only in terms of his Jansenism. While Chassebras governed the diocese from his hiding place in the tower of Saint-Jean-en-Grève, Séguier conducted a frantic search for the curé. He was probably at Port-Royal, asserted the chancellor, for "He is a noted Jansenist who acts in this case according to the advice of those at Port-Royal."[25] Roullé, who

was in a position to know, informed Mazarin of the ties among Chassebras, Hodencq, Retz, and Jansenism.[26]

These ties between Jansenists and Retz were central to the Religious
Fronde. Rapin stated that Retz was drawn to the Jansenists, not because of any belief in their doctrine, but because of his hatred for the
Jesuits, and that he hoped to use the Jansenists to avenge himself upon
Mazarin.[27] Extraordinarily enough, Hermant concurred with Rapin,
except that the former correctly dated the adherence of the Jansenists
to the cause of Retz from the time of his incarceration and later
disputed tenure as archbishop.[28] Guy Joly, secretary to Retz, claimed
that certain religious Mazarinades, such as the monitions of Chassebras and Retz's famous letter (dated 14 December 1654) to the
archbishops and bishops of France, were written at Port-Royal.[29] Even
Racine admitted that the Jansenists recognized Retz as their legitimate
archbishop, although the historiographer royal denied that this implied any disloyalty to Mazarin.[30] The rapprochement of Jansenists
and Retz was then a marriage of convenience. Retz, not a Jansenist
himself, hoped that the support of the Jansenists would be useful to
him politically and would cloak him in a mask of virtue. For their
part, the Jansenists realized that Pierre de Marca, advocate of a policy
of persecution against them, was likely to become the next archbishop
if the crown succeeded in deposing Retz.[31]

Nonetheless, historians have tended to minimize the role of Jansenism as an ingredient in the Religious Fronde in several ways: first
and most often, by ignoring the Religious Fronde and concentrating
instead on the five propositions and their aftermath;[32] by making a
fallacious distinction between ecclesiastical recognition of Retz's position as archbishop and active support in his cause; by refusing to
believe that a doctrine sustained by such devout persons as the Jansenists could be an instrument of rebellion; or, most important, by
identifying as Jansenist only those at Port-Royal. This last oversim-
plification was not made by contemporaries. They recognized that the
most ardent supporters of Retz and those most capable of effecting his
restoration in Paris were the Parisian curés, permeated with Jansenism.

But what of Mazarin, the man formulating crown policies during
the 1650s? Because the aims of the Religious Fronde were politically
similar to those of the frondeur faction during the early Frondes (that
is, changes in the high offices of government), Mazarin would have

again faced exile if the Religious Fronde had succeeded. The curés wanted Mazarin out. It is necessary, then, to know if Mazarin viewed the Jansenism of the Religious Fronde as a real danger. (At the very least, from a theological perspective, Mazarin was hostile to Jansenism. He could not accept the doctrines of predestination and of the small number of the elect, and he sympathized with the Jesuits' moral theology.)[33] Certainly, while pressing popes Innocent X and Alexander VII to cease their protection of Retz, Mazarin presented the Jansenists and Retz as inseparable. Until Retz's resignation in February 1662, during the personal reign of Louis XIV, French ambassadors and special agents in Rome since Valençay perpetuated this policy. For example, soon after Retz arrived in Rome, Father François Duneau wrote to Mazarin: "I have just talked at length to the pope's confessor about the union of the cardinal de Retz with the Jansenists. He promised to speak favorably to His Holiness."[34] After Mazarin's death, cardinal Antoine Barberini, French intermediary at the Curia, informed the king of his audience with the pope, whom he had attempted to convince of the danger of Jansenism. Barberini had told the pope that the Jansenists might win over commanders of fortresses and that "probably everything that the vicars-general and the curés of Paris have done in favor of the Jansenists was with the participation of the cardinal de Retz."[35]

Mazarin believed in the relationship among the Fronde, Retz, and Jansenism. Paule Jansen, however, rejects the notion that Mazarin feared the Jansenists and claims instead that the cardinal-minister used the Jansenist issue to influence the papacy. According to this view, Mazarin stimulated papal interest in the Jansenist question in order to turn the popes away from their pro-Spanish foreign policy to a position of benevolent neutrality and, not incidentally, to convince the popes to withdraw their support from the traitorous Retz. Jansen offers us a picture of an even more Machiavellian Mazarin, informing none of his advisors of his real intentions and utilizing the myriad and conflicting dispatches that he received in order to formulate a policy toward Jansenism of which only he was aware.[36] Implicit in Jansen's work is an explanation for the systematic persecution during the personal reign of Louis XIV of those Jansenists associated with Port-Royal. Louis XIV, obsessed with fears of Jansenism, relied on Mazarin's advisors, those who, out of their own impressions, sincerely viewed Jansenism as a cancer to be removed from the body politic.

Only Mazarin had the complete information drawn from disparate sources—and he was gone.

Jansen, nevertheless, commits the same error we have alluded to previously: a failure to distinguish between Jansenists and the "messieurs de Port-Royal." What Jansen shows is that Mazarin did not see the latter as a serious political threat, but she does not prove that Mazarin viewed with complacency others adhering to Jansenism. Quite to the contrary, Jansen demonstrates that Mazarin was preoccupied with the war against Spain and the threat of Retz's return to France. And both of these concerns were linked by the first minister to necessary tranquility in the capital, a situation endangered by Jansenists—curés—who were ready to accept the return of Mazarin's incorrigible opponent, Retz. When, scarcely a year before his death, Mazarin learned that Retz's vicar-general, Hodencq, had proposed to the other Parisian curés to take steps on behalf of the exiled archbishop, Mazarin displayed a mentality which automatically joined together the curés, Jansenism, and the return of Retz. In a letter to a confidant, Mazarin stated: "I am not surprised that the curé of St. Severin made his proposal to the other curés in favor of Retz because other than an agitator, he is a Jansenist."[37] It was significant that he joined "agitator" and "Jansenist" to a curé who pleaded for Retz. Mazarin was not mistaken in his belief that unruly curés were Jansenist.

3. The Jansenism of the Curés: As a Corporation

Just as the curés utilized elements in Richerism to confront the episcopacy, they upheld Jansenist theological positions against the Society of Jesus in an effort to retain decisive control over the religious lives of parishioners. Put another way, the struggle against the Jesuits over local religious issues was essentially part of the protracted battle of the curés to ensure their supremacy within the parish. Richerism offered the curés a set of doctrines suitable to repulse the threat of episcopal interference from above. Jansenism, by the same token, afforded the curés a moral theology and a view of the Christian life which could be employed to thwart the Jesuits and their lax casuistry. The curés realized that the rigorism of Jansenism appealed to a public already conditioned by the reformist and *dévot* qualities of the Catholic Reforma-

tion of the first half of the seventeenth century. This is not to say that
the curés felt no strong intellectual affinity for Jansenism or no visceral
hatred of laxism. The converse was true. The curés were also products
of the reforms of the preceding decades and, though it is not possible
to say with certainty, it does seem that the curés were Jansenist out of
sincere religious conviction. It must be noted, however, that during
the Religious Fronde the curés' personal and corporate interests dovetailed with their theological attitudes, as they also merged with their
political behavior. The curés were also Jansenist because it suited their
individual ambitions and those of their corps. Several issues in which
the curés acted consistently with the doctrines formulated at Port-Royal
reveal that the curés behaved corporately as Jansenists.[38]

The laxism of the Jesuits was one such issue, one brought before the
public by Pascal's *Lettres provinciales*. The Parisian curés, obsessed
with the jurisdictional encroachments of regulars, welcomed these letters, which ridiculed the Jesuits. Pascal wrote the last of the *Lettres
provinciales* in March 1657, and the curés soon followed with their
Ecrits des curés de Paris. These *Ecrits*, which were in fact the continuation of the *Provinciales*, gave the curés national—even international—
renown and linked them intimately to Jansenism.[39] Issued sporadically as were the *Provinciales*, the *Ecrits* began to appear one month
after the publication of Pirot's *Apologie* and were, for the most part,
directed against that work.

This struggle against the Jesuits' ethical teachings proved the close
ties of the curés with the great names of Port-Royal. Thomas Fortin,
who had allegedly had the *Provinciales* printed,[40] shared the responsibility for the *Ecrits* with Mazure and to a lesser extent with six
others deputed by the assemblies of the curés. Signed by these eight
commissioners and ratified by the corps of curés, the *Ecrits* were
composed by Pascal, Pierre Nicole, and Antoine Arnauld, the three
luminaries of Port-Royal. Pascal, who was in this matter "properly
and truly the secretary of the Parisian curés,"[41] wrote at least four of
these *Ecrits*.[42]

Although the curés themselves did not prepare the *Ecrits*, they did
revise them, approve them, and answer for them.[43] There was no
doubt that the curés supported wholeheartedly the contents of the
Ecrits. The curés' pursuance of the condemnation of the *Apologie*
before the Faculty of Theology, the General Assembly of the Clergy,

the vicars-general, and throughout France attested to their very real hostility to the moral theology denounced in the *Ecrits*. On the basis of the *Ecrits* alone, one could designate the Parisian curés as Jansenists.[44] Against the pernicious maxims of the Jesuits, the curés opposed "Christian morality"; to replace the new casuists, the curés offered the Church Fathers. The éclat of the *Ecrits* was aided in no small measure by the vulnerability of the Jesuits exposed by the inopportune *Apologie*. Whereas previous refutations of the *Provinciales* had used various artifices to parry Pascal's blows, Pirot agreed with the laxist doctrines castigated by Pascal. Of all the Jesuit replies to Pascal, the *Apologie* was "the most famous and the clumsiest."[45] But while the weaknesses of the *Apologie* enabled the curés to secure the censure of the hated ethical precepts of the Jesuits and to realize *gloire* through humiliation of their adversaries, the affair's outcome was not a complete success. The curés' achievement in rousing public opinion, in exposing the Jesuits as moral corruptors, and in propagating rigorist views that came increasingly to be viewed as heretical, fueled the antagonism already felt by the government toward them and so contributed to the court's decision to suppress the company of curés. The court finally issued *arrêts* against the seventh *Ecrit*—which presented a historical account of the successful campaign against the Jesuits—and the eighth *Ecrit*—which attacked Father Annat, confessor to the king, and which by its very publication defied the government. Mazarin and Le Tellier, the two most powerful figures in the government, now clearly saw the connection between the curés and Port-Royal, between sedition and Jansenism.[46]

Nonetheless, the curés of Paris achieved fame as the tenacious champions of a pure Christianity confronting the moral dilution of lax casuistry. While the curés first assailed Jesuit moral theology in 1656 in response to the appearance of the first *Provinciales*, their notoriety only blossomed later. The Parisian curés' first circular letter (of 13 September 1656) to their fellows throughout France contained a table and extract, written by Arnauld and Nicole, of thirty-eight dangerous propositions drawn from the works of the new casuists.[47] By early 1658 the combination of three factors led to a situation in which the curés' activity would receive special attention: the General Assembly of the Clergy, which ostensibly possessed the jurisdictional authority to deal with questions of moral theology, dispersed in May 1657 without resolving these issues; Pascal ceased publication of his *Provinciales* in March 1657; and the *Apologie* offered itself as an unexpected opportunity in December 1657.

Responding to the Parisian curés' request to join in the struggle against the *Apologie*, the curés of Sens recognized their singular achievements: "We share with you our joy since it is the effect of your zeal and a blessed result of these courageous actions which have won for you the glory of being the intrepid defenders of Christian morality."[48] Bishop Alphonse d'Elbene of Orléans, after issuing in his synod a condemnation of the *Apologie*, which the curés had pursued "with so much justice and so much zeal," was quick to acknowledge that "so many good curés, who are eminent in piety and in doctrine," approved of his action.[49] Similarly, the archbishop of Sens noted that "the name of the Parisian curés has everywhere become a cause of dismay for the corruptors of evangelical morality."[50] Among others, the bishop of Conserans complimented the curés for their initiative in assailing relaxed morality: "You, sirs, were the first to have been touched by the outrage which this deadly morality was going to commit upon the Church of the Son of God."[51]

The Parisian curés' success can be measured by the numerous censures obtained against Pirot, by the support forthcoming from curés of provincial cities, and by the unfavorable public reaction to the Jesuits. No one reflected the despair of the Society more poignantly than Rapin, who lashed out at those who he knew were to blame:

> . . . all the weight of the persecution of the Jesuits, who were
> held responsible for this book [Pirot's *Apologie*], came mainly
> from the Parisian curés, nearly all of whom favored the Jansen-
> ists. Those [curés] who were not Jansenist displayed a zeal for the
> hierarchy which was going to destroy the religious orders so as
> to increase the fame of the parishes. . . . As the Jesuits were of
> all the religious the most occupied with [spiritual] direction,
> it was on them that the storm began to fall with all the strength
> which a corporation as important as that of the Parisian curés . . .
> was capable of. This corporation produced writings against
> them [the Jesuits]. They [the curés] often assembled in
> order to seek the means to destroy them [the Jesuits] and
> began to discredit them in society as the seducers of consciences

through their relaxed morality. What was done then in Paris was done immediately in Rouen and in other of the most eminent cities in the kingdom. The rage against the Society was universal everywhere, but particularly in Paris where the Jansenists were permitted to breathe.[52]

Elated by these triumphs, the curés in their tenth and last *Ecrit* turned their attention to another Jesuit work of lax casuistry, that of Thomas Tamburini, published in 1659.[53] Furious that the Jesuits would repeat the maxims of the *Apologie*, which had by then been censured even by the papacy, thirty curés—that is, every participant except one in the assembly on 10 October 1659—affixed his name to the *Ecrit*, a request for the condemnation of Tamburini's book.[54] Though this solicitation did not cause the same repercussions as the previous *Ecrits*, its publication with the signatures attested to the saturation of the corporation of curés with a revulsion of lax casuistry and with a harsher view of moral imperatives traditionally associated with Jansenism.

The myriad actions of the curés from 1656 to 1659 with respect to the issue of laxism, including their conscientious effort to disseminate their moral rigorism, place them within the framework of Jansenist types elaborated by Goldmann and Namer. During these years the curés collaborated often and closely with Pascal, Arnauld, and Nicole, the three most prominent members of the moderate or centrist group of Jansenism. Pascal's *Provinciales* reflected his temporary position that rational thought and action can bring society closer to the Christian ideal. The majority of curés adhered to this position, both by their favorable reception of Pascal's message and by their further propagation of his work through the *Ecrits*. The links to Nicole and Arnauld were no less intimate. From their preparation of a series of ill-advised Jesuit propositions of moral theology for inclusion in the curés' 1656 circular letter to their role in the composition of the *Ecrits*, Arnauld and Nicole shared with the curés a working relationship and a fundamental conception of the role of the Christian in an evil world. As Goldmann argues, this centrist group viewed the world as encompassing the dialectical struggle between good and evil, truth and error, the City of God and the City of the Devil, holiness and sin. Unlike those such as Barcos who declined to act to achieve righteousness within the world, these centrists—these curés—felt that sincere Christians should attempt to alter the balance of good and evil here on earth, though theologically they believed this earthly battle to be everlasting.[55]

The decisive factor in the curés' adherence to the centrist group was their stance with respect to the first episcopal letter (*mandement*) of the vicars-general of the archbishop of Paris, dated 8 June 1661. The curés' response to this episcopal letter definitively established their posture as centrist Jansenists and constituted their final public act during the Religious Fronde.

The five-month long controversy over the episcopal letter of Jean-Baptiste de Contes and Alexandre Hodencq, curé of Saint-Severin, was occasioned by the resolution taken by the General Assembly of the Clergy on 1 February 1661, which stated in part that all ecclesiastics in France were required to subscribe to the Formulary of 17 March 1657.[56] This resolution was yet another effort to end the long controversy that had begun in 1649 when Nicolas Cornet, syndic of the Sorbonne, proposed seven propositions to the Faculty for examination. Pope Innocent X condemned five of them in his 1653 bull *Cum occasione*. Because Jansenists tried to circumvent this ruling, Alexander V in the bull *Ad sacram* attributed the five propositions specifically to the *Augustinus* of Cornelius Jansenius. The Formulary of 1657 recognized the condemnation of the five propositions and affirmed that they were indeed contained in the *Augustinus*.

Louis XIV, who unlike Mazarin did not see any differences among the Jansenists, determined after the cardinal-minister's death in March 1661 to extirpate Jansenism.[57] On 13 April, an *arrêt* of the *Conseil d'état* upheld the requirement stipulated by the General Assembly that every cleric in France sign the Formulary. On the same day, the government issued *lettres de cachet* ordering the bishops and archbishops to oversee the clergy's adherence.[58] Port-Royal also felt the effects of the king's zealotry. On 23 April, the boarders and postulants were expelled from the monastery, which was forbidden to accept new novices, and the principal directors fled to avoid the inevitable *lettres de cachet*. On 16 May, the Faculty of Theology accepted the Formulary.

It was in this atmosphere that the vicars-general promulgated their episcopal letter.[59] Perhaps written by Arnauld, this episcopal letter enunciated the solution of his centrist faction to the dilemma posed by the Formulary. Whereas the extremist group led by Le Roy refused to accept the Formulary, the centrists used the notorious distinction between "right" and "fact" to reconcile themselves to signing.[60] They agreed that the Church had the authority to condemn the five propositions, but argued that the Church could err with respect to a question of fact, such as whether the heretical propositions were actually in the *Augustinus*. By requesting, with regard to the question of "fact," merely a "complete and sincere respect," the vicars-general in effect postulated the doctrine of "respectful silence" that became so significant in the later history of Jansenism. Support from the Parisian curés was immediate. They published the episcopal letter, signed it, and compelled their parish priests to subscribe to it.[61]

Reaction from the court was also prompt, for the behavior of the vicars-general had not been unanticipated. Marca had submitted earlier a memorandum to Mazarin discussing the possibility that the vicars-general, under Retz's authority, would refuse to accede to the Formulary. The problem, according to Marca, was that the source and the strength of the Jansenists were in Paris. To prevent the spread of Jansenism, he recommended that the vicars-general be ordered to proceed with the signing of the Formulary.[62]

On 24 June, the *Conseil de conscience* (the royal council dealing with religious matters), composed of Annat, Marca, and the bishops of Rennes and Rodez, complained to the king that the episcopal letter "made the heresy of Jansenism triumphant." *Lettres de cachet* then ordered Hodencq and de Contes to Fontainebleau.[63] An assembly of court bishops held on 26 June declared the episcopal letter to be invalid and asked the king to issue an *arrêt* in support of their decision and to request the pope's aid in remedying the disorder caused in Paris and throughout France.[64] The *Conseil de conscience* tried to convince the vicars-general of the errors of Jansenism and of their episcopal letter and asked them to circulate a second one, an outline of which had been drawn up at court. The recalcitrant clerics refused.[65]

After the *Conseil de conscience* failed to resolve the affair, another assembly of court bishops stated that the episcopal letter had no legal force and urged the king to issue an *arrêt* against it.[66] The subsequent *arrêt* put the full weight of the government against the vicars-general's distinction between "right" and "fact." The *arrêt* revoked the 8 June episcopal letter and prohibited signing of the Formulary according to that episcopal letter.[67] Failure to adhere to the Formulary in the sense designated by the General Assembly now became a political, as well as an ecclesiastical offense.

The curés blatantly disobeyed the *arrêt*, throwing themselves whole-heartedly behind the vicars-general's resistance to the Formulary. In their assembly of 29 July, twenty of the twenty-two curés present signed a notarized declaration in support of the episcopal letter:

> . . . having heard with extreme satisfaction the publication made by the order of the vicars-general . . . [we] have been extremely surprised to learn that several of our lords the bishops have proclaimed that the said ordinance has scandalized Catholics. This manifestly charges the said witnesses, who have all made it public. Most have signed it and made their reluctant ecclesiastics sign it, and the others are prepared to sign it. This is why the said witnesses, having complete knowledge of the edification which all the faithful have received from it, find themselves obliged to testify to its truth. For this end they have declared unanimously in their assembly . . . that so far from the said ordinance scandaliz-ing any Catholics subject to their guidance, it has on the contrary greatly edified them as well as all the priests of their parishes. All those who have the love of peace and concord engraved in their hearts have regarded as well as them the said ordinance as the sole means of quieting the present strife and of affirming peace, harmony, and tranquility among the faithful of this diocese of Paris.[68]

As was usual since the suppression of the regular and independent assemblies of the curés in July 1659, this assembly had been convoked in the presence of the vicars-general ostensibly for the purpose of discussing certain innocuous parish problems, such as cases of con-science. In fact, the vicars-general desired reinforcement from the cu-rés in their resistance to the court and episcopacy. De Contes incited the curés with a speech denying that the episcopal letter had been designed to cause scandal or disorder in the Church; rather the vicars-general's motives were only to serve the truth, the glory of God, and the peace of the Church. The company of curés shouted in reply: "Sirs, it is the bishops who cause scandal, not your episcopal letter. We have considered it, we and all our ecclesiastics, as the holiest, the most edifying, and the most suitable [means] to bring peace which could be accomplished." As was characteristic of the curés during the Religious Fronde, their Jansenism coincided with their need to assert themselves against the episcopacy. Indignant, Nicolas de Bry, curé of Saint-Cosme, and several others remarked that it was strange that some bishops, residing at court fourteen leagues from Paris, could dare claim that the episcopal letter had scandalized everyone in that city. The curés knew the extraordinary satisfaction displayed by all the peoples of Paris at the peace reestablished in the archdiocese by this ordinance.[69]

The curés' praise of the episcopal letter constituted a rear-guard action by the centrist group.[70] Quick to sustain the curés, Arnauld, along with Noël de La Lane, published a *Défense de l'Ordonnance* defending the distinction between "right" and "fact" as legitimate, just, and necessary. They also attacked the conclusions of the bishops assembled at court and quoted from the curés' declaration to prove the beneficial effects that the episcopal letter had had in Paris.[71] On the other hand, the government greeted the curés' action with dismay. Lionne wrote to an agent in Rome that the curés had issued their declaration at the instigation of Retz, whose influence over the vicars-general was also great. The king, affirmed Lionne, interpreted these recent events as attempts of the Jansenists to preserve their sect.[72] Marca informed cardinal Barberini of the court's concern that the curés' declaration would be sent to Rome. If this happened, Marca feared, the pope might believe that measures taken against the epis-copal letter would anger the entire city of Paris.[73] To mitigate the effect of the declaration, which was sent to Rome, Barberini spoke to the pope. While emphasizing the Jansenism of the episcopal letter and of the declaration, this cardinal utilized the stratagem of contending that non-Jansenist curés had been excluded from the 29 July assembly and that the majority of the curés who subscribed to the declaration were from the suburbs, not from Paris proper (the latter claim was definitely false, as only seven of the twenty signatories possessed sub-urban cures).[74]

The crown need not have worried about any wavering in the anti-Jansenist feelings of Alexander VII. The pope sent two letters: the first reproached the vicars-general for their schismatic behavior and com-manded them to revoke their episcopal letter; the second authorized criminal proceedings against and deposition of de Contes and Hodencq if they did not yield to the papal order.[75] The affair of the episcopal letter—and the Religious Fronde—rapidly approached denouement.[76] Throughout the controversy, the resolve of the vicars-general had been fortified by the knowledge that they acted under Retz's authority and by the hope that they would receive the backing of the curés and the papacy. Now the vicars-general found themselves denounced by the pope. Still, with the curés and Retz on their side, the vicars-general did not defer to the pressure applied from the crown and from Rome.

Instead, Retz himself precipitated the capitulation of the vicars-general by tearing asunder the union of Jansenism and the political aspects of the Religious Fronde. At the time of the first episcopal letter, Retz was still preoccupied with the restoration of his archiepiscopal see. Arnauld advised Retz not to declare himself on the question of the Formulary until the court had reestablished him in all of his spiritual and temporal rights. However, coincident with the government's concern to suppress the episcopal letter were its new efforts under Louis XIV to persuade the papacy to consent to a trial of Retz under the charge of high treason. Retz's trial had been a persistent concern of the court since the outbreak of the Religious Fronde, but the problems involved in bringing a cleric to trial by a secular authority, the elevated office of cardinal, and Innocent X's antipathy to Mazarin, had frustrated French designs.

By the summer of 1661 Retz had reason to fear that he might be brought to judgment. Mazarin, himself a factor in papal policies, was replaced by a king whose personal authority was greater than that of his former first minister. Moreover, the crown utilized the problem of Jansenism and the disorder in Paris to drive a wedge between Retz and the pope. Alarmed, Retz abruptly denied in a letter to the pope that he had ever been a Jansenist, declaring that his enemies had spread that rumor. Retz affirmed that he had sworn submission to the bulls *Cum occasione* and *Ad sacram*, had declared anathema the five propositions of Jansenius, and had in his youth combatted the *Augustinus* in the Sorbonne.[77] Welcomed by Alexander, Retz's letter did forestall the government's plan to bring him to trial. The price was great. By abandoning the vicars-general, the curés, and the men of Port-Royal—all those who had supported him in the past—Retz effectively renounced all hope of realizing his goals in the Religious Fronde. Now, Retz's reinstatement could be accomplished only through reconciliation with the court.

The situation was even bleaker for his former Jansenist supporters.

As Retz had indicated that he would aid in liquidating Jansenism in Paris and as they could no longer buttress themselves on archiepiscopal authority, the curés' hopes were completely dashed. Resisting until October, the vicars-general at last submitted, consenting to publish a second episcopal letter.

This affair of the episcopal letter demonstrates the adhesion of the curés both to Jansenist positions and to Port-Royal, and the inseparability of Jansenism and the Religious Fronde. Along with the *Ecrits des curés de Paris*, the curés' declaration supporting the vicars-general's episcopal letter signified the collaboration of the assemblies of curés with the Jansenist movement.

4. The Jansenism of the Curés: As Individuals

Corporately Jansenist, then, the curés also behaved individually as Jansenists. Of the sixty-eight curés who attended the assemblies of the curés or who held cures in Paris from 1653 to 1662, thirty-eight were Jansenist or had Jansenist sympathies, twelve (that is, only 18 percent) were anti-Jansenist, while the available evidence does not permit determination for the remaining eighteen. These numbers were arrived at primarily from an examination of the curés' voting records with regard to seven ecclesiastical disputes in which Jansenism was a factor. Figure 2 indicates which curés were Jansenist, anti-Jansenist, or "unknown."[78] As the figure notes affirmative positions only, the absence of an X is not equivalent to a stance unfavorable to Jansenism. In many cases, curés were not present in the Faculty of Theology or in the assemblies of the curés when votes on these matters were recorded. There were five issues on which an affirmative position nearly always denoted Jansenism: approval of Arnauld's *Fréquente communion* in the Sorbonne in 1643; signing of the appeal to Parlement in 1649 protesting Nicolas Cornet's denunciation of the five propositions; support for Arnauld during his trial by the Sorbonne in 1655–56; affixing one's name to the *Ecrits des curés de Paris*; and attachment to the distinction of "right" and "fact" through the signing of the 1661 declaration, which sustained the first episcopal letter of the vicars-general of Paris. Thirty-three curés indicated their Jansenism by their position on these crucial issues.[79]

An affirmative stance with respect to two other indices, the 1658

FIGURE 2. *The Jansenism of the Parisian curés*

Curé	1	2	3	4	5	6	7	8
Abelly, Louis St.-Josse								A
Amyot, Edmond St.-Merry								A´
Amyot, Jacques St.-Jacques-du-Haut-Pas								U
Antin, Nicolas Ste.-Madeleine de la Ville l'Evêque					X	X	X	J
Bail, Louis Montmartre								A
Beurrier, Paul St.-Etienne-du-Mont					X	X	X	J
Blanchart, François St.-Etienne-du-Mont								A
Blondel, Jean St.-Hippolyte	X	X			X	X		J
Bourguignon de Souchaut, François Gentilly					X	X	X	J
Bréda, Antoine de St.-André-des-Arts	X			X	X	X		J
Bretonvilliers, Alexandre Le Ragois de St.-Sulpice					X			A
Bry, Nicolas de St.-Cosme					X	X	X	J
Chapelas, Pierre St.-Jacques-de-la-Boucherie								A
Chassebras, Jean-Baptiste Ste.-Madeleine		X						J
Cognet, Jacques St.-Roch							X	J
Colombet, Antoine St.-Germain-l'Auxerrois					X			U
Colombet, Pierre St.-Germain-l'Auxerrois								A
Coppin, Pierre St.-Lambert de Vaugirard		X	X					J
Cordel, Charles Cardinal Le Moyne					X		X	J

KEY:
1—Approved *Fréquente Communion*
2—Signed *appel* to Parlement against Cornet
3—Against condemnation of Arnauld
4—Signed *Ecrits des curés de Paris*
5—Signed request against *Apologie*
6—Signed request against Tamburini
7—Supported *mandement* of vicars-general
8—J = Jansenist
  A = Anti-Jansenist
  U = Unknown

Figure 2 (*continued*)

Curé	1	2	3	4	5	6	7	8
Daubé, Jean-Baptiste St.-Marine						X		U
Davollé St.-Pierre-aux-Boeufs				X	X	X		J
Degraves St.-Louis-en-l'Ile			X			X		J
Delabarthe, François St.-Jacques-du-Haut-Pas .					X	X		U
Duhamel, Henri St.-Merry	X	X						J
Dupuys, Antoine St.-Innocents				X		X		J
Du Saussay, André St.-Leu-Saint-Gilles								A
Féret, Hippolyte St.-Nicolas-du-Chardonnet								A
Fortin, Thomas St.-Christophe		X	X	X	X	X	X	J
Fresnoy, Charles du La Villette						X	X	J
Gargan, Pierre St.-Médard				X	X	X	X	J
Gobillon, Nicolas St.-Laurent							X	U
Godefroy St.-Geneviève-des-Ardents					X			U
Gosset, Nicolas Ste.-Opportune		X			X		X	J
Grenet, Claude St.-Benoît	X	X	X		X	X		J
Guyard, Louis St.-Louis-en-l'Ile								U
Hargales St.-Jean-le-Rond								U
Heu, Antoine de St.-Séverin		X						J
Hodencq, Alexandre St.-Séverin		X						J
Joly, Claude St.-Nicolas-des-Champs					X	X		A
Jutet, Jacques Ste.-Croix						X	X	J
Lespy, Henry de St.-Leu-Saint-Gilles					X	X	X	J
Le Carpentier, Lucas Ste.-Croix					X			U
Le Clerc de Lesseville, Eustache St.-Gervais								U
Le Noir, Louis St.-Hilaire			X		X	X	X	J

Figure 2 (*continued*)

Curé	1	2	3	4	5	6	7	8
Lestocq, Nicolas de St.-Laurent					X	X		U
Loisel, Pierre St.-Jean-en-Grève	X							J
Manuel, Marin Boulogne								U
Marlin, Pierre St.-Eustache			X	X	X	X	X	J
Martinet St.-Symphorien					X	X		J
Mazure, Nicolas St.-Paul	X		X	X	X	X	X	J
Méliard, Pierre St.-Josse								U
Messier, Louis St.-Landry					X	X		J
Michard St.-Sauveur					X	X		J
Mincé, Elie Du Fresne de St.-Pierre-de-Gonesse			X					J
Obry St.-Nicolas-des-Champs								J
Patu, Charles St.-Martial					X			U
Payen, Jean Ste.-Geneviève-des-Ardents			X			X	X	J
Picquet, Pierre St.-Josse								U
Pietre St.-Germain-le-Vieux								U
Poussemot St.-Martin								U
Quintaine, Nicolas St.-Pierre-de-Chaillot					X	X	X	J
Raguier de Poussé, Antoine St.-Sulpice								A
Regnier, Pierre Vaugirard							X	J
Roullé, Pierre St.-Barthélemy	X				X			A
Rousse, Jean St.-Roch		X	X	X	X			J
Rousseau, Nicolas St.-Pierre-des-Arcis						X		U
Sachot, Jacques St.-Gervais					X	X		J
Villiers, Pierre Camus de Auteuil						X	X	J

and 1659 requests for the condemnation of the works by Pirot and Tamburini, is not conclusive evidence for the presence of Jansenist sympathies, as one could in theory reject both lax casuistry and Jansenism. In deference to this possibility, adherence to a request against one, as opposed to two, of these Jesuit books is not considered proof of Jansenism. This occurred with respect to five curés (Antoine Colombet, Daubé, Godefroy, Le Carpentier, and Rousseau), whose status must be categorized as ambiguous even though there is a strong possibility that they were Jansenist. Four curés (Martinet, Messier, Michard, and Sachot) who signed both requests are listed as Jansenist.[80]

The thirty-eighth Jansenist curé, Obry, of Saint-Nicolas-des-Champs, did not vote on any of these issues. Because he resigned his cure in 1653, Obry was not involved with the curés in later Jansenist controversies. Prior to that time he evinced Jansenist sympathies. In the curés' assembly of 8 January 1652, for example, Obry defended the fervently Jansenist Duhamel against the charge made by Jean-Jacques Olier that the curé of Saint-Merry was a schismatic.[81]

Often, evidence from other sources complicates the utilization of the seven issues listed above as evidence of Jansenism. Therefore it is necessary to examine individually those curés (1) whose status was ambiguous but who voted Jansenist; (2) who we know were anti-Jansenist but who voted Jansenist; (3) who were anti-Jansenist but who voted ambiguously; and, (4) who were anti-Jansenist but who did not vote.

There were four curés whose careers seemed Jansenist, save for one instance. Delabarthe, Gobillon, Lestocq, and Patu displayed Jansenist tendencies except for their votes cast in opposition to Arnauld at his trial. While other curés decided against Arnauld, evidence for their Jansenism is overwhelming. For these four, however, lack of sufficient information determined their inclusion in the "ambiguous" category.

Both Claude Joly and Pierre Roullé were definitely not Jansenists yet seemed to adhere to Jansenist views on certain issues. Joly attended the assemblies of the curés regularly and took part in their struggles against the Jesuits. He thus signed the requests for the condemnation of the works by Pirot and Tamburini. Nonetheless, he was not, as Hermant stated, a "Disciple of Saint Augustine."[82] Although he approved Arnauld's *Fréquente communion*, Roullé in the 1650s was virulently anti-Jansenist, opposed to Retz, aligned with the government, and, unlike Joly, friendly to the Jesuits. Roullé reported to

Mazarin on Arnauld's trial in the Sorbonne and on events in the curés' assemblies. A certain indication of Roullé's bias against Jansenism was his use of the term *janséniste* in his correspondence to characterize certain of his colleagues; for example, Hodencq was a "notorious Jansenist."[83] For Roullé, "The Jansenists are the enemies of the Church and the state. . . . Their opinion is that the Church is so corrupt that it is necessary to destroy the present one and replace it with one that is pure."[84] A government informer furnished a profile of Roullé, confirming that he was "very opposed to the Jansenists and desirous of doing everything which could please the court."[85]

Although Bretonvilliers' opposition to the *Apologie* might be construed as a Jansenist action, such was not the case. The parish of Saint-Sulpice was a stronghold of anti-Jansenism in the seventeenth century. Olier, the renowned Counter Reformation figure, founder of the seminary of Saint-Sulpice and predecessor of Bretonvilliers, was rabidly antagonistic to Jansenism. In 1652 he was one of only three Parisian curés not to sustain the archbishop of Paris' condemnation of the Jesuit Jean Brisacier's book, *Le Jansénisme confondu*. Bretonvilliers himself backed his *vicaire* Charles Picoté, whose refusal to grant absolution to the duc de Liancourt because of his ties with Port-Royal prompted Arnauld to write his notorious *Lettre à une personne de condition* and, a few months later, a *Seconde lettre à un duc et pair*. Because of these two letters, the Sorbonne censured Arnauld and then expelled him on 16 February 1656. At the occasion of the bull *Ad sacram*, Bretonvilliers delivered a vigorous sermon against Jansenism.[86]

The nine curés who never wavered as adversaries of Jansenism, and whose small number could only reinforce our view of the Jansenism of the curés as a whole, were Abelly, Edmond Amyot, Bail, Blanchart, Chapelas, Pierre Colombet, Du Saussay, Féret, and Raguier de Poussé. Abelly and Chapelas were the two curés who sided with Olier in the 1652 Brisacier affair.[87] Abelly, sometime confessor of Mazarin, was also one of the most ultramontane members of the clergy, first as curé and after 1662 as bishop of Rodez. His works combined anti-Jansenism and vigorous support of papal authority.[88] No less hostile was Amyot, who denounced Jansenists as enemies of the state; persecuted his fellow curé of Saint-Merry, Duhamel, and his community of Jansenist priests;[89] supported both Cornet's designs and the condemnation of Arnauld in the Faculty of Theology; and published against the Jansenists.[90] Louis Bail also approved the condemnation of Arnauld and wrote in defense of the Society of Jesus against the Jansenists—his *De beneficio crucis* prompted the court to appoint him as superior of the two monasteries of Port-Royal in 1661. Bail's abhorrence of the Jansenists was so great, said Racine, that "his hair stood on end at the very mention of Port-Royal."[91]

François Blanchart was an anomaly both as a non-Jansenist curé and as a member of the Augustinian order who clearly took a position against Jansenist doctrine. Tied to the government as one of the first members of Mazarin's *conseils de conscience* for clerics, Blanchart rejected the opinions of those few who caused schism in the Church.[92] While general of the Congregation of Saint Augustine, he wrote in this vein to the prior of Saint-Jean de Chartres advocating the unrestricted signing of the Formulary: "When you intend to lose all of our seminaries, our studies, and our noviciates, you could not do better than to sign the Formulary with modification."[93] A Jesuit in his youth, Pierre Chapelas was the converse of a Religious Frondeur. He defended the moral theology of the Jesuits at every turn. For example, he refused to support the curés' request to the vicars-general for the censure of the *Apologie*. In fact, Chapelas rebelled against the curés' attempts to raise the authority and jurisdiction of their company—in the 5 May 1659 assembly, it was reported that Chapelas had been absent from the company for two years and had never subscribed to its statutes.[94] In 1656, Chapelas had been one of the few curés (along with Amyot and Pierre Colombet) to resist the union of the Parisian curés with those of Rouen. Finally, Chapelas regarded Retz as guilty of lese majesty and opposed the reading of Retz's letter in the curés' assembly of 5 September 1654.[95] Lauded by Rapin as a right-thinking man, Pierre Colombet was in large measure responsible for convincing François Hallier to undertake his journey to Rome for the purpose of obtaining papal denunciation of the five propositions.[96] Along with Saint-Sulpice, Saint-Germain-l'Auxerrois was noted, under Colombet, as a stronghold of anti-Jansenism. At the arrival in Paris of the bull *Cum occasione*, the Te Deum was sung at those two parishes. When several Jansenists subsequently explained to Colombet that he had misinterpreted the bull, he defended himself and accused the Jansenists of seeking to elude the papal censure.[97]

Du Saussay was more opposed to Jansenism for reasons of ambition than of temperament. Nominated to the bishopric of Toul in 1649, the curé of Saint-Leu-Saint-Gilles had to wait eight years for confirmation, principally because of disagreements between the Curia and the French government. Caught between those two powers, Du Saussay was careful not to offend: "his nomination to the bishopric to Toul put him in a position of needing everyone, and forced him not to offend the Jesuits."[98] Hippolyte Féret, though not taking an active part in the controversies of the 1650s, was a confirmed anti-Jansenist, speaking ill, Hermant said, of Port-Royal.[99] *Dévot*, inclined to Rome, Raguier de Poussé, as befitting a curé of Saint-Sulpice, was rabidly antagonistic to Jansenism. He once remarked in a letter to Le Tellier: "At Saint-Sulpice we have always opposed the damnable doctrine of the Jansenists. We have always combatted it as much as we could."[100]

These twelve anti-Jansenist curés were, then, in a small minority. The curés as a whole were overwhelmingly Jansenist. This should not surprise, as Jansenists since Saint-Cyran had exalted the priesthood.[101] For Saint-Cyran (and for his disciple Singlin) "the 'good priest' takes his place very high in the spiritual hierarchy. His vocation, his task, [and] his direct contact with the souls which he leads to God, raise him above the rich and titled prelates. The humble confessor, the parish curé, has . . . eminent authority; he represents the true Church."[102] The Parisian curés translated their centrist Jansenism into seditious activities. It was no accident that curés celebrated for their Jansenism were also Richerist and frondeurs. These currents were all potentially subversive of the theological, the ecclesiastical, and the political order. It was also not coincidental that those curés who were attached to the Jesuits did not oppose the government during the Religious Fronde. With the curés, then, Jansenism appears as part of a mentality of revolt, not as a doctrine of withdrawal from the world or from ecclesiastical politics. One is struck by the degree of involvement of the curés in the controversies of the period and by the relative unity of such a disparate group in this ten-year period. Perhaps the homogeneity of the curés with respect to Jansenism was a precondition for their attempts to remove themselves from the constraints of episcopal authority. Jansenism, it is clear, formed the glue that held the curés together in their contestations against the encroachments of the Jesuits. One wonders if a quantitative study of any other professional or social group associated with Jansenism, such as Goldmann's robe, would reveal such a high percentage of Jansenists as existed among the Parisian curés.

Because of this penetration of Jansenism among the curés during the 1650s, we must discard the exclusive identification of the Jansenist movement with Port-Royal or with the robe. Clearly, Jansenism spread beyond these groups sooner than historians have previously suspected. Furthermore, administrative correspondence reflects a fear that the curés' Jansenism, because of their control of the pulpit, was extending to parishioners. It is almost axiomatic among liberal historians that persecuted minority groups are undeservedly maltreated. This maxim does not apply to the case of the curés. It is time to reject the view of Jansenists as unjustly persecuted by a government overly concerned with doctrinal uniformity. Rather, we must view Jansenism, at least one major segment of it in the mid-seventeenth century, as a source for political revolt.

CONCLUSION

The Parisian curés should not be ignored. Though seemingly dwarfed by Retz's protracted and futile effort to replace Mazarin and by Condé's glamorous and treasonous leadership of Spanish armies, they did cause grave concern to the government. Politically, the curés posed a potential danger. The crown feared that at any time the curés, through their control of the pulpit, could incite their parishioners to open rebellion, as their counterparts during the League had done. The seventeenth century was filled with popular uprisings, and the most serious, the Day of Barricades, had only recently occurred in Paris. Another such fury might have begun more civil wars. The pope's protection of Retz and the latter's threat to use the spiritual weapons of excommunication and interdict contributed to the government's sense of instability, while international war and intermittent provincial revolt prolonged the mid-century crisis. Obviously, many of Louis XIV's policies were shaped in response to his memories of the Frondes. Louis' mentor, Mazarin, also was greatly influenced by his distrust of Paris and his fear of a renewed series of rebellions that might topple his ministeriat. By 1653, it was not yet clear that the early Frondes had resulted in a royalist victory.[1]

While the curés' political role was more traditional, their impact within the Church was potentially revolutionary. Richerism, as elaborated in the early seventeenth century, was the first set of doctrines in the history of Christianity that offered the lower clergy the opportunity to achieve significant power, and the Parisian curés constituted the first group of priests who understood, accepted, and utilized these doctrines. The curés' attempt to deny the authority of both papacy and prelacy to intervene in parochial affairs was based on an innovative interpretation of curial history and powers. Had the curés been successful, the effects on the Church would have been far-reaching. The curés knew how radical their Richerist positions were and how greatly they menaced the authority of their superiors, the bishops. The weight of Catholic tradition oppressed the curés; only the events of the

1650s, including the disorder in the archdiocese, offered the curés an opportunity to realize their aspirations.

The other side of this Richerism was an unmitigated hostility toward all regulars, especially those who posed the greatest threat, the Jesuits. The curés' preoccupation with the Society of Jesus can be seen in their violent campaigns against such Jesuits as Lingendes, Bagot, Pirot, and Maimbourg. These affairs predominated in curial assemblies. The Jesuits were rivals for control over the religious life of the parish. The curés also detested the Jesuits' lax casuistry. It would be difficult to overestimate the curés' fear of the moral consequences of ethically lax doctrines such as probabilism. Central to the curé's charge was his role as confessor, responsible for the salvation of thousands of souls, souls that the curés believed were in mortal danger from the threatened application of Jesuit teachings.

The curés' Jansenism, though not as innovative and as daring as their Richerism, was another aspect of their unorthodox behavior that made them suspect to the Church and the government. Jansenism was appealing to the individual curé because it reinforced his control over his penitent, helped him to combat his rivals, the Jesuits, and offered him a tradition of opposition.

The Parisian curés were failures. It is apparent that their audacious attempt to form a new corporation and to join with curés throughout the kingdom could not outlast that diocesan and political chaos which enabled and emboldened them to assert themselves. Indeed, the curés' position, like the magistrates' during the Parlementary Fronde, might have been untenable even in the event of victory. If the archbishop whom the curés supported had managed to topple Mazarin, it is questionable whether he would, or could, have countenanced the curés' independence or their undermining of traditional Church organization.

Their movement collapsed, primarily because the independence of the curés' assemblies was eliminated. The curés could no longer function consistently as a corporate body. The government and bishops ended the assemblies, which they perceived as too closely tied to the curés' refractory behavior. There is a parallel here with the government's suppression of the illicit assemblies of the Norman nobility in 1658, of the Company of the Holy Sacrament in 1660, and of the *élus* and *trésoriers de France* in 1661. The crown realized that dissidence could more easily be controlled by banning the secret gatherings of dangerous corporate groups.

Other causes for the decline of the curés' influence included the end of the provincial Fronde and the war against Spain. In 1659, the government had a freer hand in Paris. No longer was there a danger to the ministeriat from the union of Parisian rebels with aristocratic frondeurs and Spanish armies. Nevertheless, the Religious Fronde continued, though greatly weakened. Retz was still at large, claiming the archiepiscopal see and threatening, as always, to use his spiritual weapons. The curés may have grown impatient with Retz's inaction, but they still acknowledged him as archbishop. Finally, the curés' Jansenism continued to set them in conflict with the government. Part of the curés' movement thus could survive the end of their regular assemblies but not the events of 1661. Mazarin's death in that year removed one major source of discontent. It would have been difficult for the curés, like other dissidents, to sustain political opposition directly against a king who ruled by divine right. And Retz's repudiation of Jansenism in 1661, along with his subsequent resignation as archbishop, signaled the close of the Religious Fronde.

The Religious Fronde was not as dramatic as the earlier Frondes, nor did its participants, save Retz, behave as colorfully or belong to as high a social level. But the third Fronde was linked to the first two. Several frondeurs continued to oppose the government throughout the 1650s. None of the three Frondes constituted a revolution, though all had revolutionary elements.[2] And, lastly, all three helped shape the personal reign of Louis XIV, whose attitudes and policies toward the Parlements, the nobility, and the Church were rooted in the three rebellions that occurred during his youth.

The Sun King abhorred dissent, particularly within the Church. His persecution of Jansenism surely stemmed in part from his experiences during the Religious Fronde and from his belief that Jansenism caused disorder in a state ordered according to Louis' belief in "one God, one king, one law." Louis was correct. Theological disagreements and dissent did weaken the classical façade of his reign and the structure of the Old Regime. He was also astute in recognizing that the curés' independent and corporate behavior threatened the hierarchical organization of the First Estate. Throne was tied to altar; to sit comfortably on the former, Louis had to preserve the latter. Thus, to avoid a repetition of the "Godly Rebellion," Louis increased the power of bishops over curés. A royal edict of April 1695 solidified the jurisdictional and disciplinary authority of the prelacy over the French

Church. Parish officials in each diocese were to obey episcopal directives immediately. The bishop gained control over preaching and the administration of the sacraments and received the right to suspend or imprison any priest who disobeyed him.

These were not negligible gains, for they must be understood in light of other developments within the Church. After the Religious Fronde, the Jansenization of the Paris clergy continued,[3] and the discontent of curés seemed to spread throughout France as the spiritual movement of the Catholic Reformation and the development of seminaries elevated the priests' conception of their own dignity. At the same time curés found no means to express their dissatisfaction because of the 1659 order forbidding them to have syndics or to hold regular assemblies and because they increasingly came to be excluded from the General Assemblies of the Clergy. Curés also were not represented in the diocesan assemblies that met to allocate the taxation of the clergy. As a result, the Church taxed the curés much more heavily than it did the aristocratic upper clergy.

Disaffection among the lower clergy increased throughout the eighteenth century and again sought expression in Jansenism and Richerism. Jansenism continued to provide a mentality of opposition as it became somewhat of a mass movement. Although theologically diluted as it spread through various social strata, Jansenism received new impetus from the resurgence of Richerism during the last century of the Old Regime.[4]

The ecclesiastical watershed was the 1713 papal bull *Unigenitus*, which condemned 101 propositions from the Jansenist Pasquier Quesnel's book, *Réflexions morales*. Opposition to the bull among the lower clergy, magistrates, and others constituted an antimonarchical, antipapal, and antiepiscopal reaction. The intensity of ecclesiastical controversy reached new levels. The curés of Paris assumed a prominent role. Thirty of them petitioned their archbishop to persist in his rejection of *Unigenitus*. They demanded the convening of a diocesan synod where the lower clergy could express their grievances and campaigned throughout the diocese to win support for their proposal. The curés once more opposed royal policy, and, after the death of their archbishop, the cardinal de Noailles, who was sympathetic to Jansenism, they clamored for participation in ecclesiastical affairs and protested against episcopal despotism.[5]

The climax to the curés' espousal of their demands came with the

insurrection of the curés in 1787–89. The public debate prior to the
meeting of the Estates-General of 1789 saw an outpouring of proposals on behalf of the curés. These ideas of the curés, written for the
preparation of the *cahiers*, were infused with Richerism. Radical
though these ideas appeared at the time, they did not go beyond the
statements of the Parisian curés in the 1650s. Thus, in their pre-
Revolutionary pamphlets, curés demanded that they be recognized as
a corporation. They asserted that the government of the Church should
be held in common, and they ranted against the sloth of the upper
clergy. Like their frondeur predecessors, these curés desired better care
for their flock and a better teaching of the faith. They too used Richerism to provide a justification for their hostility toward the upper clergy
and the regulars.[6]

The pre-Revolutionary curés were not unaware of the Religious
Fronde. One pamphlet complained that since the mid-seventeenth century curés had been forbidden to organize and to assemble in order to
treat their common affairs. In the 1780s, curés had again attempted to
assemble but had been treated as rebels.[7] In 1782, the government
prohibited all curé assemblies not specifically authorized by the prelacy.

Finally, in the Estates-General, the curés were overwhelmingly represented: 203 of the 296 deputies of the First Estate were curés. Although they did not form a bloc, they were decisive in the 19 June
1789 vote to join with the Third Estate for the verification of the
electoral credentials of the deputies.[8]

Thus, the behavior and mentality of the Parisian curés during the
Religious Fronde had serious consequences for Louis XIV's policy
toward the Church and portended developments of the eighteenth
century. The fusion of Richerism and Jansenism, opposition to royal
policy, and hatred of the regular clergy—these themes of Church history in the century of Enlightenment had been played out in the 1650s.
The Parisian curés' demands, so extreme in the seventeenth century,
remained radical even in the years prior to the French Revolution. The
"Godly Rebellion" was the beginning of serious agitation on the part
of the lower clergy, but its failure meant that the dominant institutional structures of the French Church and state would suppress the
curés' demands until they were expressed in the revolutionary context
of the late eighteenth century.

ABBREVIATIONS

A.A.E. France   Archives des Affaires Etrangères. Mémoires et Documents, France.

A.A.E. Rome   Archives des Affaires Etrangères. Correspondance politique, Rome.

A.N.   Archives Nationales.

B.H.V.P.   Bibliothèque historique de la ville de Paris.

B.I.   Bibliothèque de l'Institut.

B.M.   Bibliothèque Mazarine.

B.N.   Bibliothèque Nationale.

B.N. Ms. Fr.   Bibliothèque Nationale, Manuscrits Français.

B.N. Ms. Nouv. Acq. Fr.   Bibliothèque Nationale, Manuscrits Nouvelles Acquisitions Françaises.

D.B.F.   *Dictionnaire de biographie française.* Paris, 1933–.

D.H.G.E.   *Dictionnaire d'histoire et de geographie ecclésiastiques.* Paris, 1912–.

G.E.F.   Gondi, Jean François Paul de, cardinal de Retz. *Oeuvres* (in the series *Les Grands écrivains de France*). Ed. François Régis de Chantelauze. Vol. 6. Paris, 1887.

NOTES

INTRODUCTION

1. John B. Wolf, "The Reign of Louis XIV: A Selected Bibliography of Writings since the War of 1914–1918," p. 138.

2. In approaching the Fronde, historians have usually studied the effect of the civil disturbances and the extent to which they were revolutionary, often selecting their own heroes in the struggles. For example, the roles of Mazarin and of the Parlement have been debated countless times. Thus Chéruel saw the indomitable Mazarin as leading the forces of nascent absolutism to victory. According to this view, reinforced by Madelin, the Fronde was a reaction against the strong central government that France so desperately needed. For Doolin and Moote, Parlement was the beneficent institution. Moote argued that the Parlement's legalistic *via media* enabled it to oppose both the princes and the government. In contrast with Madelin's interpretation of a *révolution manquée*, Moote contended that the Parlement succeeded in its rebellion. Kossmann disagreed with both those who admired the absolutist state and those, such as Doolin, who decried the despotism of the monarchy. Impartial in blaming princes, parlementaires, and crown, Kossmann stated that the Fronde was negative in its hopes and sterile in its effects. Mousnier, unabashedly sympathetic to the monarchy, viewed the Fronde as a revolutionary reaction to the new elements in absolutism brought about by the pressures of the war against Spain that had begun in 1635. The Parlement's pretensions were contrary to the fundamental laws and aimed to subvert the monarchy. Bonney denied Moote's interpretation of the Parlement's constitutional role and even its central position in the Fronde. He also repudiated the characterization of the nobility as arrogant freebooters intent solely on personal gain. Though disunited and self-interested, the aristocracy sought to return the crown to its forms antebellum, prior to Richelieu's and Mazarin's innovative policies. See Chéruel, *Histoire de France pendant la minorité de Louis XIV*; Madelin, *La Fronde*; Doolin, *The Fronde*; Moote, *The Revolt of the Judges*; Kossmann, *La Fronde*; Mousnier: "Quelques raisons de la Fronde: Les Causes des journées révolutionnaires parisiennes de 1648," pp. 33–78; Mousnier, "Comment les français du XVIIe siècle voyaient la constitution," pp. 9–36; Mousnier, "The Fronde," pp. 131–59; Mousnier, *Paris, capitale au temps de Richelieu et de Mazarin*, pp. 248ff.; Bonney, "The French Civil War, 1649–53," pp. 71–100; Bonney, *Political Change in France*, pp. 66–67, 284–86, 293–98.

On the other hand, Porchnev's original work on peasant revolts sparked a heated discussion as to the political role of different social groups and has no doubt influenced social and economic studies of the Fronde in Paris. Porchnev, *Les Soulèvements populaires en France de 1623 à 1648* (Paris, 1963). Flammarion published an abridged edition in 1972. See Mousnier's works, cited above, and Labatut, "Situation sociale du quartier du Marais pendant la Fronde parlementaire (1648–1649)," pp. 55–81; Bourgeon, "L'Ile de la Cité pendant la Fronde: Structure sociale," pp. 23–144. Goubert noted the fault of the traditional histories of the Fronde in ignoring social and economic behavior ("Ernst Kossmann et l'énigme de la Fronde," pp. 115–18).

Both of these strands—the conventional dichotomy of the two Frondes and the more innovative societal analyses—have understated the troubles the government encountered in Paris after the second Fronde.

3. The Treaty of Rueil, 1 April 1649, preserved the reforms wrung from the government in 1648 by the Chambre Saint-Louis, the union of the four sovereign courts of Paris (the Parlement, *chambre des comptes, cour des aides,* and *grand conseil*) that had initiated the Parlementary Fronde. Spurred by the financial crisis resulting from the continuation of the war against Spain, the Chambre Saint-Louis demanded the abolition of the office of intendant, the reduction of taxes, and an increase in the powers of the sovereign courts. Such reforms in effect stipulated a return to peacetime government.

4. Moote, *The Revolt of the Judges,* pp. 351–52; Bonney, "The French Civil War, 1649–53," p. 75.

5. See Westrich, *The Ormée of Bordeaux;* Kossmann, *La Fronde,* pp. 245–58.

6. Bonney, *Political Change in France,* pp. 229–37.

7. Porchnev, *Les Soulèvements populaires* (Flammarion edition), p. 40.

8. Dent, "An Aspect of the Crisis of the Seventeenth Century: The Collapse of the Financial Administration of the French Monarchy (1653–1661)," pp. 241–56.

9. On these assemblies and the revolt in Normandy, see below, chapter 1. Also, see Bonney, *Political Change in France,* pp. 313–17.

10. Kettering, *Judicial Politics and Urban Revolt in Seventeenth-Century Provence,* chapter 9; Pillorget, *Les Mouvements insurrectionnels,* book 2, chapter 3.

11. Méthivier, *Le Siècle de Louis XIII,* pp. 114–15.

12. Hamscher, *The Parlement of Paris after the Fronde,* chapters 4, 5, and conclusion.

13. It is interesting that the great nineteenth-century French historian Chéruel, in his nine-volume edition of Mazarin's letters, regularly omitted from the transcriptions references to the Parisian curés. Lowly curés did not seem significant to an age mesmerized by diplomacy and war.

14. It is quite possible that much material relating to the curés was in the archives of the Parisian archbishopric, consumed by fire in the nineteenth century. Also, many parish records were destroyed during the French Revolution and by the burning of the Hôtel de Ville in 1871.

15. Chantelauze was the first to use the term *Fronde ecclésiastique* to

describe Retz's opposition to the government after the Fronde of the Princes. Unfortunately, although he spent his scholarly life studying Retz, Chantelauze died before he could compose either a biography of the cardinal or his planned opus on the ecclesiastical Fronde. In his edition of Retz's works for the series *Les Grands écrivains de France*, Chantelauze did devote one volume to those documents related to the Religious Fronde. This collection clearly indicates that he conceived this last Fronde to be a quarrel between Retz and Mazarin, manifested in a war of pamphlets, pastoral letters, and briefs. On his interpretation of the ecclesiastical Fronde, see Chantelauze, *Le Cardinal de Retz et les Jansénistes*, p. 33; *Le Cardinal de Retz et ses missions diplomatiques à Rome*, pp. 6–7; *Saint Vincent de Paul et les Gondi*, pp. 74–75; and, as editor, Retz, *Oeuvres*, vol. 6. (The *Oeuvres* of Retz will be hereafter cited as G.E.F.)

Chantelauze drew much inspiration from the anonymous eighteenth-century *Histoire de la détention du cardinal de Retz*. Written from a parlementaire point of view, the *Histoire* claimed that government blunders had dominated Church-state relations during the 1650s. If the royal court had followed the process of law and allowed the Parlement of Paris to proceed with Retz's trial, the subsequent unfortunate events (which Chantelauze would term the ecclesiastical Fronde) could have been avoided. However, by keeping Retz in prison and by forcing him to resign as archbishop, the crown enabled Retz to picture himself as one unjustly persecuted by arbitrary power. As a consequence of continued government mistakes, bishops, curés, and populace took the side of Retz. The result was a long series of defeats and humiliations for the crown. [Le Paige and Du Rey de Meinières], *Histoire de la détention du cardinal de Retz*.

Champollion-Figeac (ed., *Complément des mémoires du cardinal de Retz*) covered the same period with a collection of primary materials that antedated Chantelauze's more thorough volume. And, while Chantelauze pursued his laborious research on the Religious Fronde, Gazier published his thesis on the years following the conclusion of Retz's memoirs, that is, after 1655. Gazier's view was similar to that of Chantelauze and so interpreted the period prior to 1662 as "the private Fronde of the cardinal de Retz" (*Les Dernières années du cardinal de Retz, 1655–1679*, p. 117). To Chantelauze, Gazier's work was not only incorrect at several points but also neglected to use sources, such as diplomatic correspondence, which Chantelauze deemed crucial ("Les Dernières années du cardinal de Retz" [review of Gazier's book], pp. 100–146). But Gazier's study and Chantelauze's criticisms proceeded from the same basic assumption, that the ecclesiastical Fronde centered on Retz. Everything and everyone else were important only as they impinged on the intrigues and adventures of the rebellious cardinal.

16. Labitte, *De la démocratie*, pp. 280–82; Feillet, *La Misère au temps de la Fronde*, pp. 418–22, 480–81; Jacquinet, *Des prédicateurs*, pp. 301–4.

17. Avenel, *Les Évêques et archevêques*, 1: 284; Hermant, *Mémoires*, 1: 521, 2: 131; Vallier, *Journal*, 1: 218–19.

18. "Suite chronologique des évêques et archevêques de Paris avec un abrégé de ce qui s'est passé de plus considérable pendant leur épisco-pat," B.N. Ms. Nouv. Acq. Fr. 1163, fol. 259.

19. Jourdain, *Histoire de l'université*, 1: 184.

20. Adam, *Du mysticisme à la révolte*, pp. 188–92; Chéruel, *Histoire de France sous le ministère de Mazarin*, 2: 32–33.

21. On the Contract of Poissy and the events leading up to it, see Blet, *Le Clergé de France*, 1: 141–48; Bourlon, *Les Assemblées du Clergé*, pp. 8–12; Olivier-Martin, *Histoire du droit français*, pp. 383–84. On the sixteenth-century General Assemblies, see also the concise account by Doucet, *Les Institutions de la France*, 2: 847–58.

22. For the financial system, see Cans, *L'Organisation financière du clergé*, pp. 157ff.; Serbat, *Les Assemblées du Clergé*, pp. 190ff.

23. Pierre Blet, "L'Ordre du clergé au XVIIe siècle," p. 16.

24. Blet, *Le Clergé de France*, 2: 47ff.; Cans, "Le Rôle politique de l'Assemblée du Clergé pendant la Fronde (1650–1651)," pp. 1–60; Moote, *The Revolt of the Judges*, pp. 294–97.

25. Information on the activities of clerics during the Fronde is widely dispersed. On those mentioned here as loyal to Mazarin, see Chéruel, *Histoire de France pendant la minorité de Louis XIV*, 4: 170–71, and *Histoire de France sous le ministère de Mazarin*, 1: 249, 317–18, 351, 2: 29–32; Hurel, *Les Orateurs sacrées*, 1: 16ff.; Robert, *Anthyme-Denis Cohon*, pp. 8ff.; Marca to Zongo Ondedei, 13 July 1652, A.A.E. France 883, fols. 162–63; Father Léon to Mazarin, 13 September 1652, A.A.E. France 884, fols. 314–16; Chérot, *La Première jeunesse de Louis XIV, passim*; Grand-Mesnil, *Mazarin, la Fronde et la presse, passim*.

26. Salmon, *Cardinal de Retz, passim*; Moreau, *Bibliographie des Maza-rinades, passim*; Dubois, *Henri de Pardaillon de Gondrin*, pp. 61ff.; Dethan, *Gaston d'Orléans, passim*.

27. Jean François Paul de Gondi, cardinal de Retz, *Mémoires*, p. 320. See also, pp. 136, 144, 149, 327. Historians have erred in utilizing such statements to verify the devotion of the curés, the parish priests, or the lower clergy to Retz's cause. Retz was referring simply to a few curés. See, for example Chéruel, *Histoire de France pendant la minorité de Louis XIV*, 3: 65, 132; and *Histoire de France sous le ministère de Mazarin*, 1: 356; Clément, ed., in Colbert, *Lettres, instructions, et mémoires*, 6: lv.

28. Conrart, *Mémoires*, pp. 575–76; Dulaure, *Histoire physique, civile et morale de Paris*, 3: 131.

29. Feillet, *La Misère au temps de la Fronde, passim*; Allier, *La Cabale des dévots*, p. 82.

30. Le Bras, "Paris, seconde capitale de la chrétienté," pp. 5–17.

31. Fosseyeux, "Les Revenues de l'Archevêché de Paris au XVIIe siècle," pp. 148–67.

32. Dubois, "La Carte des diocèses de France avant la Révolution," p. 680.

33. I counted 250 such "religious" Mazarinades during the period 1648–

33. Carrier, who is currently compiling a new bibliography of the Mazarinades, estimates the total number of Mazarinades as 5,000 ("Souvenirs de la Fronde en U.R.S.S.: Les Collections russes de Mazarinades," p. 27). On the most radical Mazarinades, see Golden, "Religious Extremism in the Mid-Seventeenth Century: The Parisian *Illuminés*," pp. 195–210.

34. Longnon, "L'Ancien diocèse de Paris et ses subdivisions," pp. 16–17.

35. Ferté, *La Vie religieuse*, p. 21.

36. Delumeau, *Le Catholicisme*, p. 54.

37. Ferté, *La Vie religieuse*, p. 22. See Le Bras, "Synodes et conciles parisiens," pp. 35–46.

38. There are some parishes, chapels, encompassing certain persons but no territory (Jousse, *Traité du gouvernement spirituel et temporel des paroisses*, pp. 1–2).

39. There was a distinction between the curé as such and *curés primitifs*, who kept the title but who did not function as curés when the cure was tied to a chapter or a priory. In the latter case, the one who performed the sacerdotal functions was known canonically as the *vicaire perpétuel* or the *vicaire en chef*. For practical purposes, it is suitable to label as curés those designated as such by their parishioners. That is, the curés were those who administered to the spiritual well-being of their flock. See Doucet, *Les Institutions de la France*, 2: 749; Goubert, *L'Ancien Régime*, 2: 171.

40. Jousse, *Traité du gouvernement spirituel et temporel des paroisses*, pp. 6, 268ff.

41. Ferté, *La Vie religieuse*, pp. 58–63; Crousaz-Crétit, *Paris sous Louis XIV*, 2: 12–15. The parish might also have a special priest to hold the principal crucifix and others to attend funerals and to sing all the offices.

42. Martimort, *Le Gallicanisme*, pp. 5–6; and "Comment les français du XVIIe siècle voyaient le pape," pp. 86–87.

43. Willaert, *Après le concile de Trente*, p. 369. For an interesting view of Gallicanism in a European setting, see Bouwsma, "Gallicanism and the Nature of Christianity," pp. 809–30.

44. These traditional categories ignore the Gallicanism of the lower clergy. Judge argues that there were only two Gallicanisms (of the Parlement and of the Sorbonne, the latter adhered to by many prelates). There was no royal Gallicanism because monarchical policy was opportunistic and not based on distinct theory. ("Louis XIV and the Church," pp. 245–46.)

45. Marion, *Dictionnaire des institutions de la France*, p. 21.

46. Blet argues that there was a streak of Gallicanism among French Jesuits throughout the century, particularly with regard to the king's independence and sole authority in temporal affairs ("Jésuites Gallicans au XVIIe siècle?" pp. 55–84).

47. Cynthia Dent, "Changes in the Episcopal Structure of the Church of France in the 17th Century as an Aspect of Bourbon State-Building," pp. 214–15.

48. Blond, *La Maison professe des Jésuites*, pp. 99–100.

CHAPTER ONE

1. Léon Aubineau, editor of the Jesuit Rapin's memoirs, noted that in the seventeenth century, "la dévotion du peuple de Paris, si ardente au temps de la Ligue, était encore célèbre et vivante. C'était une puissance et une force avec laquelle il fallait compter. Quelques-uns des curés sans doute employèrent au bien l'influence que leur donnait ce sentiment populaire." (Rapin, *Mémoires*, 1: xxv.)

2. "Interdit," *Dictionnaire de droit canonique*, 5: cols. 1466–67. Chantelauze, for example, believed that an interdict on Paris would have resulted in an uprising, Mazarin's exile, and Retz's return (Chantelauze, *Saint Vincent de Paul et les Gondi*, pp. 344–45).

3. For example, the fervor of the parishioners of Saint-Paul for Nicolas Mazure was well demonstrated when they protested his exile and helped secure his return following a bitter conflict between Mazure and the Jesuits. Marlin, curé of the greatest parish in Paris, Saint-Eustache, was notorious for the affection and zeal he inspired among the common people (Chérot, *La Première jeunesse de Louis XIV*, pp. 60–61). Kossmann (*La Fronde*, p. 111) notes that the populace constituted the dynamic element during the Fronde. Without their support, no group could forcefully express its discontent.

4. Ranum, *Richelieu and the Councillors of Louis XIII*; Julian Dent, "The Role of Clientèles in the Financial Elite of France under Cardinal Mazarin," pp. 41–69; Lefebvre, "Aspects de la 'fidélité' en France au XVIIe siècle: Le Cas des agents des princes de Condé," pp. 59–106; Mousnier, "Les Concepts d' 'ordres', d' 'états', de 'fidélité' et de 'monarchie absolue' en France de la fin du XVe siècle à la fin du XVIIIe siècle," pp. 289–312; Mousnier, *Les Institutions de la France*, pp. 85–93. None of these authors have ventured to study clientage within the First Estate.

5. Treuvé, *Histoire de monsieur Duhamel*, pp. 102ff. This work of Jansenist hagiography is buttressed by the account of Duhamel's *vicaire*: Matthieu Feydeau, "Mémoires pour servir à la vie de Mr Feydeau . . . ," B.M. Ms. 2486, fols. 146ff.

6. Paul Beurrier, in implementing reforms upon his accession to the cure of Saint-Etienne-du-Mont, found one group of parish priests opposed to any change (Ferté, "Saint-Etienne-du-Mont à la mi-XVIIe siècle. Mémoires d'un curé génovéfain" [Memoirs of Paul Beurrier], pp. xxvi–xxvii, 37ff. Hereafter cited as Beurrier, "Memoirs"). Pierre Gargan witnessed the same mentality among the priests of Saint-Médard when he introduced reform (Brongniart, *La Paroisse Saint-Médard*, p. 59).

7. There were thirty to forty ecclesiastics in the parish of Saint-Etienne-du-Mont and about fifty at Saint-Gervais (Beurrier, "Memoirs," p. 29; Brochard, *Saint-Gervais*, p. 273). Saint-Germain-l'Auxerrois had fifty to sixty *prêtres-habitués*, while Saint-Eustache had approximately one hundred. Saint-Sulpice had three hundred clergymen, more than any other parish (Crousaz-Crétit, *Paris sous Louis XIV*, 2: 16). Admittedly, these were some of the larger

parishes; many, especially those on the *cité*, were quite small. That of Saint-Josse, for example, included only twenty-nine homes and Saint-Marine had only twenty. Ten houses were sufficient to constitute a parish (Lebeuf, *Histoire de la ville et de tout le diocèse de Paris*, 1: 305; Bourgeon, "L'Ile de la Cité," p. 39; Jousse, *Traité du gouvernement spirituel et temporel des paroisses*, p. 2).

8. Hermant, *Mémoires*, 4: 259.

9. Ibid., 1: 659.

10. Mazarin to Le Tellier, 3 December 1652, G.E.F., 6: 451–56.

11. Moote, *The Revolt of the Judges*, pp. 223–25.

12. Chantelauze, *Le Cardinal de Retz et l'affaire du chapeau*, 1: 477.

13. On Mazarin's fears in late 1652 of an impending merger of the forces of Retz and Condé, see his letters to Abel Servien, 7 October 1652, Mazarin, *Lettres*, 5: 358; to Le Tellier, 19 November and 18 December 1652, ibid., 5: 463, 509; and to abbé Basile Fouquet, 19 December 1652, in Chantelauze, *Le Cardinal de Retz et l'affaire du chapeau*, 2: 310–11.

14. Guy Joly, *Mémoires*, p. 85.

15. Mazarin to Le Tellier, 3 December 1652, G.E.F., 6: 453–54.

16. Chantelauze forcefully asserted that Retz's arrest transgressed the terms of the amnesty (G.E.F., 6: xvii; *Saint Vincent de Paul et les Gondi*, p. 339). On the amnesty, see Chéruel, *Histoire de France sous le ministère de Mazarin*, 1: 359–60.

17. Retz, *Mémoires*, p. 768.

18. Lorris, *Le Cardinal de Retz*, pp. 203–4; Salmon, *Cardinal de Retz*, pp. 232–33; Batiffol, *Biographie du cardinal de Retz*, p. 121; Vallier, *Journal*, 4: 145–46; Chantelauze, *Saint Vincent de Paul et les Gondi*, pp. 346ff.

19. Retz, *Mémoires*, p. 770.

20. Rapin, *Mémoires*, 1: 522; Retz, *Mémoires*, pp. 47, 770; Talon, *Mémoires*, p. 515; Guy Joly, *Mémoires*, p. 86; Claude Joly, *Mémoires*, p. 165; Vallier, *Journal*, 4: 140.

21. Claude Auvry, bishop of Coutances, to Mazarin, 19 December 1652, A.A.E. France 886, fol. 244; Anonymous to Condé, 24 December 1652, ibid., fol. 290; Guy Joly, *Mémoires*, p. 86.

22. Accounts of this delegation are numerous. See, in particular, Vallier, *Journal*, 4: 140ff.; the recitation in the *Gazette* of 21 December, in G.E.F., 6: 465–66; Talon, *Mémoires*, p. 515; Anonymous to M. de la Rochefoucauld, 21 December 1652, A.A.E. France 886, fol. 267; Le Serviteur to Mazarin, 22 December 1652, ibid., fol. 285; Hermant, *Mémoires*, 1: 665. The court was aware of the archbishop's singular importance in conserving calm in Paris and was attentive to his behavior. See Le Tellier to Mazarin, 20, 28, and 30 December 1652, A.A.E. France 886, fols. 258, 336, 346; Mazarin to Le Tellier, 15 January 1653, Mazarin, *Lettres*, 5: 540.

23. On the 21 December deputation by the university, see Batiffol, *Biographie du cardinal de Retz*, p. 123; Chéruel, *Histoire de France sous le ministère de Mazarin*, 1: 389; Hermant, *Mémoires*, 1: 665–66; Jourdain,

Histoire de l'université, 1: 185–87; and, especially, the rector's report, ibid., 1: pièces justificatives, 88–89.

24. Vallier, *Journal*, 4: 142–43. The government's concern over the seditious behavior of Loisel and Duhamel was evident in Le Tellier's letters to Mazarin, 20 and 30 December, A.A.E. France 886, fols. 255, 346.

25. Cited in Rapin, *Mémoires*, 1: 518.

26. Ibid.

27. For example, Paulin, the king's Jesuit confessor, strongly approved the incarceration of Retz (Paulin to Mazarin, 25 December 1652, A.A.E. France 886, fols. 810–11).

28. "Registre et livre de ce qui a esté fait, résolu et arresté en la compagnie et assemblée de Messieurs les curez de la ville, faulxbourgs et banlieue de Paris depuis le synode de l'année 1653," B.N. Ms. Fr. 24075, fols. 55–56; Rousse, "Relation de ce qui s'est passé en l'assemblée de Messieurs les Curez de Paris le lundi 9 Iuin 1653, et au Conseil du Roy le mercredi d'après au sujet d'icelle," in Saint-Amour, *Journal*, pp. 542–46.

29. The bishops were summoned by the agent-general of the clergy, abbé Bernard Marmiesse, later bishop of Conserans, who supported Retz and upheld the curés in their campaign against the Jesuits' moral theology. Marmiesse exemplified a familiar pattern of the 1650s: clerics who favored Retz and the curés were antagonistic to both court and Jesuits. On the assembly, see Vallier, *Journal*, 4: 158 n.; Marca to Mazarin, 9 January 1653, B.N. Ms. Baluze 113, fol. 5.

30. Marca's speech of 9 January is in Duranthon, *Collection des procès-verbaux*, 4: pièces justificatives, 9–10; and in B.N. Ms. Baluze 113, fols. 2–5. For a description by an observer, see the letter by the bishop of Coutances to Mazarin, 9 January 1653, ibid., fol. 2. Marca's biographer feels that he sincerely defended ecclesiastical immunities in his speech (Gaquère, *Pierre de Marca*, pp. 279–82).

31. Marca to Mazarin, 9 January 1653, B.N. Ms. Baluze 113, fols. 7–9.

32. Guy Joly, *Mémoires*, p. 91. Mazarin's fears were not unfounded. An anonymous memorandum in the government's files reporting on the confession of one of Condé's officers proved the continual functioning of the prince's agents in Paris (5 January 1653, A.A.E. France 891, fols. 5–6). For the persistence of Mazarin's anxiety in 1653 over a merger of the forces of Condé and Retz, see his letters to M. de Febert of 12 March, 23 March, and 6 April, Mazarin, *Lettres*, 5: 574, 583, 593; and to abbé Fouquet, 27 November, ibid., 6: 97–99.

33. Korr, *Cromwell and the New Model Foreign Policy*, p. 81; Kleinman, "Belated Crusaders: Religious Fears in Anglo-French Diplomacy 1654–1655," p. 36.

34. For Mazarin's earlier relations with Innocent X, see Coville, *Etudes sur Mazarin*; Pastor, *The History of the Popes*, 30: 48ff.

35. Retz, *Mémoires*, p. 775. The same remark was noted by Guy Joly (*Mémoires*, p. 91).

36. Jansen, *Le Cardinal Mazarin*, pp. 36–37.

37. G.E.F., 6: xix, 471–72; Hermant, *Mémoires*, 2: 107; Rapin, *Mémoires*, 1: 509, 524.

38. Vallier, *Journal*, 4: 185–86; Henri-Auguste de Loménie, comte de Brienne, *Mémoires*, p. 145.

39. This is the theme of Jansen's *Le Cardinal Mazarin* (pp. 20, 193).

40. Valençay, for one, recognized the union of Jansenists and Retz as explosive. See his letters to Mazarin and Brienne, 3 February 1653, in Jansen, *Le Cardinal Mazarin*, pp. 197–200.

41. Ceyssens, *La Fin de la première période du jansénisme*, 1: v.

42. For the attitudes of Innocent, Mazarin, Anne, and the Jesuits toward the condemnation of Jansenism, see Ceyssens, "Les Cinq propositions de Jansénius à Rome," pp. 453–55.

43. Lorris, *Le Cardinal de Retz*, p. 213. Even as late as January 1654, the pope expressed bewilderment that the French government could have arrested Retz without fear of incurring excommunications and censures (bishop of Lodève to Mazarin, 4 January 1654, A.A.E. Rome 126, fol. 4).

44. 27 August 1653, B.N. Ms. Baluze 113, fols. 34–38.

45. Bishop of Coutances to Mazarin, 24 November 1653, A.A.E. France 891, fol. 340; anonymous to Mazarin, 14 December 1653, ibid., fol. 358. On Mazarin's concern over the impending vacancy, see his letter to abbé Fouquet, 18 November 1653, Mazarin, *Lettres*, 6: 87–88.

46. The death of the archbishop and events immediately subsequent to it captured the attention of contemporaries. Firsthand reports are therefore numerous and minutely detailed. See, for example, Claude Joly, *Mémoires*, p. 166; Guy Joly, *Mémoires*, pp. 92–93; Hermant, *Mémoires*, 2: 450–52; Rapin, *Mémoires*, 2: 218–23; Robert François d'Aigreville, "Histoire de l'assemblée générale du clergé de France commencée à Paris le 25 octobre 1655 et clore le 23 may 1657," A.N. G^{8}655A, fols. 60–61.

47. *Arrêt du Conseil d'état*, 21 March 1654, B.M. Ms. 2246, no. 5. An *économe* was either a cleric or a layman chosen by the king to administer the revenues of a vacant see.

48. *Arrêt de la chambre des comptes*, 18 April 1654, in G.E.F., 6: 502–4. This edict effected the seizure of the revenues of the archdiocese under the pretext that Retz had not offered the requisite oath.

49. Blet, *Le Clergé de France*, 2: 123.

50. *Prise de possession de l'archeveschè de Paris, par monseigneur l'eminentissime cardinal de Retz, passim.*

51. Memorandum from Marca to Mazarin, 7 April 1654, B.N. Ms. Baluze 113, fols. 44–50.

52. B.N. Ms. Fr. 24075, fols. 107–13.

53. Retz, *Mémoires*, p. 780.

54. Nicolas Mazure, *Oraison funèbre de feu messire Jean François de Gondy premier archevesque de Paris*, pp. 26–27.

55. Guy Joly, *Mémoires*, p. 93. In fact, relations with former frondeurs and

with Condé were renewed (see the letters from Condé to the duc de Noirmoutier, 7 April 1654, G.E.F., 6: 504–5; and from the duc de Noirmoutier to Condé, April 1654, ibid., 6: 505–6).

56. Camille de Neufville, archbishop of Lyon, was tied to Retz and had promised to support the interdict in his quality of primate of the Gauls (G.E.F., 6: xxi–xxii).

57. On the threat of an interdict and on Retz's refusal to take that enormous step, see Rapin, *Mémoires*, 2: 223; Guy Joly, *Mémoires*, p. 93; [Le Paige and Du Rey de Meinières], *Histoire de la détention du cardinal de Retz*, pp. 8–9; Salmon, *Cardinal de Retz*, p. 242; and the major works of Chantelauze: *Le Cardinal de Retz et les Jansénistes*, p. 31; *Saint Vincent de Paul et les Gondi*, pp. 344–45; *Le Cardinal de Retz et ses missions diplomatiques à Rome*, p. 5; G.E.F., 6: xxi–xxii.

58. Jourdain, *Histoire de l'université*, 1: 192.

59. G.E.F., 6: 500–502.

60. "M. le cardinal Mazarin, qui avait pris une frayeur mortelle des curés et des confesseurs de Paris, et qui, par cette considération, brûlait d'impatience de finir [i.e., to have Retz resign]" (Retz, *Mémoires*, p. 785).

61. On Retz's attempted resignation and the pope's reaction, see Claude Joly, *Mémoires*, p. 167; Guy Joly, *Mémoires*, pp. 97–98; Retz, *Mémoires*, pp. 781–90; Pastor, *The History of the Popes*, 30: 70; Lorris, *Le Cardinal de Retz*, pp. 219–29; Salmon, *Cardinal de Retz*, pp. 242–46.

62. Guy Joly, *Mémoires*, p. 105.

63. Retz, *Mémoires*, p. 793. Cf. Motteville, *Mémoires*, p. 444.

64. Abbé Antoine Arnauld, *Mémoires*, p. 539.

65. Séguier to Mazarin, 14 August 1654, B.N. Ms. Baluze 113, fol. 56. For the Parlement's agitation over *rentes* in 1653 and 1654, see Hamscher, *The Parlement of Paris after the Fronde*, pp. 72–75. For a discussion of *rentes* on the Hôtel de Ville in the seventeenth century, see also Dent, *Crisis in Finance*, pp. 46–54.

66. Chéruel, *Histoire de France sous le ministère de Mazarin*, 2: 204.

67. Knachel, *England and the Fronde*, pp. 270–71.

68. Chéruel, ed., Mazarin, *Lettres*, 6: i–vii.

69. Mazarin to M. d'Estrades, 14 August 1654, Mazarin, *Lettres*, 6: 270; Mazarin to Servien, 16 August 1654, ibid., 6: 278. For Mazarin's precautionary measures, including his reprisals against Retz's family, see also Knachel, *England and the Fronde*, p. 270; Chéruel, *Histoire de France sous le ministère de Mazarin*, 2: 207–8; Lorris, *Le Cardinal de Retz*, p. 247; Hermant, *Mémoires*, 2: 589.

70. Ranum, *Paris in the Age of Absolutism*, p. 201.

71. Hamscher, *The Parlement of Paris after the Fronde*, p. 75.

72. Laurain-Portemer, "Opposition et propagande à Paris au temps du sacre de Louis XIV," pp. 259–60.

73. Mousnier, "The Fronde," pp. 157–58.

74. Koenigsberger, "Revolutionary Conclusions," p. 395. In this article

Koenigsberger suggests the need to study societies in which revolutions did not occur.

75. The resignation and letters are in G.E.F., 6: 2–6.

76. "Response du Chapitre de Nostre Dame à la lettre du Card. de Retz par laquelle ils mandent qu'ils ont fait chanter le Te Deum de sa sortie," 14 August 1654, B.N. Ms. Fr. 15626, fol. 65.

77. On the formulation of government policy during August 1654 and on the ministers' anxiety in the face of clerical protests, see Mazarin to Séguier, 16 August, Mazarin, *Lettres*, 6: 278; Mazarin to the *surintendants* (Nicolas Fouquet and Servien), 16 August, ibid., 6: 279–80; Mazarin to Servien, 16 August, ibid., 6: 275–76; Mazarin to abbé Fouquet, 22 August, ibid., 6: 291–93; Servien to Mazarin, 21 August, with marginal notes by Mazarin, ibid., 6: 296–301; Mazarin to abbé Fouquet, 24 August, ibid., 6: 301–3; Mazarin to Brachet, 24 August, ibid., 6: 305–7; Mazarin to abbé Fouquet, 27 August, ibid., 6: 309–11; Séguier to Mazarin, 14 August, B.N. Ms. Baluze 113, fols. 56–57; Séguier to Mazarin, 15 August, ibid., fol. 58; Séguier to Mazarin, 15 August, ibid., fols. 58–59; Colbert to Mazarin, 22 August, Colbert, *Lettres, instructions, et mémoires*, 1: 227; Séguier to Mazarin, 23, 25, 26, 30, 31 August and 3 September, in Champollion-Figeac, *Complément des mémoires du cardinal de Retz*, pp. 500–505. These letters reflect the immediate concern of the government to excoriate ecclesiastical dissidence; but see Marca's learned and more reflective appraisal of this turmoil in his memoranda given to Mazarin on 22 August and to Séguier on 23 August in B.N. Ms. Baluze 113, fols. 50–55, 60–62.

78. Séguier to Mazarin, 14 August 1654, B.N. Ms. Baluze 113, fol. 56.

79. G.E.F., 6: 526–35.

80. Mazarin to Fouquet, 22 August 1654, Mazarin, *Lettres*, 6: 291; Mazarin to Servien, 23 or 24 August 1654, ibid., 6: 296–301.

81. G.E.F., 6: 535.

82. Aubineau, "Les Grands-vicaires du cardinal de Retz," 2: 506.

83. Séguier to Mazarin, 25 August 1654, in Champollion-Figeac, *Complément des mémoires du cardinal de Retz*, p. 501. Séguier repeated these same sentiments on 26 August, ibid., p. 502.

84. G.E.F., 6: xxv, 538–39.

85. Ibid., 6: xxv–xxvi, 540–42; Aubineau, "Les Grands-vicaires du cardinal de Retz," 2: 506; Guy Joly, *Mémoires*, pp. 108–9; Hermant, *Mémoires*, 2: 576–80.

86. Anonymous to Retz, 3 September 1654, B.N. Ms. Baluze 113, fols. 73–74.

87. Séguier to Mazarin, 31 August 1654, in Champollion-Figeac, *Complément des mémoires du cardinal de Retz*, p. 503.

88. Séguier to Mazarin, 3 September 1654, ibid., pp. 504–5; G.E.F., 6: 542–43.

89. *Discours sur ce qui est arrivé dans l'église de Paris, après la sortie de monsieur le cardinal de Retz de Nantes, avec la décision de la question si le*

*chapitre de Paris a pu prendre la juridiction et nommer des grands vicaires,
passim.*

90. Jourdain, *Histoire de l'université*, 1: 192.

91. The letter was published as *Lettre de monseigneur l'eminentissime
cardinal de Retz archevesque de Paris, escrite à messieurs les curez de Paris*. It
was inscribed in the 13 August 1654 register of the assemblies of the curés
(B.N. Ms. Fr. 24075, fol. 143).

92. B.N. Ms. Fr. 24075, fols. 143–45. The letter from the curés to Retz is in
A.A.E. France 1593, fols. 226–27.

93. Séguier to Mazarin, 14 August 1654, B.N. Ms. Baluze 113, fol. 56.

94. Séguier to Mazarin, 15 August 1654, ibid., fol. 58.

95. Bishop of Coutances to Mazarin, cited in Laurain-Portemer, "Opposition et propagande," p. 258.

96. For example, Mazarin had instructed his agent, the Franciscan Jean-
Dominique Ithier, to remain in Bordeaux after the failure of the Ormée
rebellion because he was a noted preacher with much influence over the
townsmen (Mazarin to Father Ithier, 31 August 1653, Mazarin, *Lettres*, 6:
12–13). On the importance of propaganda in this society, see Klaits, *Printed
Propaganda under Louis XIV*, chapter 1.

97. *Journal inédit d'un Parisien au temps de la Fronde*, G.E.F., 6: 512–13.

98. For the first minister's complicity in the use of harsh measures against
the curés, see his letters to Servien, 16 August 1654, Mazarin, *Lettres*, 6: 276;
to Fouquet, 22 August 1654, ibid., 6: 292; and to Servien, 23 or 24 August
1654, ibid., 6: 301.

99. Hermant, *Mémoires*, 2: 587. Loisel continued to provide for his parish
of Saint-Jean-en-Grève throughout his exile. See his letter to Vincent de Paul,
17 April 1659, in Vincent de Paul, *Correspondance, entretiens, documents*, 7:
495–96.

100. Servien to Mazarin, 21 August 1654, Mazarin, *Lettres*, 6: 301.

101. Mazarin to abbé Fouquet, 24 August 1654, ibid., 6: 301–2; Mazarin
to abbé Fouquet, 27 August 1654, ibid., 6: 309–10.

102. "Mémoire de ce qui s'est passé à St. Mederic le quinziesme et seiziesme
d'aoust 1654," A.A.E. France 1593, fols. 230–31; Rapin, *Mémoires*, 2: 232,
283–84.

103. Hermant, *Mémoires*, 2: 573–74; B.N. Ms. Fr. 24075, fols. 147–49.

104. Séguier to Mazarin, 23 August 1654, in Champollion-Figeac, *Complément des mémoires du cardinal de Retz*, pp. 500–501.

105. Memorandum from Marca to Mazarin, 22 August 1654, B.N. Ms.
Baluze 113, fol. 62.

106. B.N. Ms. Fr. 24075, fols. 152–56; Hermant, *Mémoires*, 2: 580–81.

107. Mazarin to abbé Fouquet, 24 August 1654, Mazarin, *Lettres*, 6: 302.

108. Chéruel, ed., Mazarin, *Lettres*, 6: 278n.

109. Cited in Rapin, *Mémoires*, 2: 283.

110. Ibid.

111. Hermant, *Mémoires*, 2: 581–82.

NOTES TO PAGES 42–46

112. Duhamel did not return to Paris until 1664. A broken man, this Jansenist and former friend of Saint-Cyran was compelled to sign the Formulary and so was ostracized by his Jansenist friends. Unpopular and unable to function effectively, Duhamel resigned his cure in 1666. (Ibid., 582–84; Treuvé, *Histoire de Monsieur Duhamel, passim.*)

113. Feydeau, "Mémoires," B.M. Ms. 2486, fols. 149–50.

114. Rapin, *Mémoires*, 2: 285. Cf. Hermant, *Mémoires*, 2: 582.

115. B.N. Ms. Fr. 24075, fols. 157–60.

116. These documents are in G.E.F., 6: 545–51.

117. Marca, "De la conciliation des deux authoritez ecclesiastique et seculaire pour la punition du crime de leze majesté commis par un cardinal ou un evesque," B.N. Ms. Baluze 113, fols. 65–67; Marca, "Mémoire pour deffendre les immunitez de l'Eglise," 27 September 1654, ibid., fols. 80–82.

118. Marca to Mazarin, 26 September 1654, ibid., fol. 78; G.E.F., 6: 551. On this controversy, see also Mazarin to Marca, 29 September 1654, B.N. Ms. Baluze 113, fol. 80; Marca to Mazarin (two letters), 10 October 1654, ibid., fols. 82–84; Mazarin to Marca, 16 October 1654, ibid., fol. 84; Marca to Mazarin, 20 October 1654, ibid., fol. 87; Relation of a conference held in Séguier's home, 20 October 1654, ibid., fols. 89–96.

119. *Arrêt du conseil d'état*, 22 October 1654, B.M. Ms. 2246, no. 10.

120. Blet, *Le Clergé de France*, 2: 231–32. The *arrêt* of 26 April 1657 is in G.E.F., 6: 641–43.

121. G.E.F., 6: 553–54, 559–62.

122. "De Monsieur de Toulouse à Paris, le mois de novembre 1654, donné à M. de Lionne envoyé à Rome par le roi," in *Recueil des instructions données aux ambassadeurs et ministres de France*, ed. Hanotaux, pp. 22–35.

123. G.E.F., 6: 563–68.

124. On Lionne's mission in Rome and on the papacy's role in the events of the Religious Fronde in 1655 and 1656, see Valfrey, *Hugues de Lionne*, pp. 163–352; Gérin, "La Mission de M. de Lionne à Rome en 1655," pp. 5–90. The latter work is more critical of Lionne's accomplishments.

125. G.E.F., 6: 710.

126. Ibid., 6: 25–71. Cf. Claude Joly, *Mémoires*, pp. 170–74.

127. Curé of Saint-Barthélemy to Mazarin, A.A.E. France 895, fol. 75.

128. Mazarin to Lionne, 20 May 1655, Mazarin, *Lettres*, 6: 475–76; Mazarin to Lionne, 17 June 1655, ibid., 6: 484–85.

129. Retz, *Mémoires*, pp. 849ff. Retz proudly indicated in his 22 May 1655 letter to the chapter of Notre-Dame that "I received from the hands of His Holiness the plenitude of the archiepiscopal power through the pallium" (G.E.F., 6: 108–9).

130. *Ordonnance du Roi, portant défense aux sujets de Sa Majesté de demeurer près du cardinal de Retz et d'entretenir aucune correspondance avec lui, soit par lettre ou autrement*, 16 April 1655, G.E.F., 6: 570–71.

131. *Lettre de Monseigneur l'Eminentissime cardinal de Retz, archevêque de Paris, écrite à Messieurs les doyen, chanoines et Chapitre de l'Eglise de*

Paris, 22 May 1655, G.E.F., 6: 92–109; Guy Joly, *Mémoires*, p. 123.

132. *Considérations sur une lettre du cardinal de Retz, écrite à messieurs les doyen, chanoines et chapitre de l'église de Paris.*

133. Séguier to Brienne, 14 June 1655, B.N. Ms. Baluze 115, fol. 104.

134. Séguier to Brienne, 17 June 1655, ibid., fol. 6.

135. Hermant, *Mémoires*, 2: 676–79; Brienne to Séguier, 18 June 1655, A.A.E. France 895, fol. 134. Throughout June, Brienne urged Séguier to act harshly and decisively with respect to the problem of the vicars-general. See his letter to the chancellor of 27 June 1655, A.A.E. France 895, fols. 156–57. Brienne was writing from La Fère on Mazarin's behalf.

136. Curé of Saint-Barthélemy to Servien, 20 June 1655, B.I. Ms. 1315, fols. 159–64.

137. Mazarin to Lionne, 17 June 1655, Mazarin, *Lettres*, 6: 488.

138. Séguier to Brienne, 21 June 1655, B.N. Ms. Baluze 115, fol. 23.

139. Servien to Mazarin, 20 June 1655, B.N. Ms. Baluze 113, fol. 111.

140. Séguier to Mazarin, 21 June 1655, ibid., fol. 112.

141. Séguier to Brienne, 30 June 1655, B.N. Ms. Baluze 115, fol. 8.

142. Hermant, *Mémoires*, 2: 679; Guy Joly, *Mémoires*, p. 124; Claude Joly, *Mémoires*, p. 176.

143. Hermant, *Mémoires*, 2: 682.

144. Brienne to Séguier, 3 July 1655, A.A.E. France 895, fol. 166; Séguier to Brienne, 5 July 1655, B.N. Ms. Baluze 115, fol. 25.

145. *Procès-verbal de Quilebeuf, huissier du conseil, contenant le commandement fait de la part du roi aux curés de Paris de ne recevoir aucun ordre de la part de M. le cardinal de Retz*, 5 July 1655, G.E.F., 6: 575–76; Séguier to Mazarin, 7 July 1655, A.A.E. Rome 128, fol. 44; Hermant, *Mémoires*, 2: 682.

146. B.N. Ms. Fr. 24075, fol. 161.

147. Hermant, *Mémoires*, 2: 684–85.

148. Séguier to Le Tellier, 10 July 1655, B.N. Ms. Baluze 113, fol. 117.

149. "Sentence du prévot de Paris, contre le sieur Chassebras, vicaire général du cardinal de Retz," B.M. Ms. 2246.

150. Séguier to Le Tellier, 7 August 1655, B.N. Ms. Baluze 113, fol. 118.

151. Séguier to Brienne, 16 August 1655, B.N. Ms. Baluze 115, fol. 13.

152. Séguier to Le Tellier, 24 August 1655, B.N. Ms. Baluze 113, fol. 119. Later Mazarin learned that Chassebras had allegedly withdrawn to Mazure's residence before leaving Paris, having been reinforced in his disobedience by the curé of Saint-Paul (anonymous to Mazarin, 28 September 1655, A.A.E. France 895, fols. 307–8).

153. Anonymous letter, August (?) 1655, A.A.E. Rome 128, fol. 232.

154. Brienne to Séguier, 23 August 1655, A.A.E. France 895, fols. 281–82.

155. Mazarin to Lionne, 19 August 1655, Mazarin, *Lettres*, 7: 60.

156. Claude Joly, *Mémoires*, p. 127.

157. *Mandement de Monseigneur l'Eminentissime cardinal de Retz, archevêque de Paris*, 28 June 1655, G.E.F., 6: 114.

158. *Mandement de Jean-Baptiste Chassebras, grand vicaire du cardinal de Rets*, 28 July 1655, G.E.F., 6: 582.

159. Claude Joly, *Mémoires*, p. 177.

160. Séguier to Brienne, 16 August 1655, B.N. Ms. Baluze 115, fol. 13. Cf. curé of Saint-Barthélemy to Mazarin, 14 August 1655, A.A.E. France 895, fols. 251–54.

161. *Monition*, 8 September 1655, G.E.F., 6: 583–86.

162. Bishop of Lodève to Mazarin, 27 September 1655, B.N. Ms. Baluze 113, fol. 122; Daubray (the *lieutenant civil*) to Mazarin, 27 September 1655, A.A.E. France 1593, fols. 305–6; G.E.F., 6: 588–90.

163. Hermant, *Mémoires*, 2: 686.

164. G.E.F., 6: 594–96; Blet, *Le Clergé de France*, 2: 128; Claude Joly, *Mémoires*, pp. 177–78. The suffragan bishops of the archbishop of Paris were those of Orléans, Chartres, and Meaux (and, in 1687, Blois).

165. *Mandement du cardinal de Retz, contre MM. Cohon, ancien évêque de Dol, et Claude Auvry, évêque de Coutances*, 25 August 1655, G.E.F., 6: 117–19; Hermant, *Mémoires*, 2: 672, 703–5; Claude Joly, *Mémoires*, pp. 174, 178; Saint-Gilles, *Le Journal de M. de Saint-Gilles*, pp. 53–54; Robert, *Anthyme-Denis Cohon*, p. 44.

166. *Avis sincère d'un évêque pieux et désintéressé envoyez au C. de Retz*, pp. 104–7.

167. *Aux fidèles du diocèse de Paris*, p. 3.

168. Guy Joly, *Mémoires*, pp. 125–27.

169. *Ordonnance de Mgr. l'Arch. de Rouen contre Mgr. l'Ev. de Coutances*, 18 September 1655, in Duranthon, *Collection des procès-verbaux*, 4: pièces justificatives, 20.

170. Séguier to Mazarin, 26 September 1655, B.N. Ms. Baluze 113, fols. 120–21; "Mémoire envoyé de la part du Roy à M. le Chancelier touchant l'affaire de M. l'Evesque de Coutances," 27 September 1655, ibid., fols. 124–26; *Conseil du roi* to Séguier, 28 September 1655, ibid., fols. 127–28; Séguier to Mazarin, 3 October 1655, ibid., fols. 131–32; Mazarin to the bishop of Coutances, 27 September 1655, Mazarin, *Lettres*, 7: 94–95.

171. Archbishop of Rouen to anonymous, 1655, A.A.E. Rome 128, fol. 226.

172. D'Aigreville, A.N. G⁸655A, fols. 125ff.; Blet, *Le Clergé de France*, 2: 129–33; [Le Paige and Du Rey de Meinières], *Histoire de la détention du cardinal de Retz*, p. 40.

173. These documents of Chassebras are in G.E.F., 6: 591ff.

174. Claude Joly, *Mémoires*, cited in G.E.F., 6: xxxviii.

175. G.E.F., 6: 600–601.

176. Brienne to Mazarin, 26 November 1655, B.N. Ms. Baluze 113, fols. 142–43; Servien to Mazarin, 26 November 1655, B.N. Ms. Baluze 115, fol. 27; Mazarin to Brienne, 27 November 1655, Mazarin, *Lettres*, 7: 153.

177. Bishop of Coutances to Mazarin, 27 November 1655, B.N. Ms. Baluze 115, fol. 31. Cf. d'Aigreville, A.N. G⁸655A, fols. 175ff.

178. Brienne to Mazarin, 28 November 1655, B.N. Ms. Baluze 115, fols. 35–36.

179. Servien to Mazarin, 1 December 1655, ibid., fol. 39.

180. Curé of Saint-Barthélemy to Mazarin, 7 December 1655, B.I. Ms. 1315, fol. 431. Detested by his colleagues for his servility to the court, Roullé had recently been attacked by men loyal to Retz. After this episode, the government offered the curé protection (Servien to Mazarin, 1 December 1655, B.N. Ms. Baluze 115, fol. 39).

181. Mazarin to the queen, 30 November 1655, Mazarin, *Lettres*, 7: 162; Mazarin to Brienne, 30 November 1655, ibid., 7: 162–63; Mazarin to Ondedei, December 1655, B.N. Ms. Baluze 113, fol. 147.

182. G.E.F., 6: 135–36. Chéruel, who favored the "establishment" and disliked what he considered to be forces of disorder, noted on Du Saussay's appointment: "L'administration du diocèse de Paris passa ainsi entre les mains d'un homme éclairé, qui s'efforça d'y rétablir l'ordre et le calme." (*Histoire de France sous le ministère de Mazarin*, 2: 237.)

183. G.E.F., 6: 154–57.

184. B.N. Ms. Fr. 15730, fols. 182–83.

185. Jansen, *Le Cardinal Mazarin*, pp. 133–34.

186. Marca to Mazarin, 22 April 1656, B.N. Ms. Baluze 113, fol. 165.

187. B.N. Ms. Fr. 15730, fols. 185–89.

188. Ibid., fols. 189–94. On this incident of Retz's episcopal letter and the papal brief for peace, see also d'Aigreville, A.N. G⁸655A, fols. 247ff.; Blet, *Le Clergé de France*, 2: 147–55.

189. Jansen, *Le Cardinal Mazarin*, p. 139; Guy Joly, *Mémoires*, p. 130.

190. G.E.F., 6: 181–216.

191. Ibid., 6: 222–23.

192. Du Saussay feared excommunication for disobeying Retz. The curé therefore begged Mazarin to permit him to be consecrated as bishop of Toul (to which he had already been nominated). Mazarin agreed. As a prelate himself, Du Saussay would be safe from Retz's revenge (Du Saussay to Mazarin, 4 July 1656, B.N. Ms. Baluze 113, fol. 208; Séguier to Le Tellier, 5 July 1656, B.N. Ms. Baluze 115, fol. 55; Du Saussay to Mazarin, 30 July 1656, B.N. Ms. Baluze 113, fol. 228).

193. *Raisons pour monstrer que mons. le cardinal de Rets a peu et deu destituer monsieur Dusaussay, evesque de Toul, de la charge de grand vicaire, et de celle d'official, passim*; *Lettre de plusieurs ecclésiastiques considérables du diocèse de Paris à monsieur le cardinal de Retz, leur archevêque, passim*; Guy Joly, *Mémoires*, pp. 129–30; d'Aigreville, A.N. G⁸655A, fol. 320. Far from rescinding its edicts against Chassebras, the government resumed the search for him after Du Saussay's commission was revoked. The curé of la Madeleine escaped the police and went to Rome where he continued to serve Retz.

194. G.E.F., 6: xlviii, 226–44. Du Saussay had been the previous *official*. Porcher was a doctor of the Sorbonne with Jansenist sympathies.

195. "Memoire sur ce qui peut estre faict pour empescher qu'aucun ne fasse la charge de grand Vicaire en larchevesché de Paris sans l'agrément du Roy," 29 June 1656, B.N. Ms. Fr. 6893, fols. 119–22.

196. Mazarin to Servien, 28 June 1656, Mazarin, *Lettres*, 7: 246–47.

197. G.E.F., 6: 604–7.

198. The abbé Dorat, who had belonged to Duhamel's community, was finally arrested in June 1657. He was still in the Bastille at the commencement of Louis XIV's personal reign (Besmaus, governor of the Bastille, to Colbert, 2 September 1661, in Depping, ed., *Correspondance administrative*, 2: 542).

199. On the abbé de Saint-Jean and the events of 19–20 June, see Duranthon, *Collection des procès-verbaux*, 4: 233–34; and the letters to Mazarin by his informants: the bishop of Séez, 19 June 1656, B.N. Ms. Baluze 113, fol. 191; abbé de Bonsy, 19 June, ibid., fols. 193–94; the bishop of Montauban, 19 June, ibid., fols. 195–97; and the bishop of Séez, 20 June, ibid., fol. 192. For the arrest of Chevalier and the threat that he represented, see M. de la Bachélerie, governor of the Bastille, to Mazarin, 1 July 1656, B.N. Ms. Baluze 114, fol. 44; Mazarin to M. de la Bachélerie, 1 July, in Champollion-Figeac, *Complément des mémoires du cardinal de Retz*, p. 541; Séguier to Le Tellier, 2 July, B.N. Ms. Fr. 6893, fols. 133–36; the interrogation of Chevalier at the Bastille, ibid., fols. 140–44; "Mémoire de ce qui s'est trouvé dans les papiers du sr. Chevallier prisonnier à la Bastille," B.N. Ms. Fr. 4233, fols. 155–60.

200. The ordinance and letter are in G.E.F., 6: 607–14.

201. B.N. Ms. Baluze 113, fol. 117.

202. D'Aigreville, A.N. G⁸655B, fols. 67–68. Mazarin was furious at Rousse's speech. See Mazarin to Marca, 9 September 1656, B.N. Ms. Mélanges de Colbert 51, fols. 256–57.

203. This assembly, prolonged on account of the atmosphere and events of the Religious Fronde, was the most extended of all General Assemblies, lasting from October 1655 to May 1657. The story of the General Assembly and Retz has been told in sufficient detail elsewhere, principally in biographies of Retz, for it to be repeated here. The account by Blet (*Le Clergé de France*, 2: book 3, chapter 4) is the best secondary work available.

204. Chéruel, *Histoire de France sous le ministère de Mazarin*, 3: 19ff.

205. M. de la Bachélerie to Mazarin, 8 July 1656, B.N. Ms. Baluze 115, fol. 45; bishop of Séez to Mazarin, 27 July 1656, B.N. Ms. Baluze 113, fol. 226.

206. Mazarin to abbé Fouquet, 19 July 1656, Mazarin, *Lettres*, 7: 283; Lair, *Nicolas Fouquet*, 1: 376ff.; Knachel, *England and the Fronde*, p. 267.

207. [Le Paige and Du Rey de Meinières], *Histoire de la détention du cardinal de Retz*, p. 72.

208. Hermant, *Mémoires*, 3: 159.

209. Clément, ed., in Colbert, *Lettres, instructions, et mémoires*, 1: 384.

210. Mazarin to Colbert, 9 September 1656, Mazarin, *Lettres*, 7: 345.

211. Mazarin to Colbert, 13 September 1656, ibid., 7: 355–61.

212. G.E.F., 6: 619–20.

213. Colbert to Mazarin, 15 September 1656, Colbert, *Lettres, instructions, et mémoires*, 1: 263; Colbert to Mazarin, 18 September, ibid., 1: 264–66.

214. G.E.F., 6: 262–63.

215. Bishop of Aire to Mazarin, 23 September 1656, B.N. Ms. Baluze 113, fol. 261.

216. Bishop of Séez to Mazarin, 23 September 1656, ibid., fol. 256.

217. Bishop of Séez to Mazarin, 25 September 1656, ibid., fol. 269.

218. Colbert to Mazarin, 28 September 1656, Colbert, *Lettres, instructions, et mémoires*, 1: 266–67; Colbert to Mazarin, 30 September, ibid., 1: 267–68.

219. "Discours pour faire voir que Monsieur le Cardinal de Retz Archevesque de Paris ne peut de son autorité mettre le Roy de France ny Paris ville capitale du Royaume en Interdit," October 1656, B.N. Ms. Fr. 17589, fols. 353–65; Marca (?), "Mémoire fait à l'occasion de l'Interdict qu'on disoit que M. le Cardinal de Retz vouloit mettre sur le diocèse de Paris," B.N. Ms. Baluze 113, fols. 318–24.

220. Hermant, *Mémoires*, 4: 81.

221. Ibid., 4: 32.

222. Dupuys, *Discours prononcé en l'Assemblée Synodale, tenue le 30 avril 1658*, p. 6.

223. Curé of Saint-Barthélemy to Mazarin, 2 December 1658, A.A.E. France 906, fol. 281.

224. Bishop of Coutances to Mazarin, 3 July 1659, A.A.E. France 907, fols. 149–50; Le Tellier to Mazarin, 9 July 1659, ibid., fol. 185; Mazarin to Le Tellier, 16 July 1659, B.N. Ms. Fr. 6895, fol. 79; Mazarin to Le Tellier, 17 October 1659, Mazarin, *Lettres*, 9: 371–72; Mazarin to the bishop of Coutances, 17 October 1659, ibid., 9: 375. See chapter two for a detailed discussion of the suppression of the curés' assemblies.

225. De Thou (the French ambassador in Holland) to Mazarin, 25 April 1658, B.I. Ms. 1322, fols. 31–32; Fouquet to Mazarin, 17 December 1658, A.A.E. France 905, fol. 537.

226. Lair, *Nicolas Fouquet*, 1: 448, 452.

227. Chéruel, *Histoire de France sous le ministère de Mazarin*, 3: 172ff.; Wolf, *Louis XIV*, pp. 96–98; Clément, ed., in Colbert, *Lettres, instructions, et mémoires*, 1: lxxvi–lxxvii; Allier, *La Cabale des dévots*, p. 346.

228. Guy Joly, *Mémoires*, p. 139.

229. Ibid.; Batiffol, *Biographie du cardinal de Retz*, pp. 191–92.

230. Logié, *La Fronde en Normandie*, 3: 148–60.

231. Stoye, *Europe Unfolding*, p. 201.

232. Mazarin to the bishop of Coutances, 18 March 1660, A.A.E. France 284, fol. 260; Hermant, *Mémoires*, 4: 403–4.

233. Moreau, *Bibliographie des Mazarinades*, 1: 4.

234. *A tous les évêques, prêtres et enfants de l'Eglise, Jean François Paul de Gondi, cardinal de Retz, archevêque de Paris*, 24 April 1660, G.E.F., 6: 321–413; Hermant, *Mémoires*, 4: 478.

235. Anonymous to Retz, 4 September 1660, B.N. Ms. Baluze 115, fols. 65–67; anonymous to Retz, 9 September 1660, ibid., fols. 67–68.

236. Hermant, *Mémoires*, 4: 479.

237. G.E.F., 6: lxx, 648–49; Chantelauze, *Le Cardinal de Retz et ses missions diplomatiques à Rome*, pp. 8–11; Salmon, *Cardinal de Retz*, pp. 318–19.

238. For Retz's involvement with the Jansenists and the affair of the episcopal letter of the vicars-general, see chapter four.

239. Hamscher, *The Parlement of Paris after the Fronde*.

CHAPTER TWO

1. Wilhelm, *La Vie quotidienne au Marais au XVIIe siècle*, pp. 277–81; Rapin, *Mémoires*, 1: 112n.; Blond, *La Maison professe des Jésuites*, pp. 107–9.

2. Rousse, *Sommaire des déclarations des curez de Paris*, pp. 17–18.

3. See Dolhagary, "Curés," *Dictionnaire de théologie catholique*, 3: cols. 2429–53, which denies the orthodoxy of the curés' pretensions. Pius IV condemned these views in the 1794 bull *Auctorem fidei*.

4. [Mazure], *L'Obligation des fidèles*, p. 17.

5. *Extrait de quelques propositions d'un livre intitulé, "Obligation des fidelles de se confesser à leur curé,"* p. 2.

6. *Sermon de Mr Jean Gerson*, p. 10.

7. "Tout son [Mazure's] dessein ne va qu'a se soustraire de la iurisdiction et de la puissance des evesques, pour se rendre aussi absolu & independant en sa Parroisse, qu'ils le sont en leurs Dioceses." (*Extrait de quelques maximes de l'Anonyme*, p. 1.) Curiously, Bagot at one point did not deny the divine origin of curés. Instead, after granting this premise, he rejected the conclusion, namely, that the curé was equal with the pope and the bishops, and that he could act independently of them (*Response du P. Bagot*, p. 35).

8. Préclin, *Les Jansénistes du XVIIIe siècle*, pp. 1–12; Préclin, "Edmond Richer," pp. 329–36. For a thorough account of the early history of Richerism, see Puyol, *Edmond Richer*.

9. Préclin, *Les Jansénistes du XVIIIe siècle*, p. 18.

10. Taveneaux, *Jansénisme et politique*, pp. 39–40; Adam, *Du mysticisme à la révolte*, pp. 19, 285ff.; Cognet, *Le Jansénisme*, pp. 83–84, 92; Tans, "Les Idées politiques des jansénistes," pp. 17–18.

11. Nicolas Le Gros, an early eighteenth-century Richerist, composed a systematic statement on the rights of the lower clergy. Significantly, a great number of his propositions mirrored the claims of the curés of Paris during the Religious Fronde. In fact, Le Gros cites from the Religious Fronde to argue against the maxim that bishops are the only judges in matters of faith ("Memoire sur les droits du second ordre du clergé," B.N. Ms. Fr. 13833).

12. Contemporaries were not unaware of the curés' efforts to exploit the Retz affair for their own purposes. For example, in the Sorbonne on 31 May

1656, a doctor complained about a curé who had ordered a penitent to confess a second time because he had confessed at first to that doctor and not to the curé. The doctor then warned the Sorbonne that "les curez de Paris font les Evesques et que quand M. le Cardinal de Retz sera informé des choses il verra que ceux qui font plus semblant de luy estre affectionnes, sont ceux qui font moins de cas de son autorité." (Abbé de Beaubrun, "Extrait des pièces qui concernent l'histoire des années 1655 et 1656, et principalement de la pretendue censure des propositions extraites de la seconde lettre de Mr. Arnauld," B.N. Ms. Fr. 13896, fol. 453.)

13. Blet, "L'Ordre du clergé au XVIIe siècle," p. 16. Although Blet is referring to the General Assemblies of the Clergy, his stress on the importance of the "droit d'assemblée" is equally applicable to the curés' assemblies.

14. B.N. Ms. Fr. 24075, fol. 76. This register of the assemblies is a principal source for the curés' activities during the Religious Fronde. For each assembly, the register contains a list of the curés present, proposals offered to the assembly, and the resolutions taken. Additionally, original materials such as letters to the assembly, reports of curés delegated to deal with a specific problem, and accounts of conferences and meetings of the curés with other groups, such as the government and Faculty of Theology, are included. Gaston seems to have been the first to see this register, although he did no more than to outline its possibilities as a source ("L'Assemblée de MM. les curés de Paris au XVIIe siècle," pp. 676–79). Ferté, in her edition of Beurrier's memoirs, used the register to supplement his account of his role in the assemblies. Neither Gaston nor Ferté seem to have been aware of two other copies of the register: B.N. Ms. Fr. 20866, fols. 118–73 (this register only includes the assemblies from 29 April 1653 through 1 March 1655), and Bibliothèque de la Société de Port-Royal, collection Le Paige 468, no. 60, "Jesuites, casuistes et reguliers, 1569–1760." Gazier, the historian of Jansenism, uncovered the latter manuscript, but did not know what to do with it, and so never utilized it. For Gazier, the register was simply "un curieux procès-verbal manuscrit" (Hermant, *Mémoires*, 2: 573n.). Although the most complete registers (B.N. Ms. Fr. 24075 and that at the Bibliothèque de la Société de Port-Royal) comprise only the records of the assemblies from 29 April 1653 to 1 March 1655 and from 3 June 1658 through 7 July 1659, other sources shed light on those between 1655 and 1658. Among these sources are government correspondence and memoranda; letters of the curés; and memoirs, particularly those of the Jansenist Hermant and of the Jesuit Rapin. Hermant is more trustworthy than Rapin, although he is as sympathetic toward the curés as Rapin is antagonistic. (For a defense of Rapin's reliability, see Dubois, "A Jesuit History of Jansenism," pp. 764–73.) Especially significant is the correspondence (which is scattered in the A.A.E. France and Rome) of Roullé, syndic of the curés, writer of the register of the assemblies, and government spy. In addition, there are the many pamphlets and publications of the curés themselves, which provide a record, although partial, of the assemblies.

15. The assembly of 2 March 1654 altered this statute. At that time, the curés resolved that each would have "séance et voix" in the assembly according to the day on which he had been admitted and received into the company of curés (B.N. Ms. Fr. 24075, fol. 104).

16. Beurrier, "Memoirs," pp. 290–93.

17. Curé of Saint-Roch to Mazarin, July 1659, B.N. Ms. Baluze 114, fol. 121. The syndics also sent out letters convoking each assembly. In January 1659, the curés resolved that it was necessary only to deliver notices for the extraordinary assemblies (B.N. Ms. Fr. 24075, fol. 28).

18. B.N. Ms. Fr. 24075, fols. 143–51.

19. Dupuys and Rousse, *Suite de l'extrait*, p. 8.

20. Hermant, *Mémoires*, 2: 573, citing the resolutions of the curés' assembly of 22 August 1654.

21. Aubineau, "Introduction," in Rapin, *Mémoires*, 1: xxv.

22. Rapin, *Mémoires*, 2: 282–83.

23. B.N. Ms. Fr. 24075, fol. 121.

24. The conflict began over the burial in the parish of Saint-Eustache of André Mondain, canon of Notre-Dame. The chapter claimed that Mondain's status of canon took precedence over his being a parishioner of Saint-Eustache, and that his body should thus be reinterred in the cathedral. The debate dragged on for years, as the curés of the "Ville, fauxbourgs, et banlieue de Paris" enthusiastically supported Marlin. The issues passed over the dead body of Mondain to the question of the curés' rights in relation to the chapter. Did the curés possess the right to administer the sacraments in the cathedral church? Or, conversely, had the cathedral been created first, and did it still maintain its jurisdiction over territory that had later been divided into parishes? (For further details, see below, chapter three.) Historically, the canons were correct, as the cathedral had been the only parish in the city until the eleventh century (Friedmann, "Notre-Dame et les paroisses de Paris au XIIIe siècle," p. 28).

25. *Sommaire du procez*, p. 22.

26. Respectively: Mazure, *Compliment de Messieurs les curés de Paris, à Monseigneur le président de Belièvre*; Mazure, *Compliment de Messieurs les curés de Paris. Fait à Monseigneur l'Eminentissime Cardinal de Retz, sur sa promotion*; Mazure, *Harangue de Mr Mazure curé de S. Paul, à la reyne de Suède, pour Messieurs les Curez de Paris* [Mazure hardly concealed the curés' pride: "Voici la compagnie des curés de Paris qui vient se presenter à V. M. pour luy rendre ses tres-humbles respects; non pas à la facon des hommes du monde par de vains complimens; mais comme des Ministres de l'Eglise de Jesus-Christ, pour luy offrir ses voeux et ses prieres" (p. 1)]; and Mazure, *Oraison funèbre de feu messire Jean François de Gondy premier archevesque de Paris*.

27. Cited in Gaston, "L'Assemblée de MM. les curés de Paris au XVIIe siècle," p. 677.

28. Hermant, *Mémoires*, 2: 636.

29. "Les curez de Paris . . . m'abandonnent par l'aversion et la haine qu'ils ont contre moy parceque Jay tousjours esté et suis tout seul contraire à leurs desseins practiques . . . Il y a longtemps que je pare aux coupes et aux orages de leurs mauvaises parolles menaces et mauvais traittements qu'ils me font tant publicquement qu'un particulier" (Curé of Saint-Barthélemy to Mazarin, 2 December 1658, A.A.E. France 906, fol. 281).

30. Hermant, *Mémoires*, 2: 635.

31. *Septième écrit des curés de Paris ou Journal de tout ce qui se passe tant à Paris que dans les Provinces. Sur le sujet de la Morale de l'Apologie des Casuistes . . .* (Paris, 1659), p. 189. For this and several of the subsequent *Ecrits des curés de Paris*, I have used the editions published in Recalde, ed., *Ecrits des curés de Paris contre la politique et la morale des Jésuites (1658–1659)*.

32. Hermant, *Mémoires*, 3: 125–26.

33. Ibid., 3: 126; *Septième écrit*, p. 190.

34. Beaubrun, B.N. Ms. Fr. 13896, fol. 510.

35. Dupuys and Rousse, *Advis de messieurs les curez de Paris*, p. 2.

36. Hermant, *Mémoires*, 3: 165.

37. Duranthon, *Collection des procès-verbaux*, 4: 230–31.

38. Hermant, *Mémoires*, 3: 171–72.

39. Rapin, *Mémoires*, 1: 484.

40. D'Aigreville, A.N. G⁸655B, fol. 109; Duranthon, *Collection des procès-verbaux*, 4: 231.

41. Rousse, *Sommaire de la harangue de messieurs les curez de Paris*.

42. D'Aigreville, A.N. G⁸655B, fols. 110–11; Duranthon, *Collection des procès-verbaux*, 4: 232.

43. Bishop of Séez to Mazarin, 25 October 1656, B.N. Ms. Baluze 113, fol. 293.

44. *Second advis, ou lettre de messieurs les curez de Paris*.

45. *Lettre circulaire de l'Assemblée générale du clergé de France*.

46. Dupuys and Rousse, *Suite de l'extrait*.

47. *Septième écrit*, pp. 197–98.

48. There were ten of these *Ecrits*. The first nine were directed against the *Apologie* and appeared between 25 January 1658 and 25 June 1659. On the curés' correspondence, see, for example, Marlin and Rousse, *Lettre de messieurs les curez de Paris, à monseigneur l'evesque d'Orléans*; Dupuys and Rousse, *Lettre de messieurs les curez de Paris à monseigneur l'archevêque de Sens*; Marlin and Rousse, *Lettre de messieurs les curez de Paris à monseigneur l'evesque de Conserans*; Marlin and Rousse, *Conclusion de messieurs les curez de Paris*.

49. For a list of these censures, see Sommervogel, ed., *Bibliothèque de la compagnie de Jésus*, 6: cols. 857–63; Marie, *Bibliographie générale des oeuvres de Blaise Pascal*, 3: 327–40.

50. Recalde, *Ecrits des curés de Paris*, p. 351.

51. *Premier écrit des curés de Paris*, in Pascal, *Les Provinciales*, pp. 404–17.

52. *Septième écrit*, pp. 198–99; Hermant, *Mémoires*, 4: 29–30. The

request to the vicars-general, drawn up by Rousse, has been published: *A Messieurs les vicaires généraux de monseigneur l'éminentissime cardinal de Rets archevesque de Paris.*

53. The *Septième écrit*, a historical record of the prosecution by the curés of lax casuistry and of the *Apologie*, ignored nonetheless their intractability after 8 February, only picking up the story again on 11 March. For details on the February events, see Hermant, *Mémoires*, 4: 29ff.

54. Hermant, *Mémoires*, 4: 57.

55. "Sa Majesté . . . a ordonné et ordonne que nouvelles deffences seront faictes a tous gentilshommes et autres, de faire cy apres aucunes associations ny assemblees sans sa permission a peine de la vie" (A.A.E. France 906, fol. 164).

56. Colbert to Mazarin, 5 June 1658, Colbert, *Lettres, instructions, et mémoires*, 1: 296.

57. *Septième écrit*, pp. 221–22.

58. B.N. Ms. Fr. 24075, fol. 11.

59. Hermant, *Mémoires*, 4: 133–34.

60. "Les Curez de Paris ont esté un peu surpris de la defense que lon a faite de publier la censure de cette apologie qui a fait tant de bruit, ils vouloyent sen plaindre en corps, ie leur ay dit qu'on ne les recognoistroit pas" (Fouquet to Mazarin, 15 August 1658, A.A.E. France 905, fol. 380).

61. Mazure to Mazarin, 10 August 1658, A.A.E. France 906, fols. 202–3.

62. Mazarin to Mazure, 28 August 1658, in Hermant, *Mémoires*, 4: 135–36.

63. B.N. Ms. Fr. 24075, fols. 12–13.

64. Marca to Mazarin, 13 September 1658, A.A.E. France 906, fols. 242–43.

65. Hermant, *Mémoires*, 4: 147–48.

66. To my knowledge, neither the assemblies of the court bishops nor this incident of opposition by the Parlement has been studied. There is a wealth of material on this subject, including the *arrêt*, memoranda, and correspondence, in B.N. Ms. Baluze 114 and in A.A.E. France 906.

67. Hermant, *Mémoires*, 4: 148.

68. Ibid., 4: 151–52.

69. B.N. Ms. Fr. 24075, fol. 16.

70. *Septième écrit*, p. 227.

71. For example, the assembly of 3 February 1659 received a request from the curés of Angers for information about the procedures of the assemblies at Paris (B.N. Ms. Fr. 24075, fols. 29–30). The register of the assemblies frequently noted the reception of correspondence from provincial curés. Moreover, curés of many provincial cities imitated those in Paris by petitioning their prelates as a corps rather than individually.

72. Dubois, *Henri de Pardaillon de Gondrin*; Le Tellier to Gondrin, 26 February 1659, in Hermant, *Mémoires*, 4: 198; Mazarin to abbé Fouquet, 1 September 1659, Mazarin, *Lettres*, 9: 264.

73. Marca, "Procez verbal de l'assemblée des prelats tenue à Paris, au Palais

Mazarin, le 22 du mois de juin 1659," B.N. Ms. Baluze 114, fol. 79.

74. The agent of the clergy officially convoked the assembly, and, besides Mazarin, was the only ecclesiastic present who was not a bishop.

75. Marca, "Procez verbal de l'assemblée des prelats . . . ," B.N. Ms. Baluze 114, fol. 79.

76. Hermant, *Mémoires*, 4: 259–60.

77. Bishop of Coutances to Mazarin, 3 July 1659, A.A.E. France 907, fols. 149–50.

78. Le Tellier to the vicars-general, 6 July 1659, B.N. Ms. Fr. 6895, fol. 36. For a description of the preparation of the ordinance, see Le Tellier's letter to Mazarin, 6 July 1659, A.A.E. France 907, fol. 163.

79. "Louis aux grands vicaires, sur les assemblées des curez de Paris," 6 July 1659, A.A.E. France 907, fols. 166–67.

80. Ibid., fol. 167.

81. "Proces-verbal des vicaires-généraux," 7 July 1659, A.A.E. France 1594, fols. 6–8; vicars-general to Le Tellier, 7 July 1659, ibid., fol. 9; Jean-Baptiste de Contes, vicar-general, to Mazarin, 9 July 1659, ibid., fols. 10–11.

82. Rousse to Mazarin, July 1659, B.N. Ms. Baluze 114, fols. 120–22; Rousse to Mazarin, 4 August 1659, ibid., fols. 122–23; [Rousse], "Avis sur les assemblées des curés de Paris," A.A.E. France 1594, fols. 24–25.

83. Abbé de Guron, bishop of Tulle, to Mazarin, 9 July 1659, A.A.E. France 907, fols. 189–90.

84. Le Tellier to Mazarin, 9 July 1659, ibid., fol. 184.

85. Séguier to Mazarin, 13 July 1659, ibid., fol. 202.

86. Mazarin to Le Tellier, 16 July 1659, B.N. Ms. Fr. 6895, fols. 79–80.

87. "Louis aux grands vicaires," 18 July 1659, A.A.E. France 907, fol. 218.

88. See, for example, the bishop of Coutances to Mazarin, 10 July 1659, A.A.E. France 1594, fols. 12–13; Le Tellier to Mazarin, 20 July 1659, B.I. Ms. 1319, fol. 200.

89. "Relation du Père Guerrier," in Pascal, *Oeuvres*, 7: 62; Lanson, "Après les *Provinciales*: Examen de quelques écrits attribués à Pascal," p. 14; Recalde, *Ecrits des curés de Paris*, p. 18.

90. Cf. Allier, *La Cabale des dévots*, p. 344.

CHAPTER THREE

1. I have of course oversimplified this intricate and important thirteenth-century quarrel. For general documentation, see Leff, *Paris and Oxford Universities*; Rashdall, *The Universities of Europe*, vol. 1.

2. Féret, *La Faculté de théologie*, 3: 158–59. Féret, especially in volumes three through five, is most valuable for regular-secular conflicts within the Faculty of Theology during the seventeenth century. See also Jourdain, *Histoire de l'université*, vol. 1; Dourarche, *L'Université de Paris et les Jésuites*. Hermant, a member of the Faculty, was an incomparable eyewitness to the struggles after 1630.

3. For these subsequent incidents, see Féret, *La Faculté de théologie*, vol. 3; Jarry and Préclin, *Les Luttes politiques et doctrinales*; and the vast secondary literature on Jansenism. No book treating Jansenism could dispense with a discussion of the antipathy of Jesuits and Jansenists and of their quarrels that involved the Faculty. Adam (*Du mysticisme à la révolte*) is particularly clear on the problem of the regulars and the significance this had for the development of Jansenism. Louis Gorin de Saint-Amour's *Journal* is excellent both for the attitudes of a Jansenist doctor toward the regulars (Jesuits) and for the quarrels themselves within the Faculty after 1648.

4. Dubois, *Henri de Pardaillon de Gondrin*, p. xviii.

5. Chesneau, *Le P. Yves de Paris*, 1: 6–9.

6. Ibid., 1: 14.

7. Duranthon, *Collection des procès-verbaux*, 4: 208–18.

8. *L'Autorité épiscopale défendue contre les nouvelles entreprises de quelques reguliers mendiants du diocèse d'Angers sur la hiérarchie ecclésiastique* (1658).

9. *La Défense de l'autorité de Notre Saint Père le Pape, de Nosseigneurs les cardinaux, les archevêques et évêques, et de l'emploi des religieux mendiants, contre les erreurs de ce temps* (Metz, 1658); cited in Blet, *Le Clergé de France*, 2: 319.

10. For the early aspects of the Angers affair, see Blet, *Le Clergé de France*, 2: 232–34; Cochin, *Henri Arnauld*; Beaubrun, B.N. Ms. Fr. 13895, fols. 390ff. For that part of the conflict after Bonichon and Vernant, see Féret, *La Faculté de théologie*, 3: 280ff.; Blet, *Le Clergé de France*, 2: 319ff.; the censures, bull, *arrêt*, and various correspondence have been collected in the B.H.V.P., *Diverses pièces* (*cote* 710 351).

11. Avranches, *Response à un escrit anonyme contre les religieux*, pp. 4–5.

12. *Response au libelle intitulé "Dom pacifique d'Avranches,"* pp. 23ff. Beaubrun dated this work in 1654 and said that it was attributed to the curé of Saint-Paul, Mazure (B.N. Ms. Fr. 13895, fol. 325).

13. *Response au libelle intitulé "Dom pacifique d'Avranches,"* cited in Hermant, *Mémoires*, 2: 565–67.

14. Ferté, *La Vie religieuse*, pp. 316, 318.

15. Cited in Watkins, *A History of Penance*, 2: 748. See also Héricourt, *Les Loix ecclésiastiques de France*, part 3, p. 25.

16. David O'Connor, "Parochial Relations and Cooperation of the Religious Clergy and the Diocesan Clergy: Canons 608–609 (Historical-Synopsis)," pp. 69–78; Wright, "The Significance of the Council of Trent," p. 358.

17. Bagot, *Défense du droict épiscopal*, pp. 9–10, 14, 19–20, 46ff., 54, 57, 91, 98.

18. Bagot, *Explication donnee par le P. Bagot*, pp. 2–3.

19. *Lettre qui respond aux falsifications d'une feuille volante*, pp. 3–4, 8. See also, Avranches, *Response à un escrit anonyme contre les religieux*, p. 4.

20. *Extrait de quelques maximes de l'Anonyme*, p. 2.

21. Des Déserts, *A Messeigneurs de l'assemblée du clergé*, p. 1.

22. See, for example, [Mazure], *L'Obligation des fidèles, passim.*; Beurrier, "Memoirs," pp. 299–300.

23. For these extremist views on the curés' right to hear confessions, see [Mazure], *L'Obligation des fidèles, passim.*; *Extrait de quelques propositions d'un livre intitulé, "Obligation des fidelles . . . ,"* p. 2; *Sermon de Mr Jean Gerson*, pp. 11–12; *Response au libelle intitulé "Dom pacifique d'Avranches,"* p. 9; *Extraict des censures de la Faculté de Théologie*, pp. 9, 13.

24. Rousse, *Sommaire des déclarations des curez de Paris*, pp. 13, 23.

25. "Quatrevingte conferences ecclesiastiques de la paroisse de St. Mederic par messieurs Henry du Hamel curé de St. Mederic . . . ," B.N. Ms. Fr. 20111, fols. 177–78. Duhamel and his priests regularly held public discussions on religious matters until his exile in 1654.

26. "De la confession annuelle," in "Articles dressés par l'Assemblée générale du clergé touchant le livre anonyme des curés de Paris et le livre du Père Bagot, jésuite," in Hermant, *Mémoires*, 3: 332–33. This text cited by Hermant has also been published under the title *Sentimens de l'assemblée du clergé de MDCLV sur le livre anonyme des Curez de Paris, et celui du Pere Jean Bagot Jesuite, pour les reguliers*, in *Recueil des actes, titres et mémoires concernant les affaires du Clergé de France . . .* , 4: cols. 681–88.

27. *Extraict des censures de la Faculté de Théologie*, p. 40.

28. B.N. Ms. Fr. 24075, fol. 30.

29. See, for example, *Lettre qui respond aux falsifications d'une feuille volante*, p. 4; Bagot, *Défense du droict épiscopal*, p. 98.

30. Beurrier, "Memoirs," pp. 297–98.

31. *Principales propositions, extraites du livre intitulé: "Defense du droit episcopal . . . ,"* in Duranthon, *Collection des procès-verbaux*, 4: pièces justificatives, 79.

32. "Articles dressés par l'Assemblée générale du clergé," in Hermant, *Mémoires*, 3: 333.

33. Schmitt, *L'Organisation ecclésiastique et la pratique religieuse*, pp. 146–47; Ferté, *La Vie religieuse*, pp. 54, 333n.

34. *Lettre instructive sur ce qui s'est passé entre les pères Jésuites et les prestres de Saint Paul.*

35. *Complainte et deffences: Pour maistre Pierre Marlin*, pp. 2–5; *Factum pour Me Pierre Marlin*, pp. 2–8.

36. Ferté, *La Vie religieuse*, p. 269n. On the frequency of attendance at the parish Mass, see ibid., pp. 285–86.

37. "Quatrevingte conferences ecclesiastiques de la paroisse de St. Mederic par messieurs Henry du Hamel curé de St. Mederic . . . ," B.N. Ms. Fr. 20111, fols. 215–17.

38. B.N. Ms. Fr. 24075, fol. 13.

39. *Septième écrit*, pp. 223–24.

40. Bagot, *Défense du droict épiscopal*, pp. 146ff.; see also Bagot, "De la messe paroissiale," in *Explication donnee par le P. Bagot*, p. 2.

41. Bagot, *Défense du droict épiscopal*, pp. 174–75.

42. Féret, *La Faculté de théologie*, 3: 170–71.

43. Ibid., 3: 169.

44. "Articles dressés par l'Assemblée générale du clergé," in Hermant, *Mémoires*, 3: 333–34.

45. Cited in [Rousse], *Extraict des propositions à examiner*, p. 7.

46. *Extraict des censures de la Faculté de Théologie*, pp. 9, 28; Bagot, *Défense du droict épiscopal*, pp. 6–8, 26ff.

47. Rapin, *Mémoires*, 1: 358, 485; Hermant, *Mémoires*, 2: 492–93.

48. *Lettre d'un advocat de la cour*, p. 3.

49. Hermant, *Mémoires*, 2: 496–98; Rapin, *Mémoires*, 1: 358, 485; Gazier, "Pascal et Jean de Lingendes," p. 298.

50. Cited in Rapin, *Mémoires*, 1: 358–59n.

51. "Portroit des docteurs de la maison de Sorbonne, de Navarre, moines, ubiquistes, & des bacheliers licentiés," B.N. Ms. Cinq cents Colbert 155, fol. 52.

52. B.N. Ms. Fr. 24075, fol. 119; Hermant, *Mémoires*, 2: 498–99.

53. B.N. Ms. Fr. 24075, fols. 119–20.

54. Hermant, *Mémoires*, 2: 500–501.

55. Ibid., 2: 501.

56. See, for example, bishop of Coutances to Mazarin, 26 April 1654, A.A.E. Rome 126, fol. 181. This bishop assured Mazarin of the good conduct of the curés since Mazure's exile.

57. B.N. Ms. Fr. 24075, fols. 120–22; Hermant, *Mémoires*, 2: 501–2.

58. Hermant, *Mémoires*, 2: 503; Gazier, "Pascal et Jean de Lingendes," p. 298.

59. Cf. l'Espine, *Lettre d'un paroissien de Sainct Paul*. This pamphlet, dated 5 July 1654, assailed Mazure, defended Jesuit views on attendance at parish Mass and on confession, and refuted the anonymous *Response d'un parroissien de S. Paul*.

60. B.N. Ms. Fr. 24075, fols. 115–25.

61. Roullé and Rousse, [*Lettre circulaire des syndics des curés de Paris, au sujet des empiétements du clergé régulier sur les droits du clergé seculier*], p. 3.

62. For this aspect of the controversy, see above, chapter two.

63. For the involvement of the Faculty of Theology in the Bagot-Mazure controversy, see Féret, *La Faculté de théologie*, 3: 166ff.; Beaubrun, B.N. Ms. Fr. 13895, fols. 315, 325, 329, 396, 418, 424–25; Hermant, *Mémoires*, 3: passim; *Extraict des censures de la Faculté de Théologie*; and chapter two, "De ce qui s'est passé dans la Sorbonne," fols. 4–9, in "Récit sommaire de ce qui s'est passé touchant l'anonyme publié par M. Mazure curé de S. Paul et la refutation de ce libelle faicte par le P. Jean Bagot de la compagnie de Jésus," B.N. Ms. Nouv. Acq. Fr. 4687. For the problems arising from the General Assembly's Episcopal Gallicanism, and the subsequent three-sided struggle among the episcopacy, government, and papacy, see Duranthon, *Collection des procès-verbaux*, 4: 228–29; Blet, *Le Clergé de France*, 2: 239–49; Jansen, *Le Cardinal Mazarin*, pp. 161–62.

64. Beaubrun, B.N. Ms. Fr. 13895, fols. 315, 325.

65. Duranthon, *Collection des procès-verbaux*, 4: 221–22.

66. These are printed in Duranthon, *Collection des procès-verbaux*, 4: pièces justificatives, 78.

67. An anonymous *Defauts pour lesquels la declaration de quelques curez* listed six propositions from *L'Obligation des fidèles* that had not been discussed by the declaration of 27 October, and even went so far as to deny that the curés of Paris could defend such a work. Similarly repudiating the curés' responsibility for *L'Obligation des fidèles*, the *Avis sur l'anonyme reformé* supported the jurisdictional and hierarchical authority of bishops against the *Sommaire* and the eleven heretical and schismatic propositions selected from Mazure's book.

68. "Response du Père Jean Bagot sur quelques propositions de son livre intitulé deffense du droict episcopal. Presentées à messeigneurs les commissaires du clergé," B.N. Ms. Nouv. Acq. Fr. 4687, fols. 13–19.

69. "Second Response du P. Bagot sur quelques articles qui luy ont esté proposés par messeigneurs les prelats touchant *La defence du droit episcopal*," ibid., fol. 26.

70. Annat's role in the ecclesiastical politics of the 1650s remains to be elucidated. Arch-enemy of the Jansenists, Annat exercised considerable influence. He led the Jesuits in the early refutations of Pascal's *Lettres provinciales* and later published against the *Ecrits des curés*. Pascal's seventeenth, eighteenth, and the fragment of the nineteenth letter were addressed to Annat, as was the *Neuvième écrit*. See Cognet, ed., Pascal, *Les Provinciales*, pp. lviiiff.; Janssen, "Un Polémiste anti-janséniste. Le Père Fr. Annat, S.J.," pp. 349–58; Ceyssens, "François Annat, S.J., avant son confessorat (1590–1654)," pp. 483–529.

71. "Esclaircissemens de quelques chefs tirés du livre du P. Bagot intitulé Deffense du droit episcopal," B.N. Ms. Nouv. Acq. Fr. 4687, fols. 19–24.

72. Des Déserts, *A Messeigneurs de l'assemblée du clergé*.

73. Ibid., p. 3.

74. *Deuxiesme chef des quatre*.

75. Bagot, *Explication donnee par le P. Bagot*; Bagot, *Response du P. Bagot*.

76. Bagot, *Response du P. Bagot*, p. 4.

77. *Extrait de quelques propositions d'un livre intitulé, "Obligation des fidelles. . . ."*

78. *Extrait de l'interpretation & vray sens*.

79. *Extraict d'un livre intitulé, "Défense du droict épiscopal. . . ."*

80. [Rousse], *Extraict des propositions à examiner*.

81. Louis Adrien Le Paige, manuscript note, Bibliothèque de la Société de Port-Royal, Collection Le Paige 468.

82. Blet, *Le Clergé de France*, 2: 239; Hermant, *Mémoires*, 3: 277–79.

83. Hermant, *Mémoires*, 3: 279–80.

84. Ibid., 3: 280–81.

85. "Articles dressés par l'Assemblée générale du Clergé," ibid., 3: 328–35; Blet, *Le Clergé de France*, 2: 240–42.

86. Hermant, *Mémoires*, 3: 347.

87. Duranthon, *Collection des procès-verbaux*, 4: 229.

88. "Lettre du president de l'Assemblée du clergé, Henry de Gondrin, archevêque de Sens, relative au differand entre les curés de Paris et les réguliers, à propos du droit de confession," B.N. Ms. Mélanges de Colbert 7, fols. 254–61.

89. Blet, *Le Clergé de France*, 2: 249–50. The letter by Mazarin can be found in Duranthon, *Collection des procès-verbaux*, 4: pièces justificatives, 79–80.

90. Mazure to Mazarin, 30 August 1659, A.A.E. France 907, fol. 357.

91. Cited in Hermant, *Mémoires*, 4: 320.

92. Bishop of Coutances to Mazarin, 27 August 1659, A.A.E. France 907, fol. 345.

93. Ibid., fol. 346; Séguier to Mazarin, 27 August 1659, ibid., fol. 347.

94. Mazure to Mazarin, 30 August 1659, ibid., fols. 356–57.

95. Bishop of Coutances to Mazarin, 1 September 1659, A.A.E. France 908, fol. 5.

96. Séguier to Le Tellier, 10 September 1659, ibid., fol. 70.

97. Bishop of Coutances to Mazarin, 17 September 1659, ibid., fol. 106; Hermant, *Mémoires*, 4: 323.

98. For the attempts at conciliation, see the letters by the bishop of Coutances to Mazarin of 22 September, 8 October, and 23 October 1659, A.A.E. France 908, fols. 121–22, 196–97, 243–44.

99. Hermant, *Mémoires*, 4: 348–49.

100. "Pièces relatives aux poursuites exercés contre le P. Maimbourg, Jésuite, à propos d'un sermon prononcé en la chapelle de la maison professe," A.N. L 428, no. 61.

101. Bishop of Coutances to Mazarin, 19 November 1659, A.A.E. France 908, fols. 340–41.

102. Bishop of Coutances to Mazarin, 26 November 1659, ibid., fol. 346.

103. Rapin, *Mémoires*, 1: 484; see also 3: 90.

104. Ibid., 1: 356, 2: 222.

CHAPTER FOUR

1. Gazier, *Histoire générale du mouvement janséniste*, 1: v. Robert Arnauld d'Andilly, one of the Port-Royal solitaries, wrote a typical disclaimer to Anne of Austria: "The crime of which I am accused, Madame, is that of being a Jansenist. I want to assure Your Majesty that this alleged Jansenism is such a 'chimère' that I swear to Your Majesty that before God and upon my salvation, I do not even know what it is . . . I am, Madame, as Catholic as it is possible to be." (Cited in Edwards, "Jansenism in Church and State," p. 2.)

2. Jacques, *Les Années d'exil*, p. x.

3. See, for example, Carreyre, "La Doctrine janséniste," 3: 515–17;

Laporte, "Le Jansénisme," pp. 91–95; Adam, *Du mysticisme à la révolte*, p. 336; Namer, *L'Abbé Le Roy*, pp. 111, 164–66.

4. See Orcibal, "Qu'est-ce que le jansénisme?" pp. 39–53.

5. Lefebvre, *Pascal*; Goldmann, *Le Dieu caché* and *Correspondance de Martin de Barcos*; Namer, *L'Abbé Le Roy*. Other historians have been careful not to confuse Jansenism with Port-Royal. See Cognet, "Etat présent des études Port-Royalistes," p. 689.

6. Goldmann, *Le Dieu caché*, p. 115.

7. For criticisms of Goldmann, see Delumeau, *Le Catholicisme*, pp. 179–80; Taveneaux, "Jansénisme et vie sociale en France au XVIIe siècle," pp. 35–37; Taveneaux, *Jansénisme et politique*, p. 21; Neveu, "Un Parlementaire parisien érudit et janséniste: Jean Le Nain (1609–1698)," p. 200. On the social and economic standing of the *officiers*, see Charmeil, *Les Trésoriers de France*, especially pp. 144–48, 446–47; Mousnier, *La Vénalité des offices*, pp. 455–578; Mousnier, *Les Institutions de la France*, pp. 177–80.

8. Mandrou, "Tragique XVIIe siècle," p. 308; Delumeau, *Le Catholicisme*, pp. 179–80.

9. Hamscher, "The Parlement of Paris and the Social Interpretation of Early French Jansenism," pp. 392–410.

10. Goldmann, *Le Dieu caché*, p. 26.

11. Ibid., p. 158. For comments on Goldmann's classification, see Taveneaux, "Jansénisme et vie sociale," pp. 38–39; Delumeau, *Le Catholicisme*, pp. 184–85; Namer, *L'Abbé Le Roy*, pp. 14, 163.

12. Namer, *L'Abbé Le Roy*, pp. 162–63; for a critique of Namer, see Deyon, "Perspectives et limites d'une 'sociologie' du jansénisme," pp. 428–34.

13. Taveneaux, "Jansénisme et vie sociale," pp. 27–29; Cognet, *Le Jansénisme*, pp. 123–24; Sedgwick, *Jansenism in Seventeenth-Century France*, pp. 193–207; Kreiser, *Miracles, Convulsions, and Ecclesiastical Politics*, chapter 1; Van Kley, *The Jansenists and the Expulsion of the Jesuits*, pp. 6–11; Préclin, "Les Conséquences sociales du jansénisme," 3: 610–35; Calvet, *La Littérature religieuse*, pp. 113–20; Ceyssens, "Le Jansénisme. Considérations historiques préliminaires à sa notion," pp. 3–32.

14. Racine, *Abrégé de l'histoire de Port-Royal*, p. 91.

15. For the political thought of the "centrist" Jansenists, see Taveneaux, *Jansénisme et politique*, pp. 25ff.

16. Cf. Tans, "Les Idées politiques des jansénistes," pp. 1–18.

17. Taveneaux, "Jansénisme et vie sociale," p. 45.

18. Moote, *The Revolt of the Judges*, p. 369.

19. Lavisse, *Histoire de France*, 7: part 1, p. 108; Edwards, "Jansenism in Church and State," pp. 237–44; Sedgwick, *Jansenism in Seventeenth-Century France*, pp. 58ff., 215; Carrier, "Port-Royal et la Fronde: Deux mazarinades inconnues d'Arnauld d'Andilly," pp. 3–29. Edwards, Sedgwick, and Carrier utilized the Mazarinades of Robert Arnauld d'Andilly to show that Jansenism provided opposition, at least on a theoretical level, to the government. But while the pamphlets of Arnauld d'Andilly may possibly be representative of

Port-Royal, Port-Royal can not be equated with Jansenism.

20. Rapin, *Mémoires*, 1: 438. See also, 1: 208, 212, 218, 363–64.

21. Hermant, *Mémoires*, 2: 110–15, 356–57.

22. Cited in Rapin, *Mémoires*, 1: 245.

23. Saint-Amour, *Journal*, pp. 293, 338–39.

24. Colbert to Mazarin, 17 September 1657, Colbert, *Lettres, instructions, et mémoires*, 1: 286.

25. Séguier to Brienne, 16 August 1655, B.N. Ms. Baluze 114, fol. 13. See also Kerviler, *Le Chancelier Pierre Séguier*, pp. 316–18, 616–21.

26. Curé of Saint-Barthélemy to Mazarin, 14 August 1655, A.A.E. France 895, fols. 251–55.

27. Rapin, *Mémoires*, 1: 160, 207–8.

28. Hermant, *Mémoires, passim*.

29. Guy Joly, *Mémoires*, pp. 113, 125.

30. Racine, *Abrégé de l'histoire de Port-Royal*, pp. 92–93.

31. Cf. Chantelauze, *Le Cardinal de Retz et les jansénistes, passim*; Gazier, *Les Dernières années du cardinal de Retz*, p. 25, and *Histoire générale du mouvement janséniste*, 1: 98; Chéruel, *Histoire de France sous le ministère de Mazarin*, 2: 108; Batiffol, *Biographie du cardinal de Retz*, pp. 188–89, 202–3; Salmon, *Cardinal de Retz*, p. 313.

32. See, for example, Cognet, *Le Jansénisme*, pp. 48ff.; Gazier, *Histoire générale du mouvement janséniste*, vol. 1; Carreyre, "La Doctrine janséniste," 3: 516; Laporte, "Le Jansénisme," pp. 92–94.

33. Dethan, "Recherches nouvelles sur la personnalité de Mazarin," p. 208.

34. Duneau to Mazarin, 12 June 1655, A.A.E. Rome 128, fol. 33.

35. Cardinal Antoine Barberini to Louis XIV, 2 September 1661, B.N. Ms. Baluze 114, fol. 234.

36. Jansen, *Le Cardinal Mazarin*.

37. Mazarin to the bishop of Coutances, 18 March 1660, A.A.E. France 284, fol. 260.

38. It is striking that recent works have noted only cursorily the phenomenon of Jansenism among curés. Four of the eight "friends" of the abbé Le Roy were curés from the Paris region, but Namer does not establish why there was such a high proportion of curés in this extremist Jansenist group. Deyon (*Amiens*, pp. 365–72, 420–21) states that, because of economic problems and jurisdictional conflicts, the curés of Amiens became sympathetic to Jansenism by the end of the seventeenth century. Elsewhere, however, he indicates that Jansenism had already made inroads among the curés by 1658 as they participated in the campaign against Pirot's *Apologie* and laxism. Ferté, in her magistral study of the curés of the Parisian countryside, mentions in passing the currency of Jansenism among this lower clergy after *Unigenitus*, but neglects to ascertain the reasons (*La Vie religieuse*, p. 195n.).

39. Several historians have parenthetically noted the adhesion of Parisian curés to Jansenism, but have neglected either to prove the observation or to see the curés' Jansenism as a means of political opposition. See Aubineau, ed.,

in Rapin, *Mémoires*, 1: xxv; Chantelauze, *Le Cardinal de Retz et les jansénistes*, pp. 29, 31; Brongniart, *La Paroisse Saint-Médard*, p. 62; Adam, *Du mysticisme à la révolte*, pp. 227, 288; Delumeau, *Le Catholicisme*, pp. 167, 178; Mandrou, *Des humanistes aux hommes de science*, p. 184.

40. "Relation du Père Guerrier," in Pascal, *Oeuvres*, 7: 62.

41. Recalde, *Ecrits des curés de Paris*, p. 30.

42. Lanson, "Après les *Provinciales*," pp. 33–34.

43. Hermant (*Mémoires*, 4: 57, 107–8, 120), reporting on various assemblies of the curés, noted their approval of the *Ecrits*. The register of the assemblies (B.N. Ms. Fr. 24075, fols. 9 ff.) also attests to the curés' endorsement of these writings.

44. Mandrou did exactly that (*Des humanistes aux hommes de science*, p. 184).

45. Bertrand, *Blaise Pascal*, p. 169.

46. See, for example, Mazarin to Le Tellier, 17 October 1659, Mazarin, *Lettres*, 9: 371; and Le Tellier's letters to Mazarin, 23 July 1659, A.A.E. France 907, fol. 240; 17 September 1659, A.A.E. France 908, fol. 104; 14 October 1659, A.A.E. France 908, fol. 213.

47. [Arnauld and Nicole], *Table et extraict*.

48. *Lettre de messieurs les curez de Sens à messieurs les curez de Paris*, p. 3.

49. Elbene, *Response de monseigneur l'evesque d'Orléans*, pp. 3–4.

50. Gondrin, *Response de monseigneur l'archevesque de Sens*, p. 3.

51. Marmiesse, *Response de monseigneur l'evesque de Conserans*.

52. Rapin, *Mémoires*, 3: 16.

53. Tamburini, *Explicatio Decalogi*.

54. *A Messieurs les vicaires généraux de monseigneur l'éminentissime cardinal de Retz*.

55. See Goldmann, *Le Dieu caché*, p. 158.

56. Duranthon, *Collection des procès-verbaux*, 4: 610.

57. On Louis XIV's attitude toward Jansenism, see his *Mémoires for the Instruction of the Dauphin*, pp. 25, 54.

58. The *arrêt* and *lettre de cachet* have been published in *Recueil des actes, titres et mémoires concernant les affaires du clergé de France*, 4: cols. 345–48.

59. *Ordonnance de MM. les vicaires généraux de monseigneur l'éminentissime et révérendissime cardinal de Retz*.

60. For the reaction of the extremist Jansenists to the episcopal letter, see Namer, *L'Abbé Le Roy*, chapter 7.

61. Jager, *Histoire de l'église Catholique en France*, 17: 140.

62. Marca to Mazarin, 13 January 1661, B.N. Ms. Baluze 114, fols. 145–46.

63. Marca, "Relation de la conference faicte par l'ordre du Roy entre Messieurs les Archevesque de Toulouse, Evesques de Rennes, & de Rhodez, d'un part, et les sieurs Jean Baptiste de Contes . . . & Alexandre de Hodencq, les XXIXe & XXXe jour de Juin 1661," ibid., fol. 163; see also the "Proces verbal de ce qui s'est passé en l'affaire du Mandement des Vicaires Generaux

de Paris pour les souscriptions au formulaire de profession de foy dressé contre le Jansenisme," ibid., fol. 150.

64. "Proces verbal de l'Assemblée des Evesques tenue à Fontainebleau," ibid., fols. 159–60.

65. "Project de second Mandement proposé à faire par Messieurs les Grands Vicaires," ibid., fol. 154; "Memoire donné par Messieurs les Grands Vicaires de Paris, contenant leur raisons pour ne point reformer leur Mandement sur la signature du formulaire de profession de foy contre les sectateurs du Jansenisme," ibid., fols. 154–58.

66. Marca, "Relation de la conference . . . ," ibid., fol. 176.

67. *Arrêt du Conseil d'Etat, portant que le mandement de MM. les grands vicaires de l'archevêché de Paris, du huitième de mois de juin dernier, pour la souscription du formulaire de profession de foi contre la doctrine de Jansenius demeurra revoqué et comme non fait. Du 9 juillet 1661.*

68. "Declaration des cures de Paris sur le Mandement de Messieurs les Grands Vicaires de Monseigneur le Cardinal de Rets," B.N. Ms. Baluze 114, fols. 183–84; cf. "Resultat de l'assemblée de Mrs les curez de Paris le 29 juillet 1661," B.M. Ms. A. 15373.

69. Hermant, *Mémoires*, 5: 181.

70. Namer, *L'Abbé Le Roy*, p. 76.

71. Arnauld and La Lane, *Défense de l'Ordonnance*, pp. 4, 40, 43–44. La Lane was a doctor of the Sorbonne who wrote prolifically defending Jansenism.

72. Lionne to D'Auberville, 6 August 1661, B.I. Ms. 1319, fols. 627–28.

73. Marca to cardinal Antoine Barberini, 12 August 1661, B.N. Ms. Baluze 114, fol. 209.

74. D'Auberville to Lionne, 30 August and 23 September 1661, B.I. Ms. 1319, fols. 648–50, 656–58.

75. Blet, *Le Clergé de France*, 2: 313–14.

76. The events from August to October, though providing an important glimpse into the issues and mechanics of seventeenth-century Church-state relationships, are too intricate for the purposes of this chapter. See, for this period, Marca's two chronological *Relations* in B.N. Ms. Baluze 114, fols. 236–45, 248–53; and Hermant, *Mémoires*, 5: 198ff. There is also a great deal of other primary material—correspondence, letters patent, etc.—in Baluze 114. Many of the sources related to the affair of the episcopal letter have been published. The *Traduction de la lettre écrite au pape par messieurs de Contes et de Hodencq . . . en suite de leur premier mandement touchant la signature du Formulaire* contains as well a letter of the vicars-general to cardinal Rospigliosi, papal secretary of state, and letters to the pope by the bishops of Vence and Angers. Equally important is the mélange published as *Arrest du conseil d'estat du roy, par lequel Sa Maiesté exhorte tous les archevesques, & evesques de son royaume, qui n'ont point encore signé ni fait signer le Formulaire, de faire leur mandement pur & simple pour proceder à la signature d'iceluy. Du 1 jour de May 1662. Ensemble le premier mandement*

de messieurs les grands vicaires de Paris; le bref de sa Sainteté sur iceluy; les lettres patentes expediées en consequence; et le second mandement desdits grands vicaires, portant revocation du premier.

77. G.E.F., 6: 432–33.

78. To my knowledge, no other such list of Parisian curés for this period exists.

79. For the approval of Arnauld's *Fréquente communion*, see Hermant, *Mémoires*, 1: 210–11; for the 1649 appeal, see Saint-Amour, *Journal*, pp. 22–23 and Jourdain, *Histoire de l'université*, 1: 197n.; for Arnauld's trial, see Beaubrun, B.N. Ms. Fr. 13896, fols. 2–3; for the *Ecrits*, see Recalde, *Ecrits des curés de Paris, passim*; and for the 1661 declaration, see above, note 68.

80. For the requests, along with the names of those curés who subscribed to them, see above, note 54, and Rousee, *A Messieurs les vicaires généraux de monseigneur l'éminentissime cardinal de Rets archevesque de Paris.*

81. Hermant, *Mémoires*, 1: 581–82.

82. Ibid., 2: 446. Hermant of course denied that anyone was a Jansenist; but his categorization of "Disciple of Saint Augustine" is a reliable indication of those traditionally labeled by historians as Jansenists.

83. Curé of Saint-Barthélemy to Mazarin, 7 December 1655, B.I. Ms. 1315, fol. 431.

84. Curé of Saint-Barthélemy to Mazarin, 14 January 1656, cited in Jansen, *Le Cardinal Mazarin*, p. 236.

85. "Portroit des docteurs de la maison de Sorbonne, de Navarre, moines, ubiquistes, & des bacheliers licentiés," B.N. Ms. Cinq cents Colbert 155, fol. 51.

86. Hermant, *Mémoires*, 3: 465.

87. Meurgey, *Histoire de la paroisse de Saint-Jacques-de-la-Boucherie*, p. 91; D.B.F., 1: col. 132.

88. See, for example, his *De l'obéissance et soumission qui est due à N.S.P. le Pape.*

89. There were two curés of Saint-Merry, alternating every week the functions of the charge.

90. D.H.G.E., 2: cols. 1377–78; D.B.F., 2: cols. 749–50. Amyot figures prominently in all of the memoirs written during the Religious Fronde; see especially those of Rapin, Hermant (who depicted Amyot as "le plus emporté de tous les defenseurs de Molina"), and Saint-Gilles.

91. Racine, *Abrégé de l'histoire de Port-Royal*, p. 127.

92. D.B.F., 6: col. 602; D.H.G.E., 9: col. 95.

93. Blanchart to the prior of Saint-Jean de Chartres, 7 October 1661, Bibliothèque Sainte-Geneviève Ms. 2560, fol. 4.

94. B.N. Ms. Fr. 24075, fol. 35.

95. Hermant, *Mémoires*, 2: 580–81, 3: 178.

96. Rapin, *Mémoires*, 1: 430.

97. Hermant, *Mémoires*, 2: 91–92.

98. Ibid., 1: 575. See also, D.H.G.E., 14: cols. 1206–7.

99. Hermant, *Mémoires*, 4: 77.

100. Curé of Saint-Sulpice to Le Tellier, 9 August 1661, B.N. Ms. Baluze 114, fol. 255.

101. Orcibal, *Saint-Cyran*, pp. 61–62.

102. Lefebvre, *Pascal*, 1: 52.

CONCLUSION

1. P. J. Coveney, *France in Crisis, 1620–1675*, pp. 37–42.

2. With respect to the Frondes not being revolutionary, see, for example, Kossmann, *La Fronde*, pp. 238–41, 259; Moote, *The Revolt of the Judges*, pp. 368–71; Richet, *La France moderne*, pp. 135–39; Shennan, *Government and Society in France*, p. 70. Moote suggests that a revolution could not occur in the seventeenth century because there were no "generalized moral and intellectual concepts undergirding grievances, dissolving habits of obedience, and articulating new aspirations," such as the Enlightenment provided by the late eighteenth century ("The Preconditions of Revolution in Early Modern Europe: Did They Really Exist?" p. 232). See also Sée, "Les Idées politiques à l'époque de la Fronde," pp. 713–38; Batiffol, "Les Idées de la révolution sous Louis XIV," pp. 97–120; Denis, "Littérature politique de la Fronde," pp. 27–93.

3. Michel, "Clergé et pastorale jansénistes à Paris (1669–1730)," pp. 177–97.

4. Préclin, *Les Jansénistes du XVIIIe siècle*; see also Williams, "The Significance of Jansenism in the History of the French Catholic Church in the Pre-Revolutionary Era," pp. 289–306.

5. Kreiser, *Miracles, Convulsions, and Ecclesiastical Politics*, pp. 44–45, 60–65.

6. Hutt, "The Curés and the Third Estate: The Ideas of Reform in the Pamphlets of the French Lower Clergy in the Period 1787–1789," pp. 74–92.

7. Ibid., p. 79.

8. See Hutt, "The Role of the Curés in the Estates General of 1789," pp. 190–220; Necheles, "The Curés in the Estates General of 1789," pp. 425–44.

BIBLIOGRAPHY

I . MANUSCRIPT SOURCES

Archives des Affaires Etrangères
Mémoires et Documents, France, 284, 883, 884, 886, 891, 895, 905, 906,
907, 908, 1593, 1594
Correspondance politique, Rome, 126, 128
Archives Nationales
G⁸655A-B—Journal of Robert François d'Aigreville on the General
Assembly of 1655–57
L428, no. 61—Maimbourg affair
Bibliothèque historique de la ville de Paris
Diverses pièces (cote 710 351)—regular-secular conflict
Bibliothèque de l'Institut
1315, 1319, 1322—various correspondence, collected by Chantelauze
Bibliothèque Mazarine
2246—material on Retz affair
2486—memoirs of Feydeau
A. 15373—assembly of the curés, 29 July 1661
Bibliothèque Nationale
Collection Baluze
113, 114, 115—various correspondence and memoranda
Fonds Français
4233—memorandum on Chevalier
6893, 6895—papers of Le Tellier
13833—Nicolas Le Gros
13895–96—memoirs of the abbé de Beaubrun
15626—material on Retz affair
15730—material on the General Assembly
17589—material on Retz affair
20111—lectures at Saint-Merry
20866—register of the assemblies of the curés
24075—register of the assemblies of the curés
Nouvelles Acquisitions Françaises
1163—archbishop of Paris
4687—Bagot-Mazure controversy
Cinq cents Colbert
155—description of members of the Faculty of Theology
Mélanges de Colbert
7—letter of Gondrin

51—administrative correspondence
Bibliothèque de la Société de Port-Royal
    Collection Le Paige 468—register of the assemblies of the curés; pamphlets
Bibliothèque Sainte-Geneviève
2560—correspondence of François Blanchart

2. PRINTED SOURCES

A Messieurs les vicaires généraux de monseigneur l'éminentissime cardinal de Retz archevesque de Paris. N.p. [1659].

Abelly, Louis. *De l'obéissance et soumission qui est due à N.S.P. le Pape en ce qui regarde les choses de la foi.* Paris, 1654.

Arnauld, Abbé Antoine. *Mémoires.* Michaud and Poujoulat collection. Paris, 1881.

Arnauld, Antoine, and La Lane, Noël de. *Défense de l'Ordonnance de messieurs les vicaires généraux de monseigneur le cardinal de Retz, archevêque de Paris, pour la signature du formulaire.* N.p., n.d.

[————, and Nicole, Pierre]. *Table et extraict de quelques unes des plus dangereuses propositions de la morale de plusieurs nouveaux casuistes, fidelement tirées de leurs ouvrages.* Paris, 1656.

Arrest du conseil d'estat du roy, par lequel Sa Maiesté exhorte tous les archevesques, & evesques de son royaume, qui n'ont point encore signé ni fait signer le Formulaire, de faire leur mandement pur & simple pour proceder à la signature d'iceluy. Du 1 jour de May 1662. Ensemble le premier mandement de messieurs les grands vicaires de Paris; le bref de sa Sainteté sur iceluy; les lettres patentes expediées en consequence; et le second mandement desdits grands vicaires, portant revocation du premier. Paris, 1662.

Arrêt du Conseil d'Etat, portant que le mandement de MM. les grands vicaires de l'archevêché de Paris, du huitième de mois de juin dernier, pour la souscription du formulaire de profession de foi contre la doctrine de Jansenius demeurra revoqué et comme non fait. Du 9 juillet 1661. Paris, 1661.

Aux fidèles du diocèse de Paris. N.p., 1655.

Avis sincère d'un évêque pieux et désintéressé envoyez au C. de Retz. . . . N.p., 1655.

Avis sur l'anonyme reformé, par les interpretations, declarations, et suplémens de quelques curez. N.p., n.d.

Avranches, Dom Pacifique d'. *Response à un escrit anonyme contre les religieux.* N.p., 1654.

Bagot, Jean. *Défense du droict épiscopal et de la liberté des fidèles touchant les messes et les confessions d'obligation, contre l'écrit d'un certain docteur anonyme, par le R.P. Jean Bagot, de la comp. de Iesus.* Paris, 1655.

————. *Explication donnee par le P. Bagot, sur les quatre chefs de son livre, qui luy ont esté proposez par messeigneurs de l'assemblée du clergé de France.* N.p. [1657].

————. *Response du P. Bagot Prestre de la compagnie de Iesus, aux plaintes qu'on fait de son livre intitulé, "Defense du Droict Episcopal, et de la liberté des fidelles touchant les messes & les confessions d'obligation."* N.p., n.d.

Brienne, Henri-Auguste de Loménie, comte de. *Mémoires.* Michaud and Poujoulat collection. Paris, 1881.

Champollion-Figeac, Aimé, ed. *Complément des mémoires du cardinal de Retz.* Michaud and Poujoulat collection. Paris, 1881.

Colbert, J.-B. *Lettres, instructions, et mémoires.* Ed. Pierre Clément. 7 vols. Paris, 1861–82.

Complainte et deffences: Pour maistre Pierre Marlin, docteur en theologie, curé de S. Eustache, demandeur, & deffendeur; et les curez de la ville, faux-bourgs, & banlieue de Paris, intervenans, & deffendeurs. Contre les venerables doyen, chanoines, et chapitre de l'église metropolitaine de Paris, deffendeurs, et demandeurs. N.p., 1651.

Conrart, Valentin. *Mémoires.* Michaud and Poujoulat collection. Paris, 1881.

Considérations sur une lettre du cardinal de Retz, écrite à messieurs les doyen, chanoines et chapitre de l'église de Paris. N.p., 1655.

Defauts pour lesquels la declaration de quelques curez, sur l'Anonyme, ne peut point estre recue par messeigneurs de l'Assemblée du Clergé de France. N.p., n.d.

Depping, G. P., ed. *Correspondance administrative sous le règne de Louis XIV.* 4 vols. Paris, 1850–55.

Des Déserts, Josselin. *A Messeigneurs de l'assemblée du clergé, sur la proposition suivante du P. Bagot au chap. 26. "Il ne faut pas se persuader, que la charge de curé précisément luy donne plus de droit, ou de grâce gratuite et de bénédiction pour la direction de ses parroissiens en la vie chrestienne et spirituelle."* N.p., n.d.

Deuxiesme chef des quatre, sur lesquels messeigneurs du clergé demandant quelque esclaircissement au Pere Bagot. N.p., n.d.

Discours sur ce qui est arrivé dans l'église de Paris, après la sortie de monsieur le cardinal de Retz de Nantes, avec la décision de la question si le chapitre de Paris a pu prendre la juridiction et nommer des grands vicaires. Paris, 1654.

Dupuys, Antoine. *Discours prononcé en l'Assemblée Synodale, tenue le 30 avril 1658. . . .* N.p., n.d.

————, and Rousse, Jean. *Advis de messieurs les curez de Paris, à messieurs les curez des autres diocèses de France; sur les mauvaises maximes de quelques nouveaux casuistes.* Paris, 1656.

————. *Lettre de messieurs les curez de Paris à monseigneur l'archevêque de Sens . . . sur la censure qu'il a faite du livre intitulé, "Apologie pour les casuistes. . . ."* N.p. [1658].

————. *Suite de l'extrait de plusieurs mauvaises propositions des nouveaux casuistes, recueillies par messieurs les Curez de Paris, et presentées à nosseigneurs de l'assemblée générale du clergé de France le 24 Novembre 1656.* Paris, 1656.

Duranthon, Antoine. *Collection des procès-verbaux des Assemblées générales du Clergé de France depuis 1560 jusqu'à présent.* 9 vols. Paris, 1767–78.

Elbene, Alphonse d'. *Response de monseigneur l'evesque d'Orléans à la lettre de messieurs les curez de Paris.* N.p., 1658.

Extraict des censures de la Faculté de Théologie de Paris. Par lesquelles elle condamne certaines propositions avancées contre la hiérarchie de l'église et renouvellées depuis peu par le P. Bagot Jésuite. . . . Paris, 1656.

Extraict d'un livre intitulé, "Défense du droict épiscopal . . . ." N.p., n.d.

Extrait de l'interpretation & vray sens que les curez de Paris donnent sur les propositions contenues dans le livre anonyme intitulé, "L'Obligation des fidelles de se confesser à leur curé." N.p., n.d.

Extrait de quelques maximes de l'Anonyme, intitulé "l'obligation des fidelles, etc." et de quelques-unes de ses sentimens; principalement contre l'autho-rité du pape & des evesques. N.p., n.d.

Extrait de quelques propositions d'un livre intitulé, "Obligation des fidelles de se confesser à leur curé." N.p., 1654.

Factum pour Me Pierre Marlin, curé de S. Eustache; et les curez de la ville . . . contre les doyen, chanoines. . . . N.p., 1651.

Ferté, Jeanne. "Saint-Etienne-du-Mont à la mi-XVIIe siècle. Mémoires d'un curé génovéfain." [Memoirs of Paul Beurrier] Unpublished thesis, Paris, 1964.

Gondi, Jean François Paul de, cardinal de Retz. *Mémoires.* Paris, Pléiade, 1956.

————. *Oeuvres.* Ed. François Régis de Chantelauze. Vol. 6. Paris, 1887.

Gondrin, Henri de. *Response de monseigneur l'archevesque de Sens, à messieurs les curez de Paris.* N.p., n.d.

Hanotaux, Gabriel, ed. *Recueil des instructions données aux ambassadeurs et ministres de France depuis les traités de Westphalie jusqu'à la Révolution française: Rome.* Paris, 1888.

Héricourt, Louis. *Les Loix ecclésiastiques de France.* Paris, 1773.

Hermant, Godefroi. *Mémoires . . . sur l'histoire ecclésiastique du XVIIe siècle (1630–1663).* Ed. Augustin Gazier. 6 vols. Paris, 1905–10.

Joly, Claude. *Mémoires.* Michaud and Poujoulat collection. Paris, 1881.

Joly, Guy. *Mémoires.* Michaud and Poujoulat collection. Paris, 1881.

L'Espine, Jean de. *Lettre d'un paroissien de Sainct Paul, à monsieur le curé.* N.p., 1654.

Lettre circulaire de l'Assemblée générale du clergé de France. N.p. [1656].

Lettre d'un advocat de la cour, à un conseiller du parlement de Rouen: Sur ce qui s'est passé dans l'Eglise de Saint Paul, le 12. du mois d'avril 1654. N.p. [1654].

Lettre de messieurs les curez de Sens à messieurs les curez de Paris. Sur la censure de "l'Apologie pour les Casuistes," faite par monseigneur l'archevesque de Sens. Avec la réponse de messieurs les curez de Paris à messieurs les curez de Sens. Paris, 1659.

Lettre de plusieurs ecclésiastiques considérables du diocèse de Paris à monsieur le cardinal de Retz, leur archevêque. N.p. [1656].

Lettre instructive sur ce qui s'est passé entre les pères Jésuites et les prestres de Saint Paul, le jour de la Saint Michel de cette presente année 1655. N.p., 1655.

Lettre qui respond aux falsifications d'une feuille volante, touchant l'obligation qu'ont les fidelles de se confesser à leurs curez, & qui prouve le pouvoir des Reguliers. N.p., n.d.

Louis XIV. *Mémoires for the Instruction of the Dauphin.* Ed. Paul Sonnino. New York, 1970.

Marlin, Pierre, and Rousse, Jean. *Conclusion de messieurs les curez de Paris, pour la publication de la censure du livre de l'Apologie pour les casuistes, faite par messieurs les vicaires generaux de monseigneur l'eminentissime cardinal de Retz, archevesque de Paris.* N.p., n.d.

————. *Lettre de messieurs les curez de Paris, à monseigneur l'evesque d'Orléans.* N.p., 1658.

————. *Lettre de messieurs les curez de Paris à monseigneur l'evesque de Conserans, sur le suite de la censure qu'il a faite avec messeigneurs les evesques d'Alet, de Pamies, de Commenge, et de Bazas, de l'Apologie des casuistes.* N.p., n.d.

Marmiesse, Bernard. *Response de monseigneur l'evesque de Conserans à la lettre de messieurs les curez de Paris.* N.p., n.d.

Mazarin, Jules. *Lettres.* Ed. Pierre-Adolphe Chéruel. 9 vols. Paris, 1872–1906.

Mazure, Nicolas. *Compliment de Messieurs les curés de Paris, à Monseigneur le président de Belièvre, sur sa promotion à la dignité de premier président. Fait par le sieur Mazure, Curé de Saint Paul, le mardy 29 d'avril 1653.* N.p., n.d.

————. *Compliment de Messieurs les curés de Paris. Fait à Monseigneur l'Eminentissime Cardinal de Retz, sur sa promotion. Par le curé de Saint-Paul.* N.p., n.d.

————. *Harangue de Mr Mazure curé de S. Paul, à la reyne de Suède, pour Messieurs les Curez de Paris.* N.p., n.d.

[————]. *L'Obligation des fidèles de se confesser à leur curé, pour respondre aux réflexions des réguliers sur le chapitre 21 du concile générale de Latran IV, tenu en l'année 1215, sous le pape Innocent III.* Paris, 1653.

————. *Oraison funèbre de feu messire Jean François de Gondy premier archevesque de Paris . . . prononcée par le sieur Mazure . . . au service . . . qui se fist . . . le 19 juin 1654 ou officierent et assisterent tous Messieurs les Curez de la ville et fauxbourgs de Paris.* Paris, 1654.

Motteville, F. B. de. *Mémoires.* Michaud and Poujoulat collection. Paris, 1881.

Ordonnance de MM. les vicaires généraux de monseigneur l'éminentissime et révérendissime cardinal de Retz, archevêque de Paris. Pour la signature du formulaire de foi dressé en exécution des constitutions de nos SS. Pères les papes Innocent X et Alexandre VII. Paris, 1661.

Pascal, Blaise. *Oeuvres.* Ed. Léon Brunschvicg et al. 14 vols. Paris, 1908–21.

———. *Les Provinciales.* Ed. Louis Cognet. Paris, 1965.

Pirot, Georges. *L'Apologie pour les casuistes contre les calomnies des jansénistes.* Paris, 1657.

Prise de possession de l'archevesché de Paris, par monseigneur l'eminentissime cardinal de Retz. N.p., n.d.

Racine, Jean. *Abrégé de l'histoire de Port-Royal.* Paris, 1909.

Raisons pour monstrer que mons. le cardinal de Rets a peu et deu destituer monsieur Dusaussay, evesque de Toul, de la charge de grand vicaire, et de celle d'official. N.p. [1656].

Rapin, René. *Mémoires du P. René Rapin. . . .* Ed. Léon Aubineau. 3 vols. Paris, 1865.

Recalde, I. de, ed. *Ecrits des curés de Paris contre la politique et la morale des Jésuites (1658–1659) avec une étude sur la querelle du laxisme.* Paris, 1921.

Recueil des actes, titres et mémoires concernant les affaires du Clergé de France. . . . 12 vols. Paris, 1768–71.

Response au libelle intitulé "Dom pacifique d'Avranches," rempli d'erreurs et de calomnies, contre la saincte memoire de feu Monseigneur l'Evesque de Belley, & contre tous les curez de Paris, composé & distribué par les Iesuites en l'an 1654. N.p., n.d.

Response d'un parroissien de S. Paul à un conseiller du parlement de Rouen, sur ce qui s'est passé dans l'Eglise de S. Paul le douzième avril. N.p. [1654].

Roullé, Pierre, and Rousse, Jean. [*Lettre circulaire des syndics des curés de Paris, au sujet des empiétements du clergé régulier sur les droits du clergé seculier*]. N.p. [1654].

Rousse, Jean. *A Messieurs les vicaires généraux de monseigneur l'éminentissime cardinal de Rets archevesque de Paris.* N.p. [1658].

[———.]. *Extraict des propositions à examiner du livre intitulé, "Deffense du droict episcopal. . . ."* N.p., n.d.

———. *Sommaire de la harangue de messieurs les curez de Paris, en l'Assemblée générale du Clergé, sur leur advis envoyé à messieurs les curez des autres dioceses, contre la fausse et pernicieuse morale du temps.* Paris, 1656.

———. *Sommaire des déclarations des curez de Paris: Sur le vray sense des onze propositions, extraictes & objectées contre le livre intitulé, "De L'Obligation des fidèles, de se confesser à leur cure." Contenant au fond la definition, les qualités, et fonctions du propre prestre. . . .* N.p., 1657.

Saint-Amour, Louis Gorin de. *Journal de Mr. de Saint-Amour. . . .* [Amsterdam] 1662.

Saint-Gilles, Antoine Baudry de. *Le Journal de M. de Saint-Gilles.* Ed. Ernest Jovy. Paris, 1936.

Second advis, ou lettre de messieurs les curez de Paris, à messieurs les curez des autres dioceses de France. Sur leur premier advis touchant la fausse & pernicieuse morale du temps. Paris, 1656.

Sermon de Mr Jean Gerson docteur en theologie, chancellier de l'université de Paris: prononcé dans l'eglise de Paris en une procession generale, faite le troisieme dimanche de careme l'annee 1409. Par le Commandement de Monseigneur l'evesque de Paris. Pour servir de Response au livre du P. Bagot Jesuite. N.p., n.d.

Sommaire du procez d'entre les Doyen, Chanoines & Chapitre de l'Eglise de Paris, demandeurs, complaignans & deffendeurs. Contre Maistre Pierre Marlin, curé de Sainct Eustache: Et les Curez de la Ville et Fauxbourgs de Paris, deffendeurs et demandeurs. N.p., 1648.

Talon, Omer. *Mémoires.* Michaud and Poujoulat collection. Paris, 1881.

Tamburini, Thomas. *Explicatio Decalogi, duabus distincta partibus.* . . . *Accesserunt etiam opuscula tria: De confessione, communione, sacrificio missae.* . . . Lyon, 1659.

Traduction de la lettre écrite au pape par messieurs de Contes et de Hodencq . . . en suite de leur premier mandement touchant la signature du Formulaire. N.p., n.d.

Vallier, Jean. *Journal.* Ed. Henri Courteault. 4 vols. Paris, 1902–18.

Vincent de Paul. *Correspondance, entretiens, documents.* Ed. Pierre Coste. 14 vols. Paris, 1920–25.

3. SECONDARY WORKS

Adam, Antoine. *Du mysticisme à la révolte. Les Jansénistes du XVIIe siècle.* Paris, 1968.

Allier, Raoul. *La Cabale des dévots, 1627–1666.* Paris, 1902.

Avenel, G.d'. *Les Evêques et archevêques de Paris depuis Saint Denis jusqu'à nos jours.* 2 vols. Paris, 1878.

Batiffol, Louis. *Biographie du cardinal de Retz.* Paris, 1929.

Bertrand, Joseph. *Blaise Pascal.* Paris, 1891.

Blet, Pierre. *Le Clergé de France et la monarchie. Etude sur les assemblées générales du clergé de 1615 à 1666.* 2 vols. Rome, 1959.

Blond, Louis. *La Maison professe des Jésuites de la rue Saint-Antoine à Paris, 1580–1762.* Paris, 1957.

Bonney, Richard. *Political Change in France under Richelieu and Mazarin, 1624–1661.* Oxford, 1978.

Bourlon, J. *Les Assemblées du Clergé sous l'ancien Régime.* Paris, 1907.

Brochard, Louis. *Saint-Gervais, histoire de la paroisse d'après de nombreux documents inédits.* Paris [1950].

Brongniart, Marcel. *La Paroisse Saint-Médard au faubourg Saint-Marceau.* Paris, 1951.

Calvet, Jean. *La Littérature religieuse de François de Sales à Fénelon.* Paris, 1956.

Cans, Albert. *L'Organisation financière du clergé de France à l'époque Louis XIV*. Paris, 1909.

Ceyssens, Lucien. *La Fin de la première période du jansénisme, sources des années 1654–1660*. 2 vols. Brussels and Rome, 1963–65.

Chantelauze, François Régis de. *Le Cardinal de Retz et l'affaire du chapeau*. 2 vols. Paris, 1878.

————. *Le Cardinal de Retz et les Jansénistes*. Paris, 1867.

————. *Le Cardinal de Retz et ses missions diplomatiques à Rome*. Paris, 1879.

————. *Saint Vincent de Paul et les Gondi*. Paris, 1882.

Charmeil, Jean-Paul. *Les Trésoriers de France à l'époque de la Fronde*. Paris, 1964.

Chérot, Henri. *La Première jeunesse de Louis XIV*. Lille, 1894.

Chéruel, Pierre-Adolphe. *Histoire de France pendant la minorité de Louis XIV*. 4 vols. Paris, 1879–80.

————. *Histoire de France sous le ministère de Mazarin*. 3 vols. Paris, 1882.

Chesneau, Charles. *Le P. Yves de Paris et son temps (1590–1678)*. 2 vols. Paris, 1948.

Cochin, Claude. *Henri Arnauld, évêque d'Angers (1597–1692)*. Paris, 1921.

Cognet, Louis. *Le Jansénisme*. Paris, 1968.

Coveney, P. J. *France in Crisis, 1620–1675*. Totowa, N.J., 1977.

Coville, Henry. *Etudes sur Mazarin et ses démêlés avec le pape Innocent X (1644–1648)*. Paris, 1914.

Crousaz-Crétit, P. de. *Paris sous Louis XIV*. 2 vols. Paris, 1922–23.

Delumeau, Jean. *Le Catholicisme entre Luther et Voltaire*. Paris, 1971.

Dent, Julian. *Crisis in Finance: Crown, Financiers and Society in Seventeenth-Century France*. New York, 1973.

Dethan, Georges. *Gaston d'Orléans: Conspirateur et prince charmant*. Paris, 1959.

Deyon, Pierre. *Amiens, capitale provinciale. Etude sur la société urbaine au XVIIe siècle*. Paris, 1967.

Dictionnaire de biographie française. Paris, 1933–.

Dictionnaire de droit canonique. 7 vols. Paris, 1935–65.

Dictionnaire d'histoire et de géographie ecclésiastiques. Paris, 1912–.

Doolin, Paul. *The Fronde*. Cambridge, Mass., 1935.

Doucet, R. *Les Institutions de la France au XVIe siècle*. 2 vols. Paris, 1948.

Dourarche, Aristide. *L'Université de Paris et les Jésuites*. Paris, 1888.

Dubois, Georges. *Henri de Pardaillon de Gondrin archevêque de Sens (1646–1674)*. Alençon, 1902.

Dulaure, J. A. *Histoire physique, civile et morale de Paris*. 4 vols. Paris, 1839.

Edwards, Tom. "Jansenism in Church and State." Unpublished Ph.D. dissertation, Harvard University, 1960.

Feillet, Alphonse. *La Misère au temps de la Fronde et Saint Vincent de Paul*. Paris, 1862.

Féret, Pierre. *La Faculté de théologie de Paris et ses docteurs les plus célèbres*. 7 vols. Paris, 1900–1910.

Ferté, Jeanne. *La Vie religieuse dans les campagnes parisiennes (1622–1695)*. Paris, 1962.

Gaquère, François. *Pierre de Marca (1594–1662), sa vie, ses oeuvres, son gallicanisme*. Paris, 1932.

Gazier, Augustin. *Les Dernières années du cardinal de Retz, 1655–1679*. Paris, 1875.

———. *Histoire générale du mouvement janséniste depuis ses origines jusqu'à nos jours*. 2 vols. Paris, 1922.

Goldmann, Lucien. *Correspondance de Martin de Barcos avec les abbesses de Port-Royal et les principaux personnages du groupe janséniste*. Paris, 1956.

———. *Le Dieu caché. Etude sur la vision tragique dans les "Pensées" de Pascal et dans le théâtre de Racine*. Paris, 1955.

Goubert, Pierre. *L'Ancien Régime*. 2 vols. Paris, 1969 and 1973.

Grand-Mesnil, Marie-Noële. *Mazarin, la Fronde et la presse*. Paris, 1967.

Hamscher, Albert. *The Parlement of Paris after the Fronde, 1653–1673*. Pittsburgh, 1976.

Hurel, A. *Les Orateurs sacrées à la cour de Louis XIV*. 2 vols. Paris, 1872.

Jacques, Emile. *Les Années d'exil d'Antoine Arnauld (1679–1694)*. Louvain, 1976.

Jacquinet, Paul. *Des prédicateurs du XVIIe siècle avant Bossuet*. Paris, 1863.

Jager, Jean-Nicolas. *Histoire de l'église Catholique en France. . . .* 20 vols. Paris, 1862–75.

Jansen, Paule. *Le Cardinal Mazarin et le mouvement janséniste français, 1653–1659*. Paris, 1967.

Jarry, E., and Préclin, E. *Les Luttes politiques et doctrinales aux XVIIe et XVIIIe siècles*. 2 vols. Paris, 1956.

Jourdain, Charles. *Histoire de l'université de Paris aux XVIIe et XVIIIe siècles*. 2 vols. Paris, 1888.

Jousse, Daniel. *Traité du gouvernement spirituel et temporel des paroisses. Où l'on examine tout ce qui concerne les fonctions, droits et devoirs des Marguilliers dans l'administration des Fabriques, des biens des Pauvres et des Ecoles de Charité. Comme aussi ce qui regarde les fonctions, droits et devoirs des Curés, et autres personnes proposées au Gouvernement et au soin des Eglises*. Paris, 1769.

Kerviler, René. *Le Chancelier Pierre Séguier*. Paris, 1874.

Kettering, Sharon. *Judicial Politics and Urban Revolt in Seventeenth-Century Provence: The Parlement of Aix, 1629–1659*. Princeton, 1978.

Klaits, Joseph. *Printed Propaganda under Louis XIV: Absolute Monarchy and Public Opinion*. Princeton, 1976.

Knachel, Philip. *England and the Fronde*. Ithaca, 1967.

Korr, Charles. *Cromwell and the New Model Foreign Policy: England's Policy toward France, 1649–1658*. Berkeley, 1975.

Kossmann, E. H. *La Fronde*. Leiden, 1954.

Kreiser, B. Robert. *Miracles, Convulsions, and Ecclesiastical Politics in Early Eighteenth-Century Paris*. Princeton, 1978.

Labitte, Charles. *De la démocratie chez les prédicateurs de la Ligue*. Paris, 1841.

Lair, J. *Nicolas Fouquet*. 2 vols. Paris, 1890.

Lavisse, E. *Histoire de France depuis les origines jusqu'à la Révolution*. Vol. 7, part 1. Paris, 1911.

Lebeuf, Jean. *Histoire de la ville et de tout le diocèse de Paris*. 6 vols. Paris, 1883–93.

Lefebvre, Henri. *Pascal*. 2 vols. Paris, 1949 and 1954.

Leff, Gordon. *Paris and Oxford Universities in the Thirteenth and Fourteenth Centuries*. New York, 1968.

[Le Paige, Louis-Adrien, and Du Rey de Meinières, J. B. F.] *Histoire de la détention du cardinal de Retz*. Vincennes, 1755.

Logié, Paul. *La Fronde en Normandie*. 3 vols. Amiens, 1951–52.

Lorris, Pierre-Georges. *Le Cardinal de Retz*. Paris, 1956.

Madelin, Louis. *La Fronde: Une Révolution manquée*. Paris, 1931.

Mandrou, Robert. *Des humanistes aux hommes de science (XVIe et XVIIe siècles)*. Paris, 1973.

Marie, Albert. *Bibliographie générale des oeuvres de Blaise Pascal*. 5 vols. Paris, 1925–27.

Marion, Marcel. *Dictionnaire des institutions de la France aux XVIIe et XVIIIe siècles*. Paris, 1969.

Martimort, A. G. *Le Gallicanisme*. Paris, 1973.

Méthivier, Hubert. *Le Siècle de Louis XIII*. Paris, 1967.

Meurgey, Jacques. *Histoire de la paroisse de Saint-Jacques-de-la-Boucherie*. Paris, 1926.

Moote, A. Lloyd. *The Revolt of the Judges: The Parlement of Paris and the Fronde, 1643–1652*. Princeton, 1971.

Moreau, Celestin. *Bibliographie des Mazarinades*. 3 vols. Paris, 1850–51.

Mousnier, Roland. *Les Institutions de la France sous la monarchie absolue*. Paris, 1974.

————. *Paris, capitale au temps de Richelieu et de Mazarin*. Paris, 1978.

————. *La Vénalité des offices sous Henri IV et Louis XIII*. Paris, 1971.

Namer, G. *L'Abbé Le Roy et ses amis. Essai sur le jansénisme extrémiste intramondain*. Paris, 1964.

O'Connor, David. "Parochial Relations and Cooperation of the Religious Clergy and the Diocesan Clergy: Canons 608–609 (Historical-Synopsis)." Unpublished Ph.D. dissertation, The Catholic University of America, 1957.

Olivier-Martin, François. *Histoire du droit français*. Paris, 1951.

Orcibal, Jean. *Saint-Cyran et le jansénisme*. Paris, 1961.

Pastor, Ludwig von. *The History of the Popes*. 40 vols. London, 1891–1953.

Pillorget, René. *Les Mouvements insurrectionnels de Provence entre 1596 et 1715*. Paris, 1975.

Porchnev, Boris. *Les Soulèvements populaires en France de 1623 à 1648*. Paris, 1963.

Préclin, E. *Les Jansénistes du XVIIIe siècle et la Constitution civile du clergé. Le Développement du richérisme. Sa propagation dans le bas clergé, 1713–1791*. Paris, 1929.

Puyol, Pierre. *Edmond Richer, étude historique et critique sur la rénovation du gallicanisme au commencement du XVIIe siècle*. 2 vols. Paris, 1876.

Ranum, Orest. *Paris in the Age of Absolutism*. New York, 1968.

———. *Richelieu and the Councillors of Louis XIII*. Oxford, 1963.

Rashdall, Hastings. *The Universities of Europe in the Middle Ages*. 3 vols. Oxford, 1936.

Richet, Denis. *La France moderne: L'Esprit des institutions*. Paris, 1973.

Robert, Charles. *Anthyme-Denis Cohon, évêque et comte de Dol. Son rôle pendant la Fronde*. Rennes, 1895.

Salmon, J. H. M. *Cardinal de Retz: The Anatomy of a Conspirator*. New York, 1969.

Schmitt, Thérèse-Jean. *L'Organisation ecclésiastique et la pratique religieuse dans l'archidiaconé d'Autun de 1650 à 1750*. Autun, 1957.

Sedgwick, Alexander. *Jansenism in Seventeenth-Century France: Voices from the Wilderness*. Charlottesville, 1977.

Serbat, Louis. *Les Assemblées du Clergé de France: Origines, organisation, développement*. Paris, 1906.

Shennan, J. H. *Government and Society in France, 1461–1661*. London, 1969.

Sommervogel, Carlos, ed. *Bibliothèque de la compagnie de Jésus*. 11 vols. Paris, 1890–1932.

Stoye, John. *Europe Unfolding, 1648–1688*. New York, 1969.

Taveneaux, René. *Jansénisme et politique*. Paris, 1965.

Treuvé, Michel. *Histoire de monsieur Duhamel*. N.p., n.d.

Valfrey, Jules. *Hugues de Lionne, ses ambassades en Italie, 1642–1656*. Paris, 1877.

Van Kley, Dale. *The Jansenists and the Expulsion of the Jesuits from France, 1757–1765*. New Haven, 1975.

Watkins, Oscar. *A History of Penance*. 2 vols. New York, 1921.

Westrich, Sal. *The Ormée of Bordeaux: A Revolution during the Fronde*. Baltimore and London, 1972.

Wilhelm, Jacques. *La Vie quotidienne au Marais au XVIIe siècle*. Paris, 1966.

Willaert, Léopold. *Après le concile de Trente. La Restauration catholique, 1563–1648*. Paris, 1960.

Wolf, John B. *Louis XIV*. New York, 1968.

4. ARTICLES

Aubineau, Léon. "Les Grands-vicaires du cardinal de Retz." In René Rapin, *Mémoires du P. René Rapin*. . . . 3 vols. Paris, 1865. 2: 505–9.

Batiffol, Louis. "Les Idées de la révolution sous Louis XIV." *Revue de Paris* 2 (1928): 97–120.

Blet, Pierre. "Jésuites Gallicans au XVIIe siècle?" *Archivum Historicum Societatis Jesu* 29 (1960): 55–84.

————. "L'Ordre du clergé au XVIIe siècle." *Revue d'Histoire de l'Eglise de France* 54 (1968): 5–26.

Bonney, Richard. "The French Civil War, 1649–53." *European Studies Review* 8 (1978): 71–100.

Bourgeon, J. L. "L'Ile de la Cité pendant la Fronde: Structure sociale." *Paris et Ile-de-France. Mémoires* 13 (1962): 23–144.

Bouwsma, William. "Gallicanism and the Nature of Christianity." In *Renaissance Studies in Honor of Hans Baron*, ed. Anthony Molho and John Tedeschi. Dekalb, Ill., 1971.

Cans, Albert. "Le Rôle politique de l'Assemblée du Clergé pendant la Fronde (1650–1651)." *Revue historique* 114 (1912): 1–60.

Carreyre, Jean. "La Doctrine janséniste." *Introduction aux études d'histoire ecclésiastique locale*, ed. Victor Carrière. 3 vols. Paris, 1934–40. 3: 513–39.

Carrier, Herbert. "Port-Royal et la Fronde: Deux Mazarinades inconnues d'Arnauld d'Andilly." *Revue d'histoire littéraire de la France* 75 (1975): 3–29.

————. "Souvenirs de la Fronde en U.R.S.S.: Les Collections russes de Mazarinades." *Revue historique* 252 (1974): 27–50.

Ceyssens, Lucien. "Les Cinq propositions de Jansénius à Rome." *Revue d'histoire ecclésiastique* 66 (1971): 449–501, 821–86.

————. "François Annat, S.J., avant son confessorat (1590–1654)." *Antonianum* 50 (July–December 1975): 483–529.

————. "Le Jansénisme. Considérations historiques préliminaires à sa notion." *Analecta gregoriana* 71 (1952): 3–32.

Chantelauze, François Régis de. "Les Dernières années du cardinal de Retz" (review of Gazier's book). *Revue des questions historiques* 21 (1877): 100–146.

Cognet, Louis. "Etat présent des études Port-Royalistes." *Critique* 8 (1952): 689–702.

Denis, M. J. "Littérature politique de la Fronde." *Mémoires de l'académie nationale des sciences, arts et belles lettres de Caen* (1892), 27–93.

Dent, Cynthia A. "Changes in the Episcopal Structure of the Church of France in the 17th Century as an Aspect of Bourbon State-building." *Bulletin of the Institute of Historical Research* 48 (November 1975): 214–29.

Dent, Julian. "An Aspect of the Crisis of the Seventeenth Century: The Collapse of the Financial Administration of the French Monarchy (1653–1661)." *Economic History Review*, ser. 2, vol. 20 (1967): 241–56.

————. "The Role of Clientèles in the Financial Elite of France under Cardinal Mazarin." In *French Government and Society 1500–1800:*

Essays in Memory of Alfred Cobban, ed. John F. Bosher. London, 1973.

Dethan, Georges. "Recherches nouvelles sur la personnalité de Mazarin." *Académie des sciences, morales et politiques. Revue des travaux* 122 (1969): 203–17.

Deyon, Pierre. "Perspectives et limites d'une 'sociologie' du jansénisme." *Annales: Economies, Sociétés, Civilisations* 21 (1966): 428–34.

Dolhagary, B. "Curés." *Dictionnaire de théologie catholique.* Paris, 1939. Vol. 3, cols. 2429–53.

Dubois, E. T. "A Jesuit History of Jansenism." *Modern Language Review* 64 (1969): 764–73.

Dubois, Jacques. "La Carte des diocèses de France avant la Révolution." *Annales: Economies, Sociétés, Civilisations* 20 (1965): 680–91.

Dubruel, Marc. "Gallicanisme." *Dictionnaire de théologie catholique.* Paris, 1915. Vol. 6, part 2, cols. 1096–1137.

Fosseyeux, Marcel. "Les Revenues de l'Archevêché de Paris au XVIIe siècle." *Bulletin de la société de l'histoire de Paris et de l'Ile de France* (1925), pp. 148–67.

Friedmann, A. "Notre-Dame et les paroisses de Paris au XIIIe siècle." *Revue d'Histoire de l'Eglise de France* 50 (1964): 27–33.

Gaston, Jean. "L'Assemblée de MM. les curés de Paris au XVIIe siècle." *Revue du clergé français* 59 (1909): 676–79.

Gazier, Augustin. "Pascal et Jean de Lingendes." *Revue politique et littéraire* 14 (9 March 1907): 297–302.

Gérin, Charles. "La Mission de M. de Lionne à Rome en 1655." *Revue des questions historiques* 26 (1879): 5–90.

Golden, Richard M. "Religious Extremism in the Mid-Seventeenth Century: The Parisian *Illuminés.*" *European Studies Review* 9 (1979): 195–210.

Goubert, Pierre. "Ernst Kossmann et l'énigme de la Fronde." *Annales: Economies, Sociétés, Civilisations* 13 (1958): 115–18.

Hamscher, Albert. "The Parlement of Paris and the Social Interpretation of Early French Jansenism." *The Catholic Historical Review* 63 (July 1977): 392–410.

Hutt, M. G. "The Curés and the Third Estate: The Ideas of Reform in the Pamphlets of the French Lower Clergy in the Period 1787–1789." *Journal of Ecclesiastical History* 8 (1957): 74–92.

———. "The Role of the Curés in the Estates General of 1789." *Journal of Ecclesiastical History* 6 (1955): 190–220.

Janssen, A. "Un Polémiste anti-janséniste. Le Père Fr. Annat, S.J." In *Mélanges d'histoire offerts à Charles Moeller.* Louvain and Paris, 1914.

Judge, H. G. "Louis XIV and the Church." In *Louis XIV and the Craft of Kingship*, ed. John Rule. Columbus, 1969.

Kleinman, Ruth. "Belated Crusaders: Religious Fears in Anglo-French Diplomacy 1654–1655." *Church History* 44 (March 1975): 34–46.

Koenigsberger, H. G. "Revolutionary Conclusions." *History* 57 (October 1972): 394–98.

Labatut, Jean-Pierre. "Situation sociale du quartier du Marais pendant la Fronde parlementaire (1648–1649)." *XVIIe siècle*, no. 38 (1958): 55–81.

Lanson, Gustave. "Après les *Provinciales*: Examen de quelques écrits attribués à Pascal." *Revue d'histoire littéraire de la France* 7 (1901): 1–34.

Laporte, Jean. "Le Jansénisme." In *Etudes d'histoire de la philosophie française au XVIIe siècle*. Paris, 1951.

Laurain-Portemer, Madeleine. "Opposition et propagande à Paris au temps du sacre de Louis XIV." In *Mélanges offerts à V.-L. Tapié*. Paris, 1973.

Le Bras, Gabriel. "Paris, seconde capitale de la chrétienté." *Revue d'Histoire de l'Eglise de France* 37 (1951): 5–17.

———. "Synodes et conciles parisiens." *Revue d'Histoire de l'Eglise de France* 50 (1964): 35–46.

Lefebvre, Pierre. "Aspects de la 'fidélité' en France au XVIIe siècle: Le Cas des agents des princes de Condé." *Revue historique* 250 (1973): 59–106.

Longnon, Auguste. "L'Ancien diocèse de Paris et ses subdivisions." *Bulletin du comité d'histoire et d'archéologie du diocèse de Paris* 1 (1863): 10–19.

Mandrou, Robert. "Tragique XVIIe siècle." *Annales: Economies, Sociétés, Civilisations* 12 (1957): 305–13.

Martimort, A. G. "Comment les français du XVIIe siècle voyaient le pape." *XVIIe siècle*, nos. 25–26 (1955): 83–101.

Michel, Marie-José. "Clergé et pastorale jansénistes à Paris (1669–1730)." *Revue d'histoire moderne et contemporaine* 27 (April–June 1979): 177–97.

Moote, A. Lloyd. "The Preconditions of Revolution in Early Modern Europe: Did They Really Exist?" *Canadian Journal of History* 7 (December 1972): 207–34.

Mousnier, Roland. "Comment les français du XVIIe siècle voyaient la constitution." *XVIIe siècle*, nos. 25–26 (1955): 9–36.

———. "Les Concepts d' 'ordres', d' 'états', de 'fidélité' et de 'monarchie absolue' en France de la fin du XVe siècle à la fin du XVIIIe siècle." *Revue historique* 247 (1972): 289–312.

———. "The Fronde." In *Preconditions of Revolution in Early Modern Europe*, ed. Robert Forster and Jack P. Greene. Baltimore and London, 1970.

———. "Quelques raisons de la Fronde: Les Causes des journées révolutionnaires parisiennes de 1648." *XVIIe siècle*, nos. 2–3 (1949): 33–78.

Necheles, Ruth F. "The Curés in the Estates General of 1789." *Journal of Modern History* 46 (September 1974): 425–44.

Neveu, Bruno. "Un Parlementaire parisien érudit et janséniste: Jean Le Nain (1609–1698)." *Paris et Ile-de-France. Mémoires* 16–17 (1965–66): 191–230.

Orcibal, Jean. "Qu'est-ce que le jansénisme?" *Cahiers de l'association internationale des études françaises* 3 (1953): 39–53.

Préclin, E. "Les Conséquences sociales du jansénisme." In *Introduction aux études d'histoire ecclésiastique locale*, ed. Victor Carrière. 3 vols. Paris, 1934–40. 3: 591–635.

_____. "Edmond Richer." *Revue d'histoire moderne* 5 (1930): 241–69, 321–36.

Sée, Henry. "Les Idées politiques à l'époque de la Fronde." *Revue d'histoire moderne et contemporaine* 3 (1902): 713–38.

Tans, J. A. G. "Les Idées politiques des jansénistes." *Neophilologus* 40 (January 1956): 1–18.

Taveneaux, René. "Jansénisme et vie sociale en France au XVIIe siècle." *Revue d'Histoire de l'Eglise de France* 54 (1968): 27–46.

Williams, William H. "The Significance of Jansenism in the History of the French Catholic Clergy in the Pre-Revolutionary Era." *Studies in Eighteenth-Century Culture*, ed. Roseann Runte. Vol. 7. Madison, Wisc., 1978.

Wolf, John B. "The Reign of Louis XIV: A Selected Bibliography of Writing Since the War of 1914–1918." *The Journal of Modern History* 26 (June 1964): 127–44.

Wright, A. D. "The Significance of the Council of Trent." *Journal of Ecclesiastical History* 26 (October 1975): 353–62.

INDEX